TALKING

pr

THE COXFORD SINGLISH DICTIONARY

The Coxford Singlish Dictionary

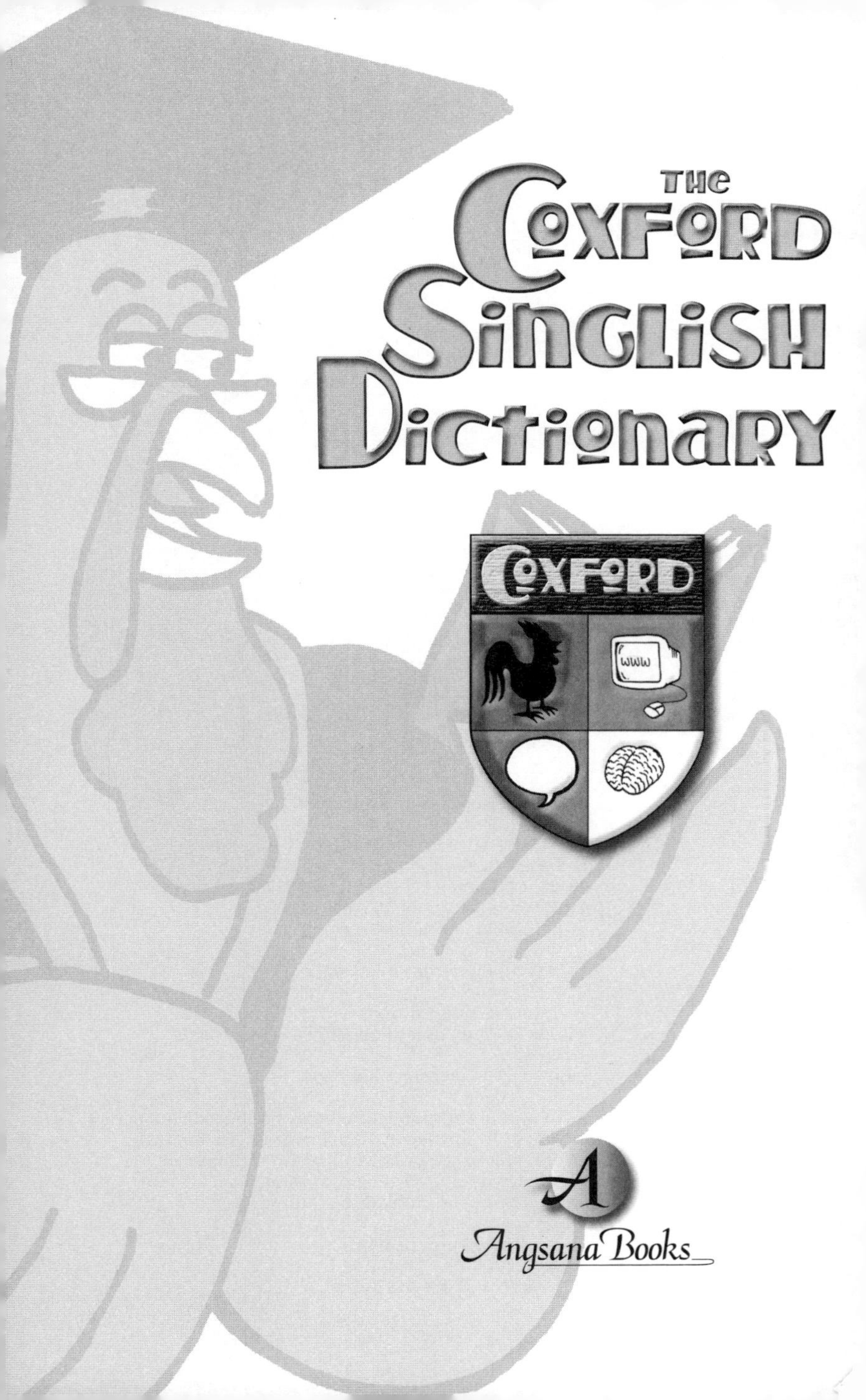

Angsana Books

Published by

Angsana Books

Angsana Books is an imprint of

FLAME OF THE FOREST PUBLISHING Pte Ltd
Blk 5 Ang Mo Kio Industrial Park 2A
#07-22/23, AMK Tech II, Singapore 567760
Tel: (65) 6484 8887, Fax: (65) 6484 2208
mail@flameoftheforest.com

www.flameoftheforest.com

Second Edition

Cover by Mangosteen Designs

Printed in Singapore

ISBN 978-981-4193-68-9

CONTENTS

Introduction to the 2nd Edition

THANK you for buying the second edition of "The Coxford Singlish Dictionary"!

It's been six whole years since our bestselling first edition, which was even praised by the Times of London as "invaluable". Neh bluff you, one! But perhaps our biggest thrill was opening the New Paper and seeing a copy of the Coxford resting on a table between the negotiating teams of the US-Singapore Free Trade Agreement. (Note: if the FTA got any cockup because of poor translation — not our pasal!)

Even though we're a bunch of loboes, we got off our pantats and decided to release a 2nd edition. This was because over the years, contributors like you have been sending us heaps of new words and phrases, as well as refinements to our existing entries. Also, with more and more new immigrants coming to Singapore, we thought it was time to update the world on the current state of Singapore's only unique cultural identifier, and also provide a comprehensive guide for those who might be learning Singlish as a second or third language.

This second edition is especially pow-ka-leow. We've added a couple of hundred new entries, a new pronunciation guide to accompany certain words, and in true Singaporean style, a PSLE (Powderful Singlish Language Exam) test paper. (If you fail it, better faster get Singlish tution!)

After the first edition of the Coxford, we're even more convinced about how important Singlish is to Singaporeans' sense of who we are (especially when we're at ease and not trying to impress anybody), and also as indisputable evidence of our humour, creativity and polyglot history.

We've also personally seen the Coxford develop as a useful text for cultural exchange. In New York, where we're currently working, we met a Singaporean woman who had an inferiority complex about Singaporean culture as compared to American culture. But with the Coxford in her hand, she became much less diffident about being able to share her world, and was soon happily introducing her American friends to words like "drama mama" and "steady pom pee pee".

Singlish is our knowledge, of which we are the experts. And we have the authority to teach others, because it is a special part of who we are. At the same time that Singlish distinguishes us from other countries, it also brings us closer to all the other societies who are being touched by the mixing of cultures and languages that is growing due to globalization.

When we were travelling around the world to promote our award-winning feature film, Singapore Dreaming, we found that audiences were fascinated by the Singlish dialogue. There were questions about it at every single screening. In Taiwan, for example, youths in the audience began repeating some of the Singlish lines and expressed envy that we Singaporeans had such a developed vernacular English of our own. In Spain and America, audiences said they were surprised at how much they could relate to the intermingling of languages. After the screening of the film on American TV, an American viewer posted this message on the station's discussion board:

Singapore Dreaming showed me how the mixture of cultures on this small island have resulted in the most imaginative language/ dialect: Singlish! It was the discovery of Singlish that made me understand just how 'globalized' Singaporeans really are AND because of its use in the film, the story and characters seemed more familiar to me.

Unfortunately, Singapore's misguided war on Singlish and dialects continues. The restrictions in the media persist, and so do the double standards: even as we are forced to chop Singlish and dialect dialogue in Singaporean productions (for instance, we had to remove phrases like "mana ooh pian" in the theatrical trailer for Singapore Dreaming), we are simultaneously inundated with Americanisms; witness American Idol's Randy Jackson and his torrent of slang terms like "dawg", "dope" and "a'ight". We still can't understand why it's "a'ight" to use other people's colloquialisms, or watch trailers in French, Japanese or Korean, but not our very own languages.

We also continue to manifest our tortured relationship with linguistic hybridity: we respond to its inherent appeal (witness the "Huayu Cool" slogan in the 2006 Speak Mandarin Campaign), yet kau peh kau bu about the erosion of the purity of English. This is bizarre, considering the mongrel origins of the English language, the ways in which it has evolved over the years, and its promiscuous borrowing of terms from other languages. One of our favourite Singlish words, "kiasu", was even added to the venerable Oxford English Dictionary lexicon in 2007.

In the past few years, a couple of novel arguments have arisen to justify continuing the war on Singlish:

(1) That the standard of English in Singapore has fallen in recent times.

Our view is that there is simply no real evidence to support this assertion. Numerically, there are definitely now more Singaporeans who are able to speak English than there were, say, in the 1970s. Further, as our newspapers never fail to trumpet, our scores in the English Cambridge examinations are always on the rise.

Yet, every year, many employers and teachers of English express concern about our young people's ability to write and speak in what they deem as "appropriate" English.

Don't be mistaken: the cause of this is NOT Singlish. Having a younger generation that writes and speaks differently is a universal "problem", experienced by many different countries, including English-speaking countries such as England and the USA. Rather, the "problem" arises from changing patterns in reading and writing. People nowadays simply spend less time reading and analysing content as we used to do. Instead, we're developing different literacies, because of the dominance of visual media, as well as rapidly changing communications technology, such as SMS or social networking software. We can see this from falling publishing revenues worldwide, and how SMS abbreviations are creeping into our writing.

> *(2) That those who advocate and support Singlish can do so only because they are able to code-switch. In other words, those who are able to speak both Singlish and English are somehow trying to prevent those who can only speak Singlish from being able to improve their English.*

Our view is that this proposition is not only confusing, it's rubbish. Ask yourself: who's keeping whom down? The people who're trying to tell you there's only one way to express yourself, or the ones who're saying, go ahead, just speak up?

We therefore fear that campaigns to denigrate and censor English are just wasting public money by barking up the wrong tree. After all, despite so many years of the Speak Good English Movement, there is no evidence that the campaign has made any significant headway. In fact we hear the same laments about the falling standards of English in the press year after year.

Worse, the attack on Singlish inhibits many people's ability to think, express and communicate. When we judge people based on linguistic ability alone, it inhibits real participation in the community — whether in schools, in civil society, in politics, in cultural activities. We'll be less inclined to speak up or share our ideas if we have to keep worrying about whether the grammar police are going to saman us for incorrect subject-verb agreement.

The ostensible aim behind the Speak Good English Movement is to improve our global competitiveness. We hear complaints from all quarters that Singaporeans are not innovative enough, not creative enough, not daring enough. How can we tell Singaporeans to be creative, daring, and innovative, but only in the right language? How can we ask Singaporeans to dare to speak their minds and take risks in order to be more globally competitive and yet silence the way in which we normally communicate?

But don't misunderstand us: we love English as much as Singlish, and believe that mastering the rules of grammar is both empowering and enjoyable. It's just that we don't believe that we have to stifle one language to boost another.

We also don't believe that the economic fate of Singapore is tied so strongly to our facility with English. Frankly, after working in New York for over 10 years, we have come to learn that one doesn't need perfect English to succeed socially or economically — the wildly varying standards of English amongst its various communities doesn't seem to have impaired New York's status as a financial and cultural capital. A great grasp of grammar is a good thing to have, but if you don't have it, dun scared, wen die.

We think Singapore society would do far better by encouraging more free expression, boosting cultural confidence and developing a questioning culture. Those traits would do us much more good than agonising over whether we're conjugating correctly before we should be allowed to open our mouths. Singaporeans should just be allowed to talk, however we talk. And when we discover for ourselves the wonders of speech and the joys of wielding language for effect, we will naturally want to improve and learn how to refine the use of our speech to connect with more and more people.

So please, by all means, speak good English. Just don't be afraid to use Singlish with friends and family, and in expressive forms such as in poetry, drama, music, TV and film. And please don't look down on people who speak Singlish. We mustn't wipe out something so full of life and laughter. We should celebrate it instead.

Exercise free speech — keep TalkingCock! (Especially in Singlish!)

Colin Goh & Woo Yen Yen
New York, January 2009

Introduction to the 1st Edition

YOU too can talk like a Hokkien peng!

- Accused of being "air-level" when you joined National Service?
- Ever been called a "keng chio kia" or banana?
- Are you a "chao ang mor" who's trying to "chee hong" an SPG?
- Accepted into NUS Law?

Worry no more! The Coxford Singlish Dictionary can help you fit in with everyday Singaporeans. Study it, and you'll soon impress your friends by swearing like a contractor!

When we decided to launch TalkingCock.com in August 2000, we decided to make the use and preservation of Singapore English — or Singlish as it is more popularly known — one of the dominant features of the site.

TalkingCock.com has since become Singapore's premier satirical humour website, and our Coxford Singlish Dictionary (originally titled "The Lexicon of Lah") is one of our most heavily-visited areas.

The reason is simple: Singlish is unique to Singapore, and listening to its mish-mash of various languages and dialects, often involving bad transliterations, is also very, very funny.

Contrary to popular belief, it is not merely badly spoken English, akin to pidgin. There is a conscious art in Singlish — a level of ingenious and humorous wordplay, as evidenced by phrases such as "pattern tzua kuay badminton" or "jangan tension", that is equalled only perhaps by Cockney rhyming slang. Singlish is to be celebrated as a cultural phenomenon, not buried, as some misguided people have been trying to do.

However, despite its massive appeal, nobody had catalogued it in a systematic manner. There have been past attempts at reflecting it (Paik Choo's seminal and still wonderfully funny "Eh Goondu" series springs to mind), and there have even been some scholarly analyses of its deviation from standard English. Nobody, however, was making a serious attempt to document the constantly-evolving patois, as well as provide a comprehensive guide to its usage in a way that celebrated, rather than condemned it. So we decided to do it ourselves.

The Coxford has since become, undoubtedly, the largest Singlish lexicon in the world and its entries continue to grow, thanks in no small part to the legions of contributors who happily email us to keep us abreast of new phrases or words.

We see the publication of the Coxford as a culturally significant event. When the world is becoming increasingly dominated by the Western media, we have to work harder to preserve the things that are uniquely our own. And we should not feel embarrassed in doing so. After all, if Londoners can speak Cockney and Liverpudlians Scouse, why shouldn't we be able to speak Singlish?

With its Speak Good English Campaign, the government has been actively campaigning for the obliteration of the use of Singlish. The erstwhile reason given is that the inability to speak or write proper English will impair our global competitiveness.

However, there is a distinct proposition between the well-intentioned aim of encouraging proper English and mandating that our arts (notably our TV programmes) also restrict the use of Singlish. What the latter has led to is that our shows do not reflect life as it is, but rather an ersatz picture of Singapore life, populated not by normal people, but by drama club poseurs who speak as if they have potatoes in their mouths. Is it any wonder that our local English programming, with very few exceptions, gives us the goose bumps?

Those who argue that our shows will sell better if they are in standard English should be reminded who their immediate audience is. What kind of message will this kind of argument send to Singaporean viewers? "We're not really interested in making shows for you; what we really want is to sell overseas." As if the people who make American sitcoms care less whether their jokes also work in Bukit Batok or Batu Pahat!

Further, those who contend that improper Singlish in the arts will encourage lower standards should be chided for their patronizing view of Singaporeans. Surely we are not so stupid that we cannot tell the difference between the kind of language acceptable in casual settings and the kind expected in business or official correspondence. (When was the last time you used "lah", "leh" or "wah piang eh" in a formal letter or report?)

After all, the British still write grammatically despite watching programmes like Eastenders, which use colloquialisms. Are Singaporeans less sophisticated than the British? Also, why do we accept programmes from the USA, with their own deviations from standard English? Why are Americanisms acceptable, but not Singlish? Why is it okay to speak like the Nanny but not Phua Chu Kang? TCS should dub over all the US imports! Fair is fair, what!

TalkingCock.com was set up to promote art that is relevant to Singaporeans, not just propaganda. Singlish is a language that is unique to us and we should celebrate it, and we hope that fellow lovers of uniquely Singaporean culture will find the Coxford Singlish Dictionary a useful and fun resource.

Supreme Cock
Editor in Chief, TalkingCock.com, and
President, The Society for the Preservation of Authentic Singlish (SPAS)
August 2001,
Coxford University,
Bukit Gorblok,
Singapore

Some Notes...

On Spelling

TRYING to devise a standard spelling for Singlish has proven to be a difficult endeavour. This is because many Singlish terms derive from different languages, in particular, Malay and the various Chinese dialects, especially Hokkien. However, there are no consistent or authoritative transliterations for most of the Chinese dialects.

Accordingly, for the moment, we have abandoned any attempt to arrive at a standardized spelling of Singlish, because that would also mean having to create a proper Romanized transliteration of Hokkien, and that would be si beh leceh, not to mention expensive.

"Wah piang! This lau pok dictionary miss out so many words, leh!"

"Aiyah, don't kau peh, lah! With a title like 'Coxford', sure got cock-up, mah!"

Instead, we have decided to adopt a spelling which is intuitive and which best approximates the way people pronounce the words and might choose to spell it, e.g. "buay" over "boey", or "chia lat" over "jia lat".

What has emerged is a spelling that borrows from both hanyu pinyin as well as its predecessor, the Wade-Giles system, and in certain instances, from Bahasa Melayu spelling as well. With some words, we have also had to acknowledge a historical pattern of spelling.

For instance, the word "chiak" (to eat in Hokkien) could be rendered as "jia" in pinyin form, and "chiah" under the Wade system. But there has been a history in Singapore of spelling it as "chiak", borrowing the Malay use of a non-explosive "k", as in "nasi lemak (nasi lema'h)" and "teruk (ter-o'h)".

For words of Chinese derivation, we have chosen to follow the Wade-Giles system a little more than hanyu pinyin. This is because the spellings are marginally more intuitive for non-Mandarin speakers, and we want to be as inclusive as possible.

We apologize if the spelling of any word runs counter to the way you believe it should be spelt. If you can't seem to find a word, try looking it up under a variant spelling.

On Pronunciation

We have supplied a simplified pronunciation guide within vertical bars for certain words whose pronunciation we feel may not be completely represented by its spelling, which, as explained above, can vary significantly. (We could have used the International Phonetic Alphabet, but it's not only leceh to key in, we also found that many of our readers see also catch no ball.)

Something that non-Singaporeans might wish to note is that because of the influence of Malay and the various Chinese languages, certain sounds which are spelled as explosives, such as in "potong", "tua", "kena" or "chiak", are not pronounced with the explosive impulse of breath that normally accompanies certain consonants in English.

"Tua" (Hokkien for "big"), for instance, would be pronounced "dtwah" — with the opening consonant somewhere between a "d" and a "t". Thus, "tua tao" (big head) would be rendered as "dtwah tao", where the "t" in "tao" is explosive, but isn't in "tua". Similarly:

- "potong" would be rendered as |pboh-tohng|
- "kena" would be rendered as |kguh-nah|
- "pak chiao" would be rendered as |pa'h tjee-ow|

Also, we have also used the symbol, "'h" at the end of certain words to indicate a glottal stop, meaning, a sudden stoppage of the flow of air. (Note: the usual phonetic symbol for the glottal stop is "ʔ" — see what we mean by catch no ball?) Thus, for words like "lemak" or "bedek", which don't end on a hard "k" but rather a glottal stop, their pronunciation would be rendered as |luh-ma'h| and |bay-de'h| respectively.

Finally, certain words which are spelled with voiced consonants, such as in "bian", "guai guai", "dao", "zi bei" are voiceless in pronunciation, so, e.g.:

- "bian tai" would be rendered as |bpian tai|
- "dao" would be rendered as |dtao|
- "guai guai" would be rendered as |gkwai-gkwai|
- "zi bei" would be rendered as |tze bpay|

Yes, it's all quite confusing, but quite understandable when you're juggling multiple languages, non-standardized transliterations, and historical representations all at the same time.

On Comprehensiveness

Singlish, like any other language, is evolving. We have endeavoured to make as many inclusions as we can, down to the last moments before publishing. However, being human, we are sure we have left some out. Don't despair, or as we say, "Dun scared!" Check out the online Coxford Singlish Dictionary at **www.talkingcock.com**, where new phrases and words are added constantly. If you think a word or phrase should be included, let us know!

On Usage

The beauty of Singlish lies in deliberate wordplay, so speakers should approach it with an irreverent sense of humour. Do not be afraid of mixing and matching words and phrases. Some of the most classic Singlish terms are an amalgam of different languages, e.g. "buay tahan" or "mana eh sai". Also, feel free to bend the rules of proper English grammar by turning nouns into verbs or adjectives or vice versa, or even English tenses to non-English words, e.g. "cabut-ed" or "balik-ing".

Acknowledgements

THE Coxford Singlish Dictionary would not have been possible without the help of our many contributors and support of the readers of TalkingCock.com. We're especially grateful to the various linguistics professionals who have provided invaluable feedback, and completely understand your request to remain anonymous! Thanks, hor!

12 O'Cock
AA
Aaron Loh
Adam
Adrian Eng
Ah Boon
Ah-Li
akm
Allan Goh
Andrew Chua
Andrew Tan
Andrew Yong
Angus
Annie Teng
Ayam Goreng
Ben Kenobi
Benny
Bernard Goh
Bernard Lee
Bernard Loo
Bernard Quek
Bertha
Brandon Seah
Bubba
Calvin Fong
Ch'ng Tuan Wee
Chan Kok Hoe
Char Kuey Teow
Chen Zhi Wei
Chris Le Yoanc
Chris Yeo
Conrad
Crab
Crow
Daniel
Daniel Hong
Desmond
edaniel
Edward Tew
Edwin
Edwin Lian
Egwin
Esther Lee
Eveline How
Feng
Foo Woon Huan
Gabriel Png
George Joseph
Grace
Hagar
Half-Cocked
Hass
Henry Tan
Hiao Cheow
Hikki Takki
Human Bear
Hume
imayoda
J Tai
James Chong
Jason
Jason Chan
Jeff
jianhui
Jimmy Yu
Joel Tan
Jonathan Ng
Joshua
JT
Justin Lee
K Ang
Kanna Kuay Kio
Karen Toh
KC
ketchup
Kevin
Kok Leong
Kok-Tong Khoo
Kwaychee
lanmao
Lee Wee Chong
Lia Tan
Lixing
Lixing Ang
Lucus Hu
Mamak Cock
Marcus Lim
Mark
Maryanne Bell
Mat
Mathias Körber
MC
Melvin Lam
Melvin Wong
Michael Witty
Mike Soo

Minglun
Mizan
Neil Yang
Noor Ashikin Mohamad Noor
Patrick Wong
Petrina
pklorius
Raphael Lee
Rene Sim
revolushun
Roger Ng
Rolland
Ronnie Gan
Samuel Tan
Scarlett
Selena
Shaun Mathew
Sherise Tan
shilie
Si Peh Eng Kia
Sian Tao Ong
SinnerLee
Sliide
Soh Sze Tiong
Stella
Stephen Tan
superflysey
Suz
Tan Tai Kwee
Terry How
thegobs
Toilet Gang
trashkore
Turd Eye
UMC-Nazzster
Varerie
Vidya Hable
viciv
Wayne "Thunder" Seah
Wayne Jamiro
Wayne Koh
Wendy Tan
Willy Ng
Woogie
Xiao Gou
Yeo Chwun Beng
Yong Kuan
You Yang
zx

Every effort has been made to trace contributors but if any of you has been inadvertently overlooked, the publishers will make the necessary acknowledgements at the earliest opportunity.

Aa

ABCDEF The acronym for "Act Blur, Completely Deaf, Extremely Forgetful". Self-explanatory epithet for a clueless, unheeding, absent-minded twit.

⊡ *"Suay ah! This project is damn important. Who go and call that ABCDEF to be the chairman?" (This is really a spot of bad luck. This project is very important. So who nominated that moron to be the chair?)*

See also **act blur, bodoh, sotong**

a-bssh! |ah-bsh| All-purpose Singaporean sound effect for being punched or thumped, similar to the English "bam!", "pow!" or "sock!"

⊡ *"And then, hor, Mike Tyson went to whack him… A-bssh! A-bssh! And then he peng san." (Then, Mike Tyson hit him — bam! pow! — and he went down.)*

See also **chibaboom / terbaboom, piak!, piang!**

a bit the A sarcastic Singlish phrase which literally means "a little", but actually means "very" or "extremely".

[1] *"Wah, you a bit the late, hor!" (My, aren't we just a little bit late!)*

[2] *"Piang eh, your skirt a bit the short, hor?" (Huh! Your skirt's a little on the short side, isn't it?)*

See also **very the**

abourit Sloppy pronunciation of "about it".

⊡ *"Aiyah, this kind of small thing, don' worry abourit." (Oh, don't worry about such small matters!)*

act {adjective} **buay** {adjective} To fail miserably at affecting a pose. Fill in your own adjective after "act" and "buay".

[1] *"Ah Beng whole life act cool buay cool, one." (Ah Beng is always trying to appear impressive, but he invariably fails at it.)*

[2] *"Wah lau, Johnson is damn condemn. Act beng buay beng. Si beh hopeless, one." (Johnson is such a failure. He wants to act like an Ah Beng, but he can't pull it off. He's hopeless.)*

See also **act cute buay cute, buay**

act blur To play innocent or feign ignorance.

⊡ *"I know you know who did it, so don't act blur!" (I know you know who did it, so don't play innocent with me!)*
See also **buat bodoh, bedek, wayang, NATO**

act cute A phrase which describes someone behaving in an exaggeratedly cute or childlike manner, often, though not always, in a coquettish or flirty fashion. Can be used as both verb and adjective.
1 *"Eh, Ah Lian is always so act cute one! She trying to be smurf, is it?" (Ah Lian is always behaving like a kid. Does she think she's a smurf or something?)*
2 *"Ah, don't care her, lah. Got boys around, she always act cute one." (Just ignore her. Whenever boys are around, she always behaves in a coquettish fashion.)*
See also **act** {adjective} **buay** {adjective}**, act cute buay cute, buay**

act cute buay cute / ACBC Describes a girl trying to flirt by behaving in a Lolita-esque fashion, but failing miserably at it.
⊡ *"Ee-yurr. I tell you, I damn buay tahan watching Ah Lian try to get Ah Beng to go kwa meenite with her. Damn ACBC one." (Ugh, I can't stand watching Ah Lian trying to get Ah Beng to watch the midnight movie with her. What a failed coquette she is!)*
See also **act** {adjective} **buay** {adjective}**, buay**

act tough To put on an act of bravado or braggadocio.
⊡ *"Aiyah, he act tough only, lah. Don't care him." (Oh, don't worry about him. It's only bravado that he's displaying.)*
See also **action**

action Behaving in a swaggering or haughty manner. Also sometimes used to describe someone as full of bluff and bluster or hot air.
1 *"Ah Beng won the CC Karaoke Idol only, hor, walk everywhere like damn action like that." (After winning the Community Centre karaoke contest, Ah Beng now walks everywhere with a swagger.)*
2 *"Aiyah, chup seow him, lah. He action only." (Oh, ignore him. He's all bluster.)*
See also **aksi / aksi borak, borak, dao, NATO, sombong, ya ya**

adey |ah-day| A popular exclamation of colloquial Tamil origin. Similar to "hey" or "dude" in meaning and tone. Often abbreviated to just "dey".
1 *"Adey, why you so like that?" (Hey, why are you behaving in this manner?)*
2 *"Dey, don't so stingy, can?" (Dude, can you please not be so stingy?)*
See also **dey**

adoi A Malay exclamation of minor pain, disgust or exasperation.
1 *"Adoi! Why you sepak me?" (Ouch! Why did you kick me?)*

2 *"Adoi... see him pok kai like that, damn poor thing, man!" (Oh dear... it's really tragic to see him become a bankrupt.)*
3 *"Adoi... this sort of thing also you can cock up!" (Oh man! How could you mess up even a simple task like this?)*
See also **alamak**

afturds Common mispronunciation of "afterwards".
1 *"I now not free. See you afturds, can?" (I'm now not free. Can I see you afterwards instead?)*
2 *"He went to school, then afturds, he went to play snooker." (He went to school, then went to play snooker afterwards.)*

again? A much more economical way of saying, "I beg your pardon?" or "Can you repeat that, please?" Can be used out of either genuine deafness, failure to understand, or incredulity.
1 *Doctor: "Mr Chao, I'm afraid you're suffering from a severe case of pneumonoultramicroscopicsilicovolcanoconiosis."*
Patient: "Ha? Again?" (Sorry, can you please repeat that to me slowly?)
2 *Beng: "Eh, yesterday I saw your wife at the Turf Club."*
Seng: "Again?" (What?! Are you sure?!)
See also **lippit, repeat again, say again**

agak-agak |ah-ga'h, ah-ga'h| "Agak" is Malay for "guess". In Singlish, it can also mean to estimate or approximate.
1 *"I think inside the building, agak-agak got 50 companies." (I think there are approximately 50 companies in the building.)*
2 *"I think her house is worth $3m. But agak-agak only." (I think her house is worth around $3m, but that's only a guess.)*
See also **agaration**

agak tarik |ah-ga'h tah-re'h| A Malay phrase literally broken down as "estimate" or "guess" (agak) and "pull" (tarik). It means to "hold back", "be charitable" or "not to go too far".
· *"Don't say him like that, lah. Agak tarik a bit and give him some face, lah." (Don't speak so ill of him. Be a little charitable and give him a break.)*
See also **give chance, panchan**

agaration |ah-gah-ray-shun| The noun form of "agak-agak", which in Malay means to guess, but in Singlish means to make a rough estimate.
· *"I arrived at the number through agaration." (I derived the number through a rough estimate.)*
See also **agak-agak**

Ah Beng An unsophisticated Chinese hoodlum, usually Hokkien. Stereotypically, he speaks gutter Hokkien and likes neon-coloured clothes, spiky, moussed or permed hair and accessories such as handphones or pagers, all of which are conspicuously displayed. He prefers squatting, even when a seat is available, and is prone to violence if stared at. Can be used as an adjective. It's common to start with "chao", meaning "smelly".

1 *"Wah lau eh, why you so chao Ah Beng one?" (Goodness, why are you such an Ah Beng?)*

2 *"I din'ch know you like this sort of Ah Beng music." (I wasn't aware that you liked this sort of Ah Beng music.)*

See also **Ah Huay, Ah Kow, Ah Lian, Ah Seng, Beng, chao Ah Beng, chao Ah Lian, cosmobeng, samseng**

Ah Beng Ah Seng A group of Ah Bengs. Also a generic pejorative term used to denote "anybody", similar to "Tom, Dick or Harry".

1 *"Why you go and make friend with those Ah Beng Ah Seng?" (Why are you associating with those Ah Bengs?)*

2 *"This sort of handphone special, meh? Any Ah Beng Ah Seng also have." (What's so special about this kind of mobile phone? Every Tom, Dick or Harry has one.)*

See also **Ah Beng, Ah Seng**

Ah Boy Generic term of affection for sons (usually but not always the youngest son) in many Singaporean Chinese families.

"Ah Boy, you better listen to your Ah Pa. Skarly he hantam you then you know." (Son, you better listen to your father, or else he might beat you.)

See also **Ah Girl, Boy-boy**

Ah Chek |ah tze'k| "Uncle", a generic Hokkien term of address for an older man.

"Ah Chek, dun anyhow kak pui, can? Very the unhygienic, leh!" (Uncle, please don't expectorate in public! It's very unhygienic!)

See also **Ah Soh**

Ah Ger Common pronunciation of "Ah Girl". See **Ah Girl, Girl-girl**

Ah Girl Generic term of affection for daughters (usually but not always the youngest daughter) in many Singaporean Chinese families.

"Ah Girl, you whole day use handphone, wait your brain kena fry then you know!" (Girl, you might fry your brains if you continue using your handphone the whole day!)

See also **Ah Ger, Girl-girl**

Ah Huay |ah hway| A pet-name which literally means, "flower". Used interchangeably with the more popular "Ah Lian". See **Ah Lian**

Ah Kau |ah gkow| A pet-name which literally means, "doggy." A

generic name given to hoodlum underlings and, of course, pet dogs.
⊡ *"Later you call your Ah Kau come and pick up your DVD, can?" (Later on, you can ask your underling to pick up your DVDs on your behalf. Will that be alright?)*

See also **Ah Beng, Ah Beng Ah Seng, Ah Ter Ah Kau**

Ah Kong Hokkien for "Grandpa".

Ah Lian A pet-name which literally means, "lotus flower". The female equivalent of an Ah Beng — an unsophisticated Chinese girl. Stereotypically dresses in neon colours, wears too much make up, and carries any number of teeth-grindingly tacky accessories.
⊡ *"Wah lau! Mary's handphone got Hello Kitty shape, one! Damn Ah Lian, man!" (Oh my god! Mary is carrying a handphone in the shape of Hello Kitty! How tacky!)*

See also **Ah Beng, Ah Huay, chao Ah Beng, chao Ah Lian**

Ah Long Hokkien for "loan shark", an illegal moneylender who imposes exorbitant interest rates and abbreviated payback periods, usually to compensate for the borrower's complete lack of collateral. Stereotypically resorts to violent or gruesome threats when demanding repayment.
⊡ *"Wah lau, last night the Ah Long go and teow one ter tau at my front door! Better faster pay him back!" (Oh my god, last night, my loanshark hung a severed pig's head at my front door. I think I'd better repay him immediately!)*

Ah Mm |ah umm| Generic name used to address an old woman.

Ah Nia |ah nee-ah| Name used to address a pretty girl.
⊡ *"Ah Nia, tonight want to go kwa meenite with me, not?" (Hello, gorgeous. Want to watch the midnight movie with me tonight?)*

See also **Ah Huay, Ah Lian**

Ah Pooi |ah bpoo-ee| Generic name given to a fat person, similar to "Fatty". A variant form is "Pooi Eh".
⊡ *"Oi, Ah Pooi! Easy on the char kway teow, leh! Wait you go NS then how?" (Hey, Fatty! Don't eat so much char kway teow! What'll happen to you during National Service?)*

See also **Fatty Bom Bom, Fei Tzai, Pooi, Pooi Eh, Pooi-Pooi**

Ah Quah |ah gkoo-ah| An offensive term for an effeminate or homosexual man. The Singlish equivalent of "faggot" or "fairy".
⊡ *"Eh, just because he want to be hairdresser, doesn't mean he Ah Quah, mah!" (Just because he wants to be a hairdresser doesn't mean he's effeminate or gay!)*

See also **ah quah tzeng, bapok, pondan**

ah quah tzeng Offensive description of someone as being effemi-

nate or effete. Literally, "like a faggot".
⊡ *"Eh? Is that Ah Beng wearing make-up? Last time he so samseng, how come suddenly so ah quah tzeng?" (Is that Ah Beng wearing make up? He used to be such a thug. How did he become so effeminate all of a sudden?)*
See also **Ah Quah, bapok, pondan**

Ah Seng Ah Beng's sidekick. Also a generic pejorative term used to denote "anybody", similar to "Tom, Dick or Harry".
⊡ *"This sort of handphone special, meh? Any Ah Seng also have." (What's so special about this kind of mobile phone? Every Tom, Dick or Harry has one.)*
See also **Ah Beng, Ah Beng Ah Seng**

Ah Soh Generic term of address for a middle-aged lady. Sometimes used to describe a woman as unsophisticated or unfashionably-dressed.
⊡ *"Our CEO is damn powderful, but she always dress like Ah Soh one." (Our CEO is a very formidable woman, but she dresses like some peasant.)*
See also **Auntie**

Ah Ter Ah Kau |ah dtuh ah gkow| Literally, "piggies and doggies" in Hokkien. Collective term for Ah Kaus, i.e. the underlings of hoodlums. See **Ah Kau**

ah then? / arbo / arbuthen |ah-buh-den| The Singlish equivalent for "of course!" or "duh!". "Ah then?" is the sarcastic response given to blindingly obvious questions or statements. Somehow, it evolved into "arbuthen" sometime during the 1980s (possibly a deliberate mispronunciation of "ah, but then?"), and has now been abbreviated even further to "arbo".
[1] *Ah Beng: "Eh, your void deck so clean and new, your constituency kena upgrading, ah?" (Hey, your void deck is so clean and new. Is your constituency undergoing upgrading?)*
Ah Seng: "Ah then?" (Of course! What do you think?)
[2] *Ah Lian: "Wah, you wear until so pretty! Tonight you and Johnson go pak tor, ah?" (Wow, you're dressed prettily. Do you have a date with Johnson tonight?)*
Ah Hway: "Arbuthen?" (What else?)
[3] *Ali: "Wah, you so free, exam finish oreddy, is it?" (You seem very free. Are your exams over?)*
Ah Lee: "Arbo!" (Of course! Isn't it blindingly obvious?)

ai kia steady mai? |ai gkee-ah steady muy| Hokkien for "do you wish to go steady with me?" The mating call of Ah Bengs everywhere.

See also **stead**

ai lai mai sua |aye lie muy soo-a'h| A Hokkien expression which translates as "If you want it, come and get it. If you don't, then consider it settled!" The nearest English equivalent is "take it or leave it".

⊡ *"Nowsaday recession, employer all got one kind of ai lai mai sua attitude." (With the recession nowadays, employers all have a "take it or leave it" attitude.)*

See also **sua**

ai pee, ai chee, ai tua liap nee Teochew saying which literally translates as "want cheap, want pretty, want big breasts!" It is used to describe someone who wants the earth, i.e. someone with unrealistic or unreasonable demands or expectations.

⊡ *"Singaporeans all very hard to please, one. They all ai pee, ai chee, ai tua liap nee." (Singaporeans are all very hard to please. They want the earth.)*

ai si |ai see| Literally, Hokkien for "want to die". Courting disaster.

⊡ *"Aiyoh, you want to chiak hong in Iraq? Ai si, ah?" (What? You're going on holiday in Iraq? Do you want to die?)*

See also **chuay si**

ai tzai |ai tzah-ee| A Hokkien exhortation to calm down. Literally, "you want to be steady!"

⊡ *"This exam not counted, one. Ai tzai!" (These exam results are not taken into account. Relax!)*

See also **steady, tzai**

air lebber The local, and deliberately sarcastic, pronunciation of "A" level, the Cambridge-administered high school examinations taken by Singaporean students enrolled in junior college or pre-university centres. Can be used as both noun and adjective.

1 *"Wah, you got air lebber means you bee tang chiak beh leow, lah!" (Wow, with your "A" level qualifications, you'll never starve!)*

2 *"What, you think you air lebber only can ya ya, is it!" (Don't think that just because you have "A" level qualifications means you have the right to be arrogant!)*

See also **orh lebber**

ak kah ak chiew |a'h kah a'h chee-ew| Hokkien phrase literally meaning "duck legs, duck hands". Used to describe someone's extremely poor coordination. "Ak kah" and "ak chew" can be used separately.

1 *"Don't ask him to help you set up the stage. He very ak kah ak chew, one." (Don't ask him to help you set up the stage. He's very clumsy.)*

2 *"Wah lau, like that also cannot score! The player is damn ak kah, one!" (Oh my god, he couldn't even score with such a clear opportunity! What a lousy player!)*

See also **chui kana kah, kah kana lum pah**

ak kah liao / ak |a'h gkah lee-ow| Hokkien for being extremely close friends with someone. Can be abbreviated to just "ak".

1 *"Ah Beng and the boss are damn ak kah liao, so he sure can find you lobang one." (Ah Beng and the boss are really tight, so I'm sure he can find a job opening for you.)*

2 *"I din'ch know you and your MP were so ak, one." (I didn't know you and your Member of Parliament were so chummy.)*

akan datang Malay for "coming soon". Seen in movie trailers and some advertisements, but less so nowadays.

"Eh, relac, ah! My report akan datang!" (Hey, relax! My report will be issued soon!)

akasai A pejorative description of something or someone as nauseatingly cutesy and girlish. Possibly a contraction of "act cute until like sai" (act cute until like shit).

"Aiyoh, Priscilla wear the Hello Kitty hairclips, so akasai!" (Ugh, check out Priscilla with her Hello Kitty hairclips! They're nauseatingly cute!)

See also **act cute, act cute buay cute**

aksi / aksi borak |ek-see/ek-see bo-ra'h| To be arrogant with no basis. "Aksi" is Malay for "action", and is believed to be derived from the Dutch "actie". Meanwhile, "borak" means "bunkum" in Malay. An "aksi borak" is an unjustifiably arrogant person.

1 *"Just because you pass your 'N' level, no need to be so aksi borak, okay?" (Just because you passed your "N" level exams, does not give you any reason to be arrogant, alright?)*

2 *"He get into NUS law fac only, suddenly became this aksi borak." (Once he made it into the NUS law faculty, he suddenly became this haughty fool.)*

See also **action, borak, dao, NATO, sombong, ya ya**

alamak |ah-lah-ma'h| An Malay expression of dismay, surprise or alarm that has long been rumoured to mean "Allah's mother" but more likely comes either from the Arabic "Allah Ma'ak", meaning, "God be with you" or "Allah maaf kar" meaning "God forgive you". It is thus used to denote a situation or action of such calamity or stupidity that God's intervention is necessary.

1 *"Alamak! Why you go and do this sort of stupid thing?" (Oh my God! Why did you do such a stupid thing?)*

2 *"Alamak! I think so I forgot to off my oven! I better go home and*

check!" (Oh God, I think I forgot to turn my oven off! I better go home and check on it!)

Ali Baba No doubt a reference to the Forty Thieves more than Ali Baba, it means to steal or cheat.

[1] *"You don' act blur, okay! I know you Ali Baba my fries when I went to the toilet!" (Don't play innocent! I know you stole some of my French fries when I went to the toilet!)*

[2] *"Don't try and Ali Baba, okay! I saw you take another ace of spades out of your pocket!" (Don't try and cheat us! I saw you take another ace of spades out of your pocket!)*

all fart and no shit Used to describe someone who is full of empty promises.

[3] *"Ah, shaddup lah. Everyday say you wan' to treat me go lunch. You all fart and no shit only." (Ah, shut up. You tell me everyday that want to treat me to lunch. But you're just full of empty promises.)*

See also **NATO**

all over the shop The Singlish equivalent of the English idiom "all over the place", describing something as disorganised, messy or confused, and is not limited to physical spaces, retail outlets or the main work space in a factory, i.e. the "shop floor". Why "shop" is used instead of the more general "place" is unknown.

[1] *"Aiyoh! Why your office so messy, got paper throw all over the shop?" (Dear me! Why is your office so messy, with paper strewn all over the place?)*

[2] *"Why you do maths, your working all over the shop, one?" (Why is it when you're solving mathematical problems, your working is in such a mess?)*

See also **haywire all over the shop**

also |oh-so| In Singlish usage, "also" retains its traditional meaning of "in addition", or "likewise", but is often also used interchangeably with "even".

[1] *"He damn kiasu. I go and buy that stock, he also go and buy." (He's so competitive. When I bought that stock, he also did likewise.)*

[2] *"Ha? Like that also can, ah?" (You mean even that is acceptable?)*

[3] *"He so kiam, one cent also do'wan to donate." (He's so stingy, he won't even donate one cent.)*

amacam |ah-mah-chahm| A contraction of the Malay greeting, "apa macam" which is the Malay equivalent of "what's up?" or "what's happening?"

[·] *"Eh, Ramli! Long time no see! Amacam?" (Hey, Ramli! Long time no see! What's happening?)*

See also **apa macam**

an chua |ahn choo-ah| Hokkien for "what's the matter?", "what's up?" or "how are things?" Heard very often as the first or second phrase used on a mobile phone. It's sometimes used more aggressively, as in "what's your problem?"

1 *"Hallo? Ah Beng? An chua?" (Hallo? Ah Beng? What's up?)*

2 *"Eh! Why you stare at me? An chua? Kiam pak, ah?" (Hey! Why are you staring at me? What's your problem? Want to get beaten up?)*

See also **kua si mi?**

aneh |ah-nair| A racist term for Indians.

• *"Eh, how come got so many aneh lawyers, ah?" (Why are there so many lawyers who are of Indian descent?)*

See also **apu neh neh, bhai, mama, mamak, mungalee, thambi**

aneh kuan |ah-nay kwahn| Hokkien for "like that" or "that kind".

1 *"Oi! Careful, leh! You cannot aneh kuan wash car! Wait you scratch the paint, then how?" (Hey, be careful! You can't wash the car like that! You may scratch the paint!)*

2 *"Don't care Ah Beng this type. Whole life aneh kuan." (Don't trouble yourself over people like Ah Beng. They're just that kind of people.)*

ang moh / ang mor / ang moh lang / ang moh nang |ahng maw/ahng maw lahng/ahng maw nahng| Hokkien for "red-hair" and red-haired people. A once pejorative, now generic term used to describe Caucasians. To be pejorative, it's common to add "chao", meaning "smelly" or "kwee", meaning devil.

1 *"I heard Ah Lian last night kena buaya by some ang moh." (I heard that some Caucasian was trying to put the moves on Ah Lian last night.)*

2 *"Cricket Club got a lot of ang moh lang, one." (The Cricket Club has a lot of Caucasian members.)*

See also **ang moh gao, ang moh kwee, chao ang moh, mat salleh, orang putih**

ang moh gao |ahng maw gkao| Hokkien for "red haired monkey", a pejorative reference to Caucasians.

• *"Wah lau, their rugby team got so many ang moh gao, so tua chiak. How to win them?" (Oh man, their rugby team has so many big-sized Caucasians. How on earth are we to beat them?)*

See also **ang moh, mat salleh, orang putih**

ang moh kwee |ahng maw gkoo-ee| A pejorative term used to describe Caucasians. Literally, "red haired devils".

• *"That firm, the partners all ang moh kwee, one. Asian employees all boh pian hentak kaki." (The partners in that firm are all Cauca-*

sians, so there's a glass ceiling for Asian employees.)
See also **ang moh, ang moh kwee, chao ang moh, mat salleh, orang putih**

ang moh pai A term used to describe Singaporeans who are more proficient in English than their native tongue, or Anglophiles in general. Not quite as derogatory as "keng chio kia".

▣ *"Wah! Damn buay tahan them, so ang moh pai, one! Whole day chiak kantang!" (I really can't stand them. They're such colonized people, always speaking in fake Westernised accents.)*
See also **keng chio kia**

ang moh tua kee |ahng maw too-ah gkee| A Hokkien phrase that literally means, "the red haired ones have bigger sticks", meaning that Caucasians are better endowed. This phrase is usually uttered sarcastically, in bitter resignation at the fact that Caucasians continue to get preferential treatment even in a supposedly post-colonial society.

▣ *"James got promoted over Ah Seng? You surprise, meh? Ang moh tua kee, what." (Are you really surprised that James was promoted instead of Ah Seng? Caucasians always get preferential treatment.)*
See also **ang moh**

ang tao chuloot |ahng tau choo-loot| Literally, "red-headed cigar" in Singapore Hokkien. A graphic reference to the erect male member. "Chuloot" is a mispronunciation of "cheroot", an English word for "cigar", derived from the Tamil "curuttu", which means "roll of tobacco".

▣ *"Eh, zip up your pants, lah. You want whole world to see your ang tao chuloot, is it?" (Hey, zip up your pants. Do you want the whole world to see your male appendage?)*

angkat bola / angkat bodek |ahng-kaht boh-lah / ahng-kaht boh-de'h| Malay term meaning to curry favour or be sycophantic. Literally, to "carry balls". "Bola" is Malay for spherical objects, while "bodek" is a colloquial term for the testicles.

1 *"Boh pian, want promotion, means must angkat bola oreddy." (There's no choice in the matter: if you want to be promoted, you have to suck up to the bosses.)*

2 *"Aiyah! That chao recruit, hor, whole day angkat the Inche's bola!" (Ugh! That smelly recruit is always trying to curry favour with the Warrant Officer!)*
See also **por, sah kah**

anoneh |ah-nor-neh| A Japanese expression similar to "well..." or "if that's the case..." In Singlish, however, this has come to be a generic racist term for any Japanese person.

[1] *"Wah lau, see that anoneh! Her dressing damn solid one." (Wow, check out that Japanese chick! She sure knows how to dress!)*
[2] *"I got some friends in Pasir Ris, they are all anoneh working for airline, one." (I have some friends who live in Pasir Ris; they're all Japanese working for an airline.)*

anyhow To behave in a haphazard or reckless fashion
[·] *"Eh, now you join bomb disposal unit this kind of job, cannot anyhow one, you know!" (Hey, now that you've joined a sensitive profession like the bomb disposal unit, you can't behave in a reckless manner.)*

any o how Same as "anyhow". The "o", which stands for "old", is added for emphasis. See **anyhow**

apa macam |ah-pah mah-chahm| The Malay equivalent of "what's up?" or "what's happening?"
[·] *"Eh, brudder! Apa macam, man?" (Hey, dude! What's happening?)*
See also **amacam**

apu neh neh Childish and racist term for Indian men, used primarily by Chinese people.
[1] *"Why you go and join the hockey team? There mostly apu neh neh, right?" (Why did you join the hockey team? Aren't they predominantly Indian?)*
[2] *To a child: "Don't go out by yourself! Skarly the apu neh neh catch you then you know!" (Don't go out by yourself. The Indian bogeyman might catch you!)*
See also **aneh, bangali, bhai, mama, mamak, mungalee, thambi**

arbuthen See **ah then**

argly |aah-glee| The Singlish pronunciation for "ugly".
[·] *"Wah lan, check out Ah Beng's shirt. It's damn argly." (Will you take a look at Ah Beng's shirt? It's really ugly!)*

arrow To delegate a task to somebody. Generally used only if the task is unpleasant, troublesome or boring. Derives from the old army or civil service practice of

"Donno why also, but the new Head of North American Affairs is very clever to arrow people."

stamping a tiny arrow next to the name of persons in official documents.

1 *"I don't know why I always kena arrow by the Inche to wash the jamban." (I don't know why the Warrant Officer is always getting me to wash the toilets.)*

2 *"So suay, I just step into the office, and he immeelly arrow me to type his document." (What bad luck! I just stepped into the office, and he immediately stuck me with typing his document for him.)*

arse luck Used to describe extremely bad luck. Originally idiomatic in England, but increasingly popular in Singlish.

• *"Ah Hock just got his driving license and straightaway kena saman for speeding. Arse luck, man!" (Ah Hock just obtained his driving licence and immediately got fined for speeding. What bad luck!)*

"No wonder people say that opera is damn atas. Our seats are so high up, I kena nosebleed, man!"

atas |ah-tahs| Malay for "upstairs" or "higher level", it describes someone as snobbish, hoity-toity, affected or arrogant.

• *"Wah, you nowsaday do'wan to eat ikan bilis, only eat caviar. Become damn atas oreddy!" (Whoa, nowadays eating anchovies isn't good enough for you, you only crave caviar. You've become really snooty, haven't you!)*

auntie A generic appellation for any woman old enough to be your aunt, though the person need not actually be your aunt. Depending on the context, it can be either respectful (i.e. as an acknowledgment of a person's age and seniority) or pejorative (i.e. describing a woman as old and unfashionable).

1 *"Boy-boy, come and call Auntie Bee Leng. She's your Mummy's classmate, know." (Son, come and greet Auntie Bee Leng. She's Mummy's classmate, you know.)*

2 *"Not say I say what, hor, but Nancy dresses very auntie, one." (Don't quote me, but Nancy dresses like a middle-aged woman.)*

See also **Ah Soh, uncle**

aw buay kong |ow bway kong| Literally, Hokkien for "to talk behind", an exhortation to resolve a dispute, invariably with violence. The local equivalent of "let's finish this outside!"

⊡ *"See what? You buay song, is it? Okay! Aw buay kong!" (What are you looking at? Are you dissatisfied with something? Let's settle this out the back!)*

See also **settle**

aw buay ooh kwee |ow bway ooh gkwee| Hokkien phrase meaning, "There's a ghost behind you." Often shouted when playing football or hantam bola, to warn someone that an opposing team member is behind them.

ayam |ah-yahm| Malay for "chicken". Used to describe a task as easy, or someone as hopeless or easily intimidated.

① *"Relac, ah! That test is damn ayam. Jangan tension!" (Relax, the test is really easy. Don't get uptight.)*

② *"Man U sure win. The other team damn ayam one." (Manchester United is sure to win. The other team is hopeless.)*

See also **chicken / chicken feed**

Bb

BCC See **bin chao chao**

BGR |bee jee ah-rer| Acronym for "Boy Girl Relationship".

⊡ *"Today, I suay-suay kena lecture by the principal on BGR." (Today, I was unfortunate enough to be hauled before the principal for a lecture on boy-girl relationships.)*

bah long long Of indeterminate origin, this term is used to describe someone as lackadaisical, lethargic or aimless. Often said in disgust. There has been some suggestion that the term is somehow connected to a mispronunciation of "buah kedondong", the Malay name for a fruit known variously as the ambarella, Tahitian quince or great hog plum *(Spondias dulcis)* but this has not been verified, and it is unclear what the tart-tasting fruit's connection to lethargy might be.

⊡ *"See him, so bah long long, whole day just hang out at the kopi*

tiam." (What a bum he is, spending the whole day hanging out at the coffee shop.)
See also **nuah, slack**

bak chew tah stamp |ba'h chee-ew ta'h stem| Classic Singlish hybrid of Hokkien and English. Literally translates as "eyes have been pasted over with a stamp", meaning to be blind.
⊡ *"How can you step right onto that big pile of kao sai? You bak chew tak stamp, is it?" (How could you step right onto that big pile of dog shit? Are you blind or what?)*

bak chew tah sai |ba'h chee-ew ta'h sai| Hokkien for "eyes smeared with excrement", meaning blind. A ruder version of "bak chew tah stamp" (above).
⊡ *"She so jude, her boyfriend look like chichak. She bak chew tah sai, ah?" (She's so pretty, while her boyfriend looks like a lizard. What is she — blind?)*

bakero |bah-kay-row| A Singapore corruption of the Japanese swear word "baka yarou", which loosely means "stupid neanderthal". Erroneously thought to mean "bastard".
⊡ *"Wah lau, the principal is a damn bakero, man!" (Man, the principal sure is a twit!)*

balik |bah-le'h| Malay for "to return". Can sometimes be used in the sense of "come again?", i.e. a request to backtrack or repeat.
1 *"Aiyah! I left my diary in the office! I better balik and pick it up." (Oh darn, I left my diary in the office. I better go back and pick it up.)*
2 *"5 o'clock and you balik-ing orreddy ah?" (It's only 5 o'clock and you're already going home?)*
3 *"Balik, balik, say again? Ah Beng had a sex change operation?" (Whoa, back up and repeat that again! Ah Beng had a sex change operation?)*
See also **chao, lippit, repeat again, say again**

balik kampong |bah-lay'h kahm-pohng| Literally, Malay for "return to the village". Used in the sense of "fuck off" or "get lost", or more accurately, "go back where you came from." Chants of "balik kampong" can usually be heard at the National Stadium by Singaporean fans trying to scare the visiting soccer team. (But we ALL know who's really going to "balik kampong" in the end.)
⊡ *"Aiyah, why you go and listen to him? Just tell him to balik kampong, lah!" (Why on earth are you listening to him? Just tell him to get lost!)*

balu |bah-loo| A Hokkien term derived from the Malay word "baru" (new), meaning "recently".

□ *"I balu buy this handphone and it's oreddy koyak." (I bought this handphone only recently and it's already broken.)*

bang **[1]** Onomatopoeic term denoting exasperation or frustration.
□ *"I expected to win the lottery, instead I kena fine. Damn bang, man." (I expected to win the lottery, but instead, I got fined. How frustrating.)*
See also **bang balls, heng kao kan, lum pah pah lan, pek chek, giah lum pah chu lai tom to'teng**
[2] |bahng| Short for "'abang", Malay for "elder brother".

bang balls Essentially the Anglicized version of the Hokkien phrase "lum pah pah lan", which describes the frustration of having a plan or action backfire on you.
□ *"Wah lan! When I heard I kena saman that time, I damn bang balls, drop on floor, bounce three times!" (Oh man! When I heard that I got fined, I was really aggravated!)*
See also **bang, heng kao kan, lum pah pah lan, pek chek, giah lum pah chu lai tom to'teng**

bangali |bahng-gah-lee| A corruption of "Bengali", which has come to be a racist reference to Sikhs or Northern Indians. See also **bhai, mungalee**

bangla Racist abbreviation of "Bangladeshi".
□ *"Those two Bangla very hardworking, day in day out never stop working one." (Those two Bangladeshis are very hardworking. They work round the clock.)*

bangsat |bahng-saht| From the Malay word "bangsat", for "scoundrel", in Singlish it refers to someone who resorts to unfair tactics or cheating.
□ *"I do'wan to play with you. You all bangsat, one!" (I don't want to play with you guys! You're all cheats!)*
See also **chao kuan, mungsat, play cheat**

bapok |bah-po'h| Pejorative Malay term for "transvestite" or "transsexual". See also **ah quah, pondan**

barang barang |bah-rahng bah-rahng| Colloquial Malay for "chattels", or "personal property or belongings". Sometimes abbreviated to just "barang".
□ *Sergeant: "OK, we're moving off to Peng San Hill in 10 minutes time. You all got your barang-barang ready, not?" (Sergeant: We'll be moving off to Peng San Hill in 10 minutes. Have you got all your belongings ready?)*

basket |bahs-kate| An exclamation denoting frustration or anger, similar to "damn!" which has nothing to do with woven receptacles.

A term of uncertain origin, but the general consensus is that it was once a euphemism for "bastard". (How this probably came about was that the Peranakan term "berbakul-bakul", meaning "to heap abuse upon", and the Malay word "bakul", which means "basket", somehow merged to become a single epithet.)

⊡ *"Basket! Five minute only dun put coupon, kena saman!" (Damn! I left the car without using a parking coupon for only five minutes, and I got fined!)*

bayi Common erroneous spelling of "bhai". See **bhai**

because the sky is so high, the bird shit in your eye This phrase is essentially an annoyed retort to being asked "why", and conveys the meaning that the questioner ought to mind his or her own business. Popular in the mid-70s, its usage began to decline in the early 80s and is rarely heard these days.

⊡ *Sally: "Eh, Jasmine, how come I never see you with Roger anymore?"*
Jasmine: "We oreddy break up, lah!"
Sally: "Why?"
Jasmine: "Because the sky is so high, the bird shit in your eye!"

bedek / action bedek / bedek kacang |bay-de'h/ek-shuhn bay-de'h/bay-de'h kah-chang| Derived from the Malay word "membidik", meaning "to aim at", it has come to be used to describe someone who is acting dishonestly or disingenuously, or who is full of hot air, or who pretends to be capable but is in reality a failure. Can also be used as a verb in the sense of "to bluff" or "mislead". Tagging on "action" or "kacang" (peanuts) is merely for emphasis.

1 *"Oi, you make sure you can really do it, ah! Don't anyhow bedek me, okay!" (Hey, make sure you can really do it. Don't you dare bluff me!)*

2 *"I saw you pontang school today, you don't come and bedek kacang with me, okay?" (I saw you playing truant today, don't you act innocent with me!)*

3 *"Wah! That S-League player really want to score, sia! But open goal still can fall down! So action bedek one, man!" (Huh! That S-League player seemed like he really wanted to score, but despite an open goal, he still fell down! What a fraud!)*

See also **act blur, aksi borak, buat bodoh, wayang**

bee tang chiak buay liao |bee tahng tjia'h boo-ay lee-ow| Hokkien idiom which literally means "the rice bin from which one will never be able to finish eating", i.e. a rice bin that will never be depleted of rice. The Hokkien equivalent of finding the goose that lays golden eggs. It means attaining a position or status which is eternally secure and lucrative.

☐ *"Wah, you President Scholar, means you bee tang chiak beh leow, lah!" (Wow, as you've earned a President's Scholarship, your future is really secure!)*

See also **chiak buay liao**

beh |bay| Hokkien for "not" or "un–". Also pronounced "buay".

[1] *"Eh, his speech damn beh saht, leh." (His speech wasn't very impressive, was it?)*

[2] *"Wah lau, how come he walk beh steady, one?" (Hey, how come he's walking in an unsteady manner?)*

See also **buay**

belakang mari |blah-kahng mah-ree| Literally, Malay for "going by the rear". Used to describe situations where an alternative (often covert) approach is employed when the obvious has failed.

☐ *"Wah, that guy super saht man! Cannot get in first time, then belakang mari second time can oreddy!" (Wow, he's cool! He couldn't get in the first time, but by acting sneakily the second time, he managed to do it!)*

beng Contraction of "Ah Beng". Compares a person or object to an Ah Beng and his unsophisticated ways.

☐ *"Why you dress so beng one?" (Why have you dressed in such an Ah Beng manner?)*

See also **Ah Beng**

bengkok |beng-ko'h| Malay for "bent" or "crooked".

☐ *"Adey! Your wall that painting a bit the bengkok, leh." (Hey, that painting on your wall is a little crooked.)*

See also **senget**

beo |bee-oh| To ogle and survey people, usually comely women.

☐ *"I free that time, like to go Orchard Road and beo the babes." (When I'm free, I like to go to Orchard Road to ogle the pretty girls.)*

berak |bay-ra'h| Malay for the act of defecation. (The Malay word for faeces is "tahi".)

☐ *"Eh, you all wait awhile for me, hor, I need to berak." (Please wait for me, I need to take a shit.)*

See also **do business, number two, pang sai**

bhai |bah-yee| Racist way of addressing a Sikh gentleman. The term "bhai" in Punjabi is innocuous and means "brother". But this has since taken on racist connotations in Singapore.

☐ *"Bhais are si beh powderful at hockey." (Sikhs are very adept at hockey.)*

bhai si mi sek "Bhai what colour?" A racist game played by churlish Chinese people. It involves pinching your companion whenever you spot a Sikh gentleman, and not letting go till your companion shouts out the colour of his turban. See also **bhai**

bian tai |bpian tai| In Mandarin, "bian tai" means an abnormal metamorphosis, usually into a pervert or lecher.

☐ *"Ah Beng see so many blue movie until he bian tai oreddy." (Ah Beng watched so many pornographic films, that he eventually became a pervert.)*

See also **chee ko pek, se lang, ter kor**

bilis See **no bilis**

bin chao chao / BCC |bin chow chow| Hokkien phrase literally meaning, "smelly face". Used to describe someone with a grumpy look and sour disposition. Often abbreviated to "BCC".

☐ *"I do'wan to talk to him, lah. He always so bin chao chao, one." (I don't want to talk to him. He's always so grouchy.)*

See also **chi teh bin**

bising |bee-seng| Malay for "noisy".

☐ *"Alamak, every Saturday night, my upstairs neighbour throws a karaoke party. Damn bising, sia!" (Oh my God, my neighbour upstairs throws a karaoke party every Saturday night. It's bloody noisy, man!)*

blanco "Blanco" is the trademarked name of a long-established brand of whitening liquid. It has now become a generic term for applying white correction fluid over an error.

☐ *"No need to get me a new form. I'll just blanco over the old names."*

blanja |blahn-jah| From the Malay word "belanja", meaning "expense" or "cause for spending money". In Singlish it has come to mean "treat".

☐ *"Eh, today I blanja you lunch, okay?" (Hey, let me treat you to lunch today, okay?)*

See also **spend**

blarder Ah Beng pronunciation of "brother". Contrary to popular belief, does not mean "bladder".

bluff |blahf| As with its English counterpart, this means to mislead or deceive someone. However, unlike its English counterpart, this does not carry any connotation that the deception was achieved through an act of strength, boldness or self-confidence. In Singlish, "bluffing" is merely lying.

☐ *"Ah seng said today got test, but he bluff me one." (Ah Seng told me there would be a test today, but he was only lying.")*

See also **dun bluff**

blur Used to describe someone as unclear, inept and in a world of his own. May also be used to describe the feeling of being dazed. A common usage is "blur like sotong".
1 *"Such a simple thing also cannot do. Why you so blur?" (You can't do even this simple task? Why are you so incompetent?)*
2 *"Wah lau, I do maths, do until blur, man." (Ugh, I've been doing so many mathematics problems, I'm now in a daze.)*
See also **act blur, blur like fuck, blur like sotong, blur toad, concuss, gong gong, mong cha cha, sotong**

blur like fuck The rude version of "blur like sotong".
"All new recruits, hor, all blur like fuck." (All new recruits are invariably bewildered and confused.)
See also **blur, blur like sotong, blur toad, sotong**

blur like sotong A riff on "blur", this is one of Singapore's most colourful and popular similes. "Sotong" is Malay for squid, and its blurness comes from the cloudy ink that squids squirt. The meaning is identical to "blur", i.e. it is used to describe someone as unclear, inept and in a world of his own, and may also be used to describe the feeling of being dazed. Often reduced to just "sotong".
"Wah lau eh, I got this tuition student, hor, blur like sotong. Explain to him donno how many times also, he still catch no ball." (Oh my god, I have this student who's really dense. No matter how many times I explain things to him, he still doesn't get it.)
See **blur, blur like fuck, blur toad, sotong**

blur toad A common variant of "blur like sotong", i.e. someone who's dumb and inept. Of uncertain origin.
"Don't ask him to help, he's such a blur toad." (Don't ask him to help, he's a such a big dope.)
See also **blur, blur like fuck, blur like sotong, sotong, toad**

bobo / bobo king / bobo shooter Used to describe a soldier who frequently misses his shooting target. Possibly derived from a common military term used at the shooting range, "W/O W/O" (wipe-out), when no hits are achieved at all. Can be transposed into the civilian sphere to describe someone who can't attain his objectives.
1 *"Eh, it's that bobo shooter again, always cross lane one." (Oh no, it's that inept shooter again, always shooting into another's firing lane.)*
2 *"Recruit Beng is super bobo king one. Last time at the range, he accidentally shot his OC." (Recruit Beng is a really bad marksman. The last time he was at the range, he accidentally shot his officer-in-charge.)*

③ *"Wah lau, Ah Seng went disco, and every girl he try to buaya also tell him to fly kite. When he become so bobo, ah?" (Man, Ah Seng went to the disco and every girl he tried to pick up blew him off. When did his judgment get so skewed?)*

bodoh Malay for "stupid" or "fool".

① *"Ah Beng is damn bodoh, man. Simple thing also can cock-up like that." (Ah Beng is really stupid. He messes up even simple tasks.)*

② *"Salim is a real bodoh. He light his cigarette that time, his eyebrows can catch fire." (Salim is such an idiot. When he lit his cigarette, he managed to set his eyebrows on fire.)*

See also **dungu, goondu, gorblok**

boh Hokkien word denoting the lack of something. When placed before any word, it means that that quality or object is missing. Thus, calling someone "boh chup" means he is insufficiently "chup", and "boh chee" means a person has a deficiency of "chee". Its antonym is "ooh".

① *"Eh, you got cigarette, not?" (Do you have any cigarettes?) "Boh." (No, I don't.)*

② *"I air lebber poon boh, how to become scholar?" (As I lack even "A" level qualifications, how am I to get a scholarship?)*

See also **ooh**

boh bah ti |boh ba'h tee| Hakka admonishment meaning "ignorant of death". Used when someone is audacious and cavalier about consequences. The Hokkien equivalent is "mm tzai si".

⊡ *"Why you go and make fun of Ah Beng's tattoo? Boh bah ti!" (Why did you make fun of Ah Beng's tattoo? Do you have a death wish?)*

See also **tzai si, mm tzai si**

boh beh chao |boh bay tzao| Hokkien term which literally translates as "no horse running". It is used to describe something or someone with such excellent qualities that there's no competition.

⊡ *"Wah lau eh, that Tiger Woods really boh beh chao, man! Si peh tok kong ah!" (Wow, that Tiger Woods is really beyond compare! Excellent!)*

boh chee / boh ji |boh tjee| Hokkien for "no balls", denoting a lack of courage or conviction.

⊡ *"Eh, like that also dun dare try. He damn boh chee, lah." (Huh, he doesn't dare to try even something like that? What a wuss!)*

See also **boh lum pah chee**

boh cheng hu |boh tzeng hoo| A Hokkien term literally meaning, "to lack governance". Means lawlessness or chaotic.

⊡ *"Wah, boss go on leave, this whole place boh cheng hu orreddy."*

(With the boss on leave, the office is without control.)

boh chiak png |boh chee-a'h bpng| Literally, Hokkien for "have not eaten rice". Used to describe someone as physically weak.

▣ *"Wah lau, like that also cannot carry! You boh chiak png, ah?" (Oh my god, you can't even manage to carry that? Are you starving or something?)*

boh chup |boh chahp| As an adjective, it means nonchalant, cavalier, relaxed or phlegmatic. As a verb, it means to ignore.

1 *"He's very boh chup about his work." (He has a very relaxed attitude towards his work.)*

2 *"Aiyah, boh chup him, lor." (Ah, just ignore him.)*

See also **chup seow**

boh eng Hokkien term literally meaning "not free". Used to convey how busy you are.

1 *"Go East Coast to swim? Boh eng lah!" (You want me to follow you to East Coast Park for a swim? I'm not free!)*

2 *"Today I boh eng, cannot go see show with you." (I'm really not free today, so I can't go to see a movie with you.)*

See also **eng, mana ooh eng, chiak sior eng**

boh her hae mah ho |boh hur hay mah ho| A Hokkien proverb which translates as "If there is no fish, prawns are just as good." It is unclear if this is meant to be said in resignation at having to accept one's second choices, or if it is a cheerfully pragmatic way of dealing with situations where you do not get what you originally intended. Perhaps a little of both.

▣ *"You couldn't get tickets to the Stefanie Sun concert, so you bought us seats for the Bukit Pantat Community Centre Angklong Orchestra performance? Oh well, boh her hae mah ho."*

boh hew / don't hew Hokkien for "don't give a damn". It's not entirely clear what "hew" translates to on its own, but it's invariably used in the negative. A slightly more vehement variant of "boh chup".

1 *"Aiyah, this small-small thing, just boh hew, can oreddy." (Oh, these trivial matters! It's alright to just ignore them.)*

2 *"It's not worth fighting him over this kucing kurap stuff. Don't hew him, better." (It's not worth fighting him over such small matters. It's better to just ignore him.)*

See also **boh chup, chup seow**

boh lang ai / boh nang ai |boh lahng ai/boh bahng ai| Hokkien for "nobody wants", meaning "useless".

▣ *"This sort of free gift, boh lang ai one lah." (Nobody wants this sort of free gift.)*

boh lat |boh laht| Hokkien for "lacking in strength". Can mean weak or exhausted.

1 *"Yesterday, I went gym. Today, I damn boh lat, man." (Yesterday, I went to the gym. Today, I'm completely exhausted.)*

2 *"This kind of light-light thing also cannot carry? How come you so boh lat?" (You can't carry such light things? How come you're so weak?)*

See also **boh chiak png**

boh liao |boh lee-ow| Hokkien for "nothing better to do". Dangerously idle. In Mandarin, it's "wu liao".

"What for he go and do that sort of thing? Must be damn boh liao." (Why did he do that? He must have nothing better to do!)

See also **wu liao**

boh lui |boh looi| Hokkien phrase literally meaning "no money". Commonly heard from students, NSmen, and people aspiring to Mercedes Benzes.

"Eh, tonight cannot treat you all to karaoke. I boh lui liao!" (Tonight, I can't treat you to a karaoke session, because I'm broke.)

See also **pok kai**

boh lum pah chee |boh lahm pah tjee| Hokkien for "no testicles/balls/guts", it is used to admonish someone for being a coward. A more aggressive variant of "boh chee".

"You don't dare print this entry in the Coxford, you boh lum pah chee." (If you don't dare print this entry in the Coxford Singlish Dictionary, you're a gutless wonder.)

See also **boh chee, boh tah boh lum pah**

boh pakay |boh bpah-kay| See **pakay, sorry boh pakay**

boh pian |boh bpee-en| Hokkien for "can't do anything about it" or "no choice." To be at wit's end.

1 *"Go this launge must pay cover charge. Boh pian one." (We have no choice but to pay a cover charge if we wish to enter this lounge.)*

2 *"I every year also boh pian must go and pay taxes." (Every year, I have no choice but to pay my taxes.)*

boh say Hokkien phrase meaning "doesn't have the look".

"That kind also can be occifer ah? Damn boh say, leh!" (You mean even he could make officer? He just doesn't look the type!)

See also **ooh say**

boh tah boh lum pah |boh dtah boh lahm pah| Literally, Hokkien for "If it's not dry, you've got no balls." A dare issued to someone to drink up something unpleasant.

☐ *"You say you can tahan spicy food? Then drink that whole bowl of laksa, lah! Boh tah, boh lum pah!"* (You say you can take spicy food? Then drink that whole bowl of laksa! If it's not drained till it's dry, you've got no guts!)

See also **boh ji, boh lum pah chee**

boh tai ji |boh dtai tjee| Hokkien for "nothing's the matter" or "nothing's wrong".

1 *"Here everything boh tai ji, why you itchy backside come and listurb?"* (Everything was just fine. Why did you have to mess things up?)

2 *"Eh, dun fight, leh. Boh tai ji."* (Hey, don't fight. Everything's cool.)

See also **tai ji**

boh tak chek |boh ta'h che'h| Hokkien for "no schooling", i.e. uneducated.

☐ *"You ah, boh tak chek one, how can get cheng hu kang?"* (What? How did an uneducated lout like you get into the civil service?)

boh tao boh buay |boh tau boh bway| Hokkien term which literally translates as, "no head, no tail", meaning "incomprehensible".

☐ *"Wah lau eh, that movie was damn boh tao boh buay."* (Man, that movie was really incomprehensible.)

See also **no head no tail**

boh tua boh suay |boh too-ah boh soo-ay| Hokkien phrase literally meaning "no big, no small". Used to admonish someone for not knowing his place or being disrespectful of one's superiors. Famously used by PM Goh Chok Tong in a National Day Rally speech.

☐ *"You talk like that to your father? Si noong kia! Damn boh tua boh suay!"* (You dare speak in that manner to your father? Accursed child! You don't know your place!)

boleh |boh-lay| Malay for "can" or "possible".

1 *"Can fix my computer, not?"* (Can you fix my computer?) *"Boleh!"* (Of course I can!)

2 *"You do my way, sure boleh one."* (If you follow my instructions, you can do it.)

bopeng Peranakan for "pockmarked".

☐ *"He so bopeng also can get married."* (He could get married despite his face being so pockmarked.)

borak |boh-ra'h| Malay for "bunkum" or "nonsense". Can be used as both verb and adjective.

1 *"Dun borak me, man, you only pay two loler for this?!"* (Don't feed me that crap, man! How could you pay only two dollars for this?)

2 *"Aiyah, he's such a big borak. Don't care him, lah!"* (Ah, he's such

a big bullshitter. Ignore him!)
See also **aksi / aksi borak, talk cock**

borrow For some reason, in Singlish this means "to lend".
⊡ *"Eh, can borrow me your book?" (Can you lend me your book?)*

boss Nothing to do with one's superiors, this is a deliberately sloppy pronunciation of "balls". Used at the end of sentences for emphasis. Interestingly, it does not add any obscene overtones to the sentence or subject.
1 *"Did you see the shirt Ah Beng was wearing? Can go blind, boss." (Did you see the shirt Ah Beng was wearing? It can make you go blind.)*
2 *"I just read that book by that opposition politician. Fierce, boss." (I just read that book by that opposition politician. It was really hard-hitting.)*

botak / botak head |boh-ta'h| "Botak" is Malay for bald. "Botak head" is used to describe a bald person, a skinhead or even someone with a short crew-cut.
1 *"Eh, Botak! How come you buy shampoo?" (Hey, Baldie! Why are you buying shampoo?)*
2 *"Which one is Mr Tan? He's that botak head sitting over there." (Which one is Mr Tan? He's that bald person sitting over there.)*

Boy-boy More affectionate variant of "Ah Boy" See **Ah Boy, Girl-girl**

buat bodoh |bua'h boh-doh| In Malay, literally, "to play dumb". To feign ignorance or play innocent.
⊡ *"Oi, I know you know who did it, so don't buat bodoh, okay!" (I know you know who did it, so don't feign ignorance!)*
See also **act blur**

buay |bway| Hokkien for "not" or "un–". Also pronounced "beh".
1 *"Eh, his speech damn buay saht, leh." (His speech wasn't very impressive, was it?)*
2 *"Wah lau, how come he walk buay steady, one?" (Hey, how come he's walking in an unsteady manner?)*
See also **beh**

buay gam |bway gahm| A Hokkien term describing something as inconsistent, or being an imperfect match.
⊡ *"Why did I break up with Ah Lian? Aiyah, she and I just buay gam lor." (Why did I break up with Ah Lian? I guess we were just incompatible.)*

buay heow |bway hee-ow| Hokkien for "to be ignorant of something".
1 *"Aiyah, why you ask him? He sure buay heow one!" (Don't bother asking him about it, he's sure not to know.)*
2 *"If you buay heow fix the computer, just say so, lah!" (If you don't*

know how to fix the computer, just say so!)

buay heow bai |bway hee-ow buy| Literally, not to know what ugliness is. Not embarrassed easily.

⊡ *"His voice cannot make it still go and sing so much, damn buay heow bai."* (*Despite his awful voice, he sings a lot. He really doesn't know how bad he is!*)

See also **buay pai seh, thick skin**

buay kan |bway gkahn| Hokkien for, literally, unable to fuck. An especially crude term used to describe an utterly incompetent person. Applies only to extreme cases.

⊡ *"Wah lau eh, this fler so buay kan, if we put him in charge, sure cock-up one."* (*Oh my god, this fellow is such a loser. If we put him in charge, he's bound to screw things up!*)

buay kan tan |bway gkahn dtahn| Hokkien phrase meaning "not easy". Also used to describe someone as complicated or complex, in the sense of being wily or having too many ambitions or abilities.

1 *"Dun anyhow rush. This sort of thing, buay kan tan, one."* (*Don't run off half-cocked. These matters are complicated.*)

2 *"Dun see him look so innocent. Acherly, he buay kan tan one."* (*Don't be fooled by his innocent looks. He's actually a complex fellow.*)

buay kantang |bway kahn-tahng| Literally, "to sell potatoes". A hybrid of the Hokkien phrase "buay kan tan", meaning "not easy" and the Malay word "kentang", for potato, this phrase means that there is more than meets the eye in a given situation.

⊡ *"Don't anyhow rush. This sort of thing, ah, buay kantang one."* (*Don't run off half-cocked. There's more than meets the eye with these matters.*)

See also **buay kan tan**

buay kia |buay gkee-ah| Hokkien for "unable to walk or move". Also used to denote the implausibility of a plan or strategy.

1 *"Eh? How come your car buay kia, leh?"* (*Huh? Why isn't your car able to move?*)

2 *"Not say I say what, but that policy sure buay kia, one."* (*If you ask me, that policy is a non-starter.*)

See also **tak jadi**

buay kia nang too lan |bway gkee-ah nahng dtoo lahn| Hokkien phrase which means to do things unabashedly, or unashamed of doing things others might disapprove of.

⊡ *"Wah lau, this sort of voice also can cut album. Damn buay kia nang too lan!"* (*Huh! He dares to record an album with such a lousy voice? He sure isn't scared of pissing people off!*)

See also **buay heow bai, buay pai seh, thick skin**

buay kum guan |bway kahm goo-ahn| Hokkien for "unwilling" or "reluctant".

☐ *"Aiyah, ask him to help you damn no use, lah. He sure damn buay kum guan, one." (Ah, it's no use asking him to help. He's bound to be reluctant.)*

buay pai seh |bway pai say| Literally translated as "not shy", it means to be thick-skinned, i.e. unashamed or unembarrassed by one's own actions. The term also usually connotes insensitivity.

1 *"Wah lau, you everyday let her buy you drink, buay pai seh, meh?" (Wow, you let her buy you drinks everyday? Aren't you embarrassed?")*

2 *"See him dancing all over the bartop like some monkey, damn buay pai seh, man." (Look at him dancing on the bartop like some monkey. He sure is thick-skinned!)*

See also **pai seh, buay tze tong**

buay sai |bway sah-ee| Hokkien for "cannot" or "incapable". Can be used in many forms.

1 *"You want Ah Beng to help you with your maths? Buay sai!" (Impossible! or You can't!)*

2 *"You want Ah Beng to help you with your maths? He damn buay sai one!" (But he's incapable!)*

3 *"Ah Beng buay sai help you with your maths." (Ah Beng cannot help you with your maths.)*

See also **cannot make it**

buay sior |bway see-or| Hokkien for "not thinking".

☐ *"How come Ah Beng join the Raffles Town Club? Because he buay sior, lah! Arbuthen?" (Why on earth did Ah Beng join the Raffles Town Club? Because he wasn't thinking, that's why!)*

See also **sior**

buay song Hokkien for "not satisfied". Usually said with a belligerent tone.

1 *"You stare at me for what? Buay song ah?" (Why are you staring at me? What's your problem?)*

2 *"Ah Beng supposed to be my peng yew, yet he treat me like this. Now I damn buay song him." (Ah Beng was supposed to be my good friend, yet he treated me like this. Now I'm really unhappy with him.)*

buay steady A hybrid Hokkien/English phrase that literally means "not steady". However, it does not denote unsteadiness, but rather is used to describe people as being dubious, unfair or incompetent.

1 *"Important job cannot send him, one. He damn buay steady, sure cockup." (You can't send him on important assignments. He's really incompetent and is bound to mess things up.)*
2 *"Wah lau, I go outside two minute and you sapu all the prawn! Damn buay steady, ah, you!" (Holy cow, I left the place for two minutes and you hoarded all the prawns for yourself! How unethical of you!)*

buay swee Hokkien phrase literally meaning "not pretty". It is used to denote a person's actions as suspicious, biased or unfair.
"I treat you so well, and you sabo me in front of the boss! You damn buay swee, leh!" (I treat you so well, and yet you humiliated me in front of the boss! You're really underhanded!)

buay tah han / beh tah han |bway tah hahn/bay tah hahn| A hybrid Hokkien-Malay term meaning, "I can't stand it" or "I can't deal with it". (Hokkien for cannot is "buay" and "tahan" in Malay is "endure".)
1 *"Why must he speak with that accent? Damn beh tahan!" (Why must he speak with that accent? I can't stand it!)*
2 *"Aiyah, sometimes I really buay tahan him!" (Argh, sometimes I really can't stand him!)*

buay tzai |bway tzah-ee| Hokkien for "not calm". Used to describe someone as nervous and unsteady.
"Do this sort of thing is very easy. Why you so buay tzai one?" (These tasks are very easy. Why are you so nervous?)
See also **ai tzai, tzai**

buay tze tong |bway tz tong| Hokkien phrase referring to an inconsiderate person or someone who lacks initiative. Literally, "does not know how to move by oneself."
"He see her got so many things to carry then still donno how to go and help. Damn buay tze tong, leh!" (Despite seeing the woman struggling with so many packages, he didn't help her. How inconsiderate!)

buaya |bwah-yah| Malay for "crocodile". Means "lothario" or wolf, i.e. a sleazy pick-up artist. May also be used as a verb.
1 *"Saturday night, that club, ah, full of buaya, one." (On Saturday night, that club is packed with men on the prowl.)*
2 *"Johnny's buaya-ing Jane, even though he's supposed to be Jenny's stead. What a chao buaya." (Johnny's trying to pick Jane up, even though he's supposed to be going steady with Jenny. What a sleazebag.)*

bully kichi |bully kee-chi'h| To pick on someone smaller or less powerful than oneself. "Kichi" is a common mispronunciation of the Malay word "kechil" (small).

⊡ *"Eh, dun think just because you become assistant manager, you can bully kichi, okay!" (Don't think that just because you've been promoted to assistant manager, you can push your subordinates around!)*

bung kah tio lum pah |bahng kah tee-o'h lahm pah| Literally meaning "mosquito biting the testicles", this is a term used to describe a painful dilemma, where all options carry dire consequences. Similar in spirit to "Hobson's Choice", "to be caught between a rock and a hard place" and "to be caught between Scylla and Charybdis", it means that one has no real choice at all. Believed to have originated in rural China, by farmers who had to relieve themselves in mosquito-infested fields.

⊡ *"I don'ch whack him, he sure damn ya ya one. I whack him, he sure report me to police. Wah lan eh, this is damn bung kah tio lum pah!" (If I don't hit him, he'll be swaggering insufferably. Yet, if I do hit him, he's sure to report me to the police. Man, this is really to be caught between a rock and a hard place!)*

bungkus |boong-koos| Malay for "wrap up" or "bundle". In Singlish, its use is almost exclusively limited to take-away meals.

⊡ *"Bang, gimme one nasi lemak, one mee rebus. Bungkus, yah?" (Bro, one order of nasi lemak and one order of mee rebus to go, please.)*

See also **tar pao**

buruk |boo-ro'h| Malay adjective meaning "evil" or "wicked". Used in the Malay style, i.e. after the noun.

⊡ *"Rahman has become this lawyer buruk." (Rahman has become an evil lawyer.)*

busok |boo-so'h| Derived from "berbau busuk", Malay for "smelly". Used to accuse someone of either having body odour or being a cheat.

1 *"Wah lau, you whole month never bathe, ah? Damn bleddy busok!" (Holy cow, did you not bathe for a month or something? You really stink!)*

2 *"I dun friend you, you play mahjong very busok one." (I'm not going to be your friend; you cheat when you play mahjong.)*

See also **bangsat, chao, chao kuan, chao kah, mungsat**

Cc

cabut |chah-bote| Derived from "cabut", the Malay word for "abstract", "remove" or "to take out", in Singlish it has come to mean "flee" or "escape", and is often used where the context of flight is urgent or unexpected.

[1] *"If the teacher comes, we all cabut, OK?" (If the teacher comes, we're all going to take off, okay?)*

[2] *"I tried to find him, but he cabutted already." (I tried to find him, but he already fled.)*

calefare |care-lare-fare| Colloquial Cantonese for "movie extra", it is also used to describe people as idle hangers-on or layabouts. Can also be used as a verb, as in "to calefare".

[1] *"Eh, next week my company got product launch for TV. If got time, come and calefare, lah." (Hey, next week, my company is launching a product on television. If you're free, come and be an extra.)*

[2] *"Since he kena retrenched, he whole day go kopi tiam and calefare around." (Since he was retrenched, he spends the entire day hanging around the coffee shop.)*

call To greet someone. From the Hokkien word "kio" which can mean either "call", or "greet".

[•] *"Boy-boy, faster come and call Auntie Bee Leng." (Son, hurry over here and greet Auntie Bee Leng.)*

can [1] Monosyllabic answer denoting one's ability to fulfil a requested task. "No problem."

[•] *Beng: "Eh, Seng, lend me your car, leh." (Hey, Seng, can I borrow your car?)*
Seng: "Can." (Sure.)

[2] An adjective used to praise one for one's abilities.

[1] *"Wah, you got so many A-stars! You damn can, hor?" (Wow, you scored so many A-stars! You're really capable!)*

[2] *"Of course he'll solve the problem. He very can one!" (Of course he'll solve the problem. He's really ingenious.)*

can die An exclamation of simultaneous despair and horror.

[1] *"Wah lau, this new 'A' level syllabus damn can die one!" (Man, this new "A" level syllabus is horrific!)*

[2] *Beng: "How's work?" (How's work?)*
Seng: "Can die, man." (Horrible!)

can I hepchu? |can I hep-choo?| Common pronunciation of "can I help you?", especially in department stores.
[·] *Salesgirl: "Can I hepchu?" (Can I help you?)*
Customer: "Sorry, my name not Choo." (Sorry, my name is not Choo.)
(Clearly this joke doesn't work in English — Ed.)
See also **can you help me**

can or not? Asking whether something is permissible. This is the Anglicized version of the Hokkien phrase "eh sai bo?"
[1] *"Today after school follow me go downtown, can or not?" (Today, after school has been dismissed, would you be willing to follow me downtown?)*
[2] *"Eh, borrow me $5 today, tomorrow I return you, can or not?" (Hey, would you be able to lend me $5 today? I'll return it to you tomorrow.)*
See also **eh sai / eh sai boh**

can you help me While this seems like a regular plea for assistance, in Singapore, "Can you help me…" is often a specific request for one to take over the task completely, while the pleader does something else. Very rarely is it a request for one to work alongside the pleader. E.g. "Can you help me wash the car?" doesn't mean "Please assist me by washing the car together with me." Rather, it means "Please help me by washing the car for me while I do something else entirely." See also **can I hepchu**

cannot make it / CMI To try, but fall far short of any acceptable standard. An exclamation denoting resignation and despair, it is often abbreviated to its initials. Applicable to both people and objects.
[1] *"One beer only concuss already! His drinking skill damn cannot make it, man!" (Only one beer and he's passed out! His drinking skills are really substandard.)*
[2] *"His new car two weeks old only, oreddy spoil three times. I told him already, Proton Saga: cannot make it." (His two week old car has already broken down three times. I've already told him that Proton Sagas are rubbish.)*
[3] *"Aiyah, almost 5am oreddy and still haven't finish studying for the exam. CMI liao, lah!" (Argh, it's almost 5am and I still haven't finished studying for the exam. I'm doomed!)*
See also **buay sai**

cartoon Used to describe someone or something as funny or silly.
[·] *"Aiyah, he's never serious; always damn cartoon one." (Oh, he's*

never serious. He's always such a clown.)

catch no ball The literal translation of the Hokkien phrase "liak boh kiew". Means to completely not understand.

1 *"Wah, that movie was so cheem, I totally catch no ball, man!" (Wow, that movie was so deep, I completely didn't understand it.)*

2 *"His accent is so powderful, I completely catch no ball." (His accent is so strong, I totally don't understand what he's saying.)*

See also **liak boh kiew**

catching The Singaporean name for the game of "Tag".

"Chewren that time we play catching, hor, Ah Beng always play cheat one." (When we were kids, Ah Beng always cheated whenever we played "Tag".)

See also **chope, pasang**

cha si lang / cha si nang |cha see lahng/cha see nahng| Hokkien term which translates as "annoying people to death". It is used to admonish noisy people.

"I'm trying to study! Can you karaoke somewhere else, not? Cha si lang!" (I'm trying to study! Can you go and perform your karaoke somewhere else? You're driving me round the bend with your noise!)

challen The Singlish pronunciation of "challenge".

"Next week, I challen you go MacRitchie and run." (Next week, I challenge you to a race at MacRitchie Reservoir.)

cham |chum| A Hokkien word meaning "pitifully disastrous", it is usually uttered with a sad shake of one's head.

1 *"His girlfriend ran off with his grandfather? Aiyah, damn cham one." (His girlfriend ran off with his grandfather? Oh, what a disaster.)*

2 *"Why you so cham, every day kena sai from your teacher one?" (Why are you so unlucky, getting crap from your teacher everyday?)*

cham siong |chum see-ohng| To negotiate or come to an agreement in order to get out of a spot of trouble.

1 *"Officer, no need to fine me leh. Cham siong, can or not?" (Officer, is fining me totally necessary? Can we come to some sort of alternative arrangement?)*

2 *"Aiyah, he not so bad, lah. Cham siong-cham siong sure can, one." (Oh, he's not so bad. I'm sure you'll be able to come to some arrangement where you're let off the hook.)*

champion A term describing the unbelievable actions of a person. Usually used in a sarcastic and somewhat derogatory manner.

Ah Beng: "Wah lau! You never hear! Ah Seng is in hospital! His finger kena bitten off by his hamster!" (Holy cow! Did you hear? Ah

Seng is in the hospital! His finger was bitten off by his hamster!,
Ah Meng: "Serious ah? He damn champion, man!" (Are you serious? That really takes the cake!)

chankyewp / chankyewps Common pronunciation of "thank you".

Channel Five To speak in English or be an Anglophile.
⊡ *"Ha? He go see Hong Kong movie? I thought he very Channel Five one?"* (He went to watch a Hong Kong movie? I'm surprised, as I thought he was an Anglophile.)
See also **Channel Eight**

Channel Eight To speak in Mandarin or be very Chinese-educated.
⊡ *"Brudder, Channel Eight, can? My kaki all helicotter one, you slang like that, they catch no ball."* (Brother, would you mind speaking in Mandarin? My friends here are all Chinese educated, and with your thick Western accent, they have no idea what you're saying.)
See also **Channel Five**

chao [1] |tsao| Hokkien for "to run". Can also mean to dodge or skive. Curiously, nowadays, it's also sometimes used very much like "goodbye" a la the Italian "ciao", which sounds very similar.
1 *"Got mad dog chase you — chao like siao, man!"* (If a mad dog chases you — run like crazy!)
2 *"Want to chao class today?"* (Do you want to skip class today?)
3 *Beng: "Eh, see you tomorrow."* (See you tomorrow.)
Seng: "OK. Chao liao!" (Okay. I'm off!)
See also **pontang, siam, tuang**

[2] |chow| Hokkien for "smelly". Used to add emphasis to one's unsavoury traits, similar to "damn" or "bloody". Can also be used to describe someone as unethical.
1 *"Wah lau! You one month never bathe, is it! Damn chao, man!"* (Holy cow! Have you gone an entire month without bathing or something? You stink!)
2 *"Don't play mahjong with him. He always play damn chao, one."* (Don't play mahjong with him. He's always playing dirty.)
3 *"He's such a chao lawyer! Whole life cannot get straight answer from him, one."* (He's such a bloody lawyer! One can never get a straight answer from him.)
See also **bangsat, busok, chao kuan, chao kah, mungsat**

chao Ah Beng / chao Ah Lian / CAB Quintessential examples of Ah Bengs or Ah Lians. Sometimes abbreviated to "CAB".
1 *"Wah lau eh, your ringtone, hor, is damn chao Ah Beng one."* (Man, only a real Ah Beng would have a ringtone like yours.)
2 *"Eh, don't go to that launge lah. That place full of CABs one!"*

(Please don't go to that lounge. It's full of louts.)
See also **Ah Beng, Ah Lian**

chao ang moh |chow ahng maw| Literally, Hokkien for "smelly red hair". A pejorative reference to Caucasians.
⊡ *"Betty always por chao ang moh, one." (Betty is always sucking up to those smelly Caucasians.)*
See also **ang moh, ang moh gao, ang moh kwee, mat salleh, orang putih**

chao chui |chow choo-ee| Hokkien for speaking ill of others. Describes someone who never has anything good to say.
⊡ *"Every time I meet Ah Beng, he always say I put on weight. He damn chao chui, one!" (Every time I meet Ah Beng, he always says I've put on weight. He really can't seem to be able to say anything nice.)*
See also **chee bye mouth**

chao kah Literally, Hokkien for "smelly feet". A bad loser or cheat.
⊡ *"Don't go and play mahjong with him. He damn chao kah one." (Don't play mahjong with him. He always plays dirty.)*
See also **cheaterbug, play cheat**

chao keng |chao gkeng| To act or pretend in order to either impress others or escape being given extra duties.
1 *"Don't chao keng lah, we know you very good leow." (You can dispense with your act. We already know how good you are.)*
2 *"No need to chao keng anymore... the other guy oreddy kena arrow." (You can stop putting on your act. The other guy's already been stuck with the task.)*
See also **wayang**

chao kuan |chow koo-ahn| Literally, Hokkien for "smelly-type". Used to describe a cheat or devious person.
⊡ *"Don't go and buy from him. He damn chao kuan one." (Don't patronize his store. He's a dirty dealer.)*

chap cheng |tzahp tz'eng| Hokkien for "mixed kind", a derogatory term used to refer to people of mixed racial origins, such as Eurasians.
⊡ *"A lot of chap cheng chewren all quite swee, hor." (Many children of mixed racial parentage are quite attractive.)*
See also **geragok, serani**

chap chye |tzahp chai| A popular Hokkien dish of stewed mixed vegetables. Is sometimes used as an adjective to describe something as being of an indeterminate or inharmonious mix.
⊡ *"Gahmen say we must stop speaking chap chye Mandarin." (The government says we should stop incorporating non-Mandarin words when we speak Mandarin.)*

See also **rojak**

chap sar tiam |tzahp sah dtee-ahm| Literally, "13 o'clock". A Hokkien expression describing something as half-baked or incompetent.

1 *"Don't go and ask Ah Seng to do it. He very chap sar tiam one." (Don't ask Ah Seng to do it. He's incompetent.)*

2 *"Wah lau eh, what kind of chap sar tiam company is this? Even fax machine also don't have!" (What kind of crappy company is this? They don't even have a fax machine!)*

See also **half past six, kucing kurap**

chapalang |chahp'lahng| An indiscriminate mix of odds and ends, or sometimes even people. It usually connotes a lack of class

1 *Tai Tai: "These all diamond one, ah?" (Are these all diamonds?) Salesman: "No, just chapalang, one." (No, they're just a mix of this and that.)*

2 *"Got all sorts of chapalang people working in the nightclub industry." (There are all sorts of low lifes working in the nightclub industry.)*

See also **humpalang**

char bor |tzah-baw| Hokkien for "woman" or "female".

"Char bor can be very hiong, one. Don't anyhow play-play, okay!" (Hell hath no fury like a woman scorned.)

char tao |tsah tau| Hokkien for "wooden head". Similar to "idiot". Can be either an adjective or noun.

1 *"Don't ask Ah Seng to do it. He damn char tau, one." (Don't ask Ah Seng to do it. He's such a moron.)*

2 *"How many times must I explain! Why you so char tau one?" (How many times must I explain this to you? Why are you so idiotic?)*

See also **gorblok**

cheat my money To be tricked into something. Often used when there is no overt fraud, but when feeling upset at having entered into an imprudent bargain.

"Wah lau, kway teow $25 one plate? Eh, hotel, no hotel, this is damn cheat my money one!" (What, $25 for a plate of kway teow? I know this is a hotel, but the prices are a real rip-off!)

cheaterbug Local epithet for cheaters, usually used by children. Of uncertain provenance.

"Ah Beng copy my homework! He's such a cheaterbug!" (Ah Beng is copying my homework! He's such a cheater!)

chee bye |chee bai| One of the rudest terms in Singlish. Essentially, "vagina", though not confined to clinical gynaecological circumstances. The English equivalent would be "cunt".

1 *"I this week spend over $700 on 4D, but never touch! Chee bye!" (Despite spending over $700 on lottery tickets this week, none of them won. Damn!)*

2 *"Oi, chee bye! Come here! Why you go and scratch my car?" (Hey! Come here, you cunt! Why did you scratch my car?)*

chee bye mouth A very rude way to describe someone who goes around saying bad things about others.

▪ *"That Madam Tan, ah, is a damn chee bye mouth! Whole day go round telling people I kena arrested!" (That Madam Tan keeps spreading all these disgusting rumours! She's been going around telling people that I've been arrested!)*

See also **chao chui**

chee hong The even ruder version of "pok". Used in an identical way. See also **buaya, pok**

chee ko Hokkien for "lewd", "lascivious" and "lecherous".

▪ *"When you go into Mr Tan office that time, hor, be careful. He can be a bit chee ko, one." (When you enter Mr Tan's office, be careful. He can be quite lecherous.)*

See also **chee ko pek, hum sup loh, lao ter kor, ter kor**

chee ko pek |tjee gkoh pe'h| Hokkien for "dirty old man". An elderly lecher.

▪ *"Wah lau, look at that uncle, whole day sit by the public pool beo char bor. What a chee ko pek." (Look at that old man! He spends the whole day ogling girls at the public pool. What a lecher!)*

See also **hum sup loh, lao ter kor, se lang, ter kor**

cheebilised A sarcastic and crude way of saying "civilised". Obviously a fusion of "chee bye" and civilised.

1 *"Wah! Every time see you wear clothes until kana sai. Today wear until so cheebilised for what?" (Whoa! Your dress sense is usually so bad, so how come you're all sophisticated today?)*

2 *"Every time come out all the four-letter word! You very cheebilised, hor!" (You're always swearing. How civilized of you!)*

cheem Hokkien term meaning something is profound or deep or intellectual.

1 *"You study philosophy? Wah lau, damn cheem, man!" (You're studying philosophy? Whoa, that's deep stuff, man!)*

2 *"Aiyoh, that Jacques Derrida, hor, is si beh cheem. I read until gong-gong." (Man, that Jacques Derrida is really deep. Reading his stuff makes me giddy.)*

cheemkology / cheeminology A hybrid English-Hokkien word meaning that something is written in a bombastic or excessively intellectual fashion, such that it is completely incomprehensible.

☐ *"Eh, when you write essay that time, can cut down on the chee-ni-nology or not?" (Hey, when writing your essays, can you avoid using highfalutin language?)*

See also **cheem**

cheena A pejorative term used, mostly by uppity English-educated Singaporeans, to describe someone who exhibits the unrefined and unsophisticated behaviour they associate with nouveau riche or arriviste Chinese people, such as opportunism, rudeness, boorishness and a predilection for the tacky.

1 *"Wah lau, did you check out Mr Tan's luminous yellow Mercedes? Damn cheena, man!" (Have you seen Mr Tan's luminous yellow Mercedes? It's hideous!)*

2 *"Why you go and download such a cheena ring tone? Super cheena beng, man!" (Why did you download such a tacky ring tone? It's really too gross!)*

See also **beng, ching chong, cheenagerk, cheenapiang, sinkek**

cheenagerk |cheena-gu'h| A pejorative term used by Peranakans (Straits-born Chinese) to distance themselves from their fresh-from-the-mainland cousins, who are seen as lower class, vulgar, unsophisticated, and tacky. Probably derived from the Malay word "Cina" for "China".

☐ *"Alamak, why Auntie Poh Neo go and buy that cheena Versace dress? She looks so cheenagerk!" (Oh dear, whatever possessed Auntie Poh Neo to buy that garish Versace dress? She looks so tacky!)*

See also **cheena, cheenapiang, obiang**

cheenapandi A racist term that Indians use to describe Chinese. "Pandi" means pig in Tamil, and Singaporean Indians perceive a strong association between Chinese people and their consumption of pork. See also **cheenapiang, munjen**

cheenapiang / cheenapok A ruder version of "cheena". Is both a noun and a verb.

1 *"Wah lau! He's super cheenapiang, man. Hear how he speak English!" (Whoa, how much more Chinese can he get? Listen to the way he speaks English!)*

2 *"Mr Chen is a real cheenapok. Look at him with his perm, gold chains and long last fingernail!"*

See also **cheena, cheenagerk, munjen**

cheng hu |tzeng hoo| Hokkien for "government".

☐ *"Why you so goondu, go and believe everything cheng hu tell you?" (Why are you so dumb, believing everything the Government tells you?)*

See also **gahmen, boh cheng hu**

cheng hu kang |tzeng hoo gkahng| Hokkien for "government job". In the old days, it was seen as an honour and privilege to work for the civil service. So Chinese parents would always tell their children to go and "chuay cheng hu kang" (find a job with the government).

cheo |tzee-oh| An informal invitation to some activity.

☐ *"Wah lau! You all yesterlay go Zouk neh cheo me one." (Hey! You guys all went to Zouk yesterday. How come you didn't include me?)*

cher |tcher| Not to be confused with the surgically-enhanced American singer, this is just a short and snappy way to address one's teacher.

☐ *"Eskew me, cher, can go toilet?" (Excuse me, teacher, please may I go to the toilet?)*

chey / chey! / cheyyyyyy |chay| Of uncertain origin, "chey" is a popular expression of contempt, disdain, or derision towards a person, object, or situation, especially when high hopes have been crushed. Two common variants in pronunciation exist, to convey varying degrees of negativity. **[1]** "Chey!" — expresses scorn or contempt. **[2]** "Cheyyyyyy" — longer-drawn out variant of the above, expressing disappointment or regret.

[1] *"Chey! Lai dat only?? You say until so good, I thought what. Waste my money!" (Damn! You mean that's it? You described it so well, I was expecting a lot more. What a waste of money!)*

[2] *"Eh!! Over there got chio bu!" (Hey, check out the hot chick!) And upon getting a closer look: "Cheyyyyyy, face damn hojjiber. Look good from behind only." (Ugh, what an awful face. She only looks good from behind.)*

chey bah! Not to be confused with "chey" (above), this is an expression of encouragement and admiration.

☐ *"I heard your noong kia won the Baby Contest? Chey bah!" (I heard your child won the Baby Contest? Well done!)*

See also **steady**

chi teh bin |tzee dtay bin| Literally translates from Hokkien as "a piece of face". Describes someone who displays a sour face, suggesting he is arrogant or spoiling for a fight.

☐ *"Wah lau, I do'wan to work with Ah Beng, ah. He everyday also damn chi teh bin." (Man, I don't want to work with Ah Beng. Everyday, he's got that sour face on."*

See also **bin chao chao**

chia |tchee-ah| Hokkien for "to treat", i.e. to pay for another's entertainment, food or drink.

1 *"You yesterday tio beh pio, today must chia, lah!" (As you won money at the race track yesterday, you should give us all a treat today!)*

2 *"Come, I chia you go eat ice kacang!" (Come, let me treat you to an ice kacang!)*

See also **blanja, spend**

chia lat |tjee-ah laht| Hokkien adjective literally meaning "to eat strength". It means that a task is onerous and consumes one's energy. Often also used to denote being in trouble. Is sometimes used to denote the overpowering nature of something horrible.

1 *"Wah, doing my income tax is damn chia lat." (Filing my income tax return is very difficult.)*

2 *"You three years neh file your income tax? Wah lau eh, you damn chia lat liao." (You haven't filed your income tax returns for three years? Boy, you're in trouble!)*

3 *"Wah piang! Your BO, hor, damn chia lat, man!" (Oh man, your body odour is really powerful!)*

See also **fierce, garang, hiong, powderful, siong, terror**

chiak |tjee-a'h| Hokkien for "eat". Is also the Hokkien equivalent of "bon appetit" at the dinner table, i.e. an invitation to commence eating.

1 *"Chiak pah buay? If not, we can go Geylang and whack." (Have you eaten? If not, we can go to Geylang and get something to eat.)*

2 *"Today I touch 4D, so I chia you all chiak, lah!" (I won the lottery today, so I'm buying everyone a meal!)*

3 *"Everyone dun pai seh, hor! Chiak, chiak, chiak!" (Please, everyone, don't stand on ceremony! Tuck in!)*

See also **makan**

chiak buay liao |tjee-a'h bway leow| Hokkien phrase meaning "unable to finish eating". It means to have come into great, unending fortune.

"Wah, your father now Minister. Lai dat, you chiak buay liao, lah!" (Wow, with your father now a Minister, you'll never starve!)

See also **bee tang chiak buay liao**

chiak chao |tjee-a'h ts'ao| Hokkien phrase which literally means "eating grass". It is used to describe impoverishment, and having to forego luxuries.

"I go casino, suay-suay lose everything, so now I have to chiak chow till payday." (Unfortunately, I lost everything at the casino,

so I'm on an austerity drive till payday.)

chiak chua |tjee-a'h tzoo-ah| Hokkien term literally meaning, "to eat snake". Means to goof off or skive.

⊡ *"Just because you outstation doesn't mean you can chiak chua, okay?" (Just because you're stationed overseas doesn't mean you can goof off, alright?)*

See also **keng, tuang**

chiak hong |tjee-a'h hong| A Hokkien phrase which literally translates as "eating wind". It means to go on a holiday.

⊡ *"Last week, I went Hong Kong chiak hong." (Last week, I went to Hong Kong for a holiday.)*

chiak kantang |tjee-a'h kahn-tahng| Literally, "eating potatoes", this is a classic Singlish mix of local languages. "Chiak" in Hokkien means "eat", while "kentang" is Malay for "potato". A pejorative expression used to describe an Asian who speaks with a Western accent.

⊡ *"He go Cambridge one year, come back only chia kantang." (He went to study in Cambridge for only a year, yet returned with a Western accent.)*

chiak kuay-kuay |tjee-a'h koo-eh koo-eh| Literally translated from Hokkien as "to eat over and over", this phrase is used to describe achieving a crushing victory, and is often said with a mixture of confidence and arrogance.

⊡ *Beng: "Wah lau, today's maths paper si beh siong, leh." (Man, today's maths paper was really difficult.)*

Seng: "Ai tzai lah, I got study, chiak kuay-kuay one." (Relax. I studied, so I think I'll ace it.)

See also **sure can one**

chiak lang |tjee-a'h lahng| Hokkien phrase literally translated as "eating people". It is used to describe someone as exploitative.

⊡ *"I always kena overtime, but never get overtime pay. My company damn chiak lang, man!" (I'm always working overtime without overtime pay. My company is really exploitative!)*

chiak leow bee |tjee-a'h lee-ow bee| Hokkien phrase literally meaning to "a waste of rice". It describes someone as useless, or having wasted time or resources.

⊡ *"Spend so much money on tuition and still always fail your exam? You damn chiak leow bee!" (You're spending so much money on tuition and yet you're always failing your exams? You're really wasting your money!)*

chiak lui |tjee-a'h looi| Hokkien phrase that literally translates as "eating money". It is used to describe someone as a con man or cheat.

⊡ *"You invest money with Ah Long must be careful. Skarly he chiak lui, then you know." (If you're thinking of investing with that loan shark, you must be careful, as he might cheat you of your money.)*

chiak pah boh sai pang |tjee-a'h pah boh sai pbahng| Hokkien expression which literally translates as "finished eating, no shit to excrete". A phrase used to denote that someone is frivolous and has too much time on one's hands.

⊡ *"Why you always come and disturb me? Chiak pah boh sai pang!" (Why must you always come over and annoy me? You must have nothing better to do!)*

chiak pah pak ka chng |tjee-a'h bpah pa'h kah ts'ng| Hokkien phrase literally meaning "eat till full, hit backside". It means to be able to enjoy without paying.

⊡ *"Eh, you think this your grandfather restaurant, can chiak pah pak ka chng, is it?" (Hey, do you think this is your grandfather's restaurant or something, where you can just eat without paying?)*

chiak sior eng |tjee-a'h see-or eng| Hokkien expression meaning, "too free".

⊡ *"Play golf on a weekday?! Chiak sior eng ah?!" (Playing golf on a weekday? You must be too free!)*

See also **chiak pah boh sai pang, eng**

chiam see tong With all due respect to opposition MP Mr Chiam See Tong, this phrase is actually Hokkien for "endure for the moment" (which ironically may be of some comfort to Mr Chiam).

⊡ *"Wah lau, my this job damn hojjiber, but boh pian. Must chiam see tong, wait until can find better job." (Man, my present job is horrible, but I have no choice. I must endure for the moment, until I can find a better job.)*

chibaboom! / terbaboom! Singaporean sound effect denoting an explosion.

1 *"Then ah, the bomb essploded… CHIBABOOM!" (The bomb then exploded — boom!)*

2 *"Wah lau, wha'ppen to your hair? Terbaboom like that." (Hey, what happened to your hair? It looks like it exploded.)*

See also **a-bssh! piak! piang!**

chichak |chee-cha'h| From the Malay word "cicak", meaning lizard. Generally taken to refer to the household gecko.

⊡ *"Why you tsk-tsk-tsk at me? You chichak, is it?" (Why are you clucking your tongue at me? Are you a gecko?)*

chickabong Of indeterminate origin, this mean spirited term is used to describe an overweight and unattractive girl.
▣ *"Last night you got see Ah Beng, not? He got drunk and went to pok this super chickabong." (Did you see Ah Beng last night? He got drunk and went to seduce a very fat woman.)*

chicken / chicken feed In traditional English, the term "chicken feed" refers to a trifling amount of money, e.g. "I'm earning chicken feed compared to most lawyers." In Singlish, its use has been expanded to include tasks that are ridiculously easy to accomplish. It is also commonly mispronounced "chicken feet" and very often abbreviated to just "chicken".
1 *Ah Beng: "Eh, how? Maths test hard or not?" (Hey, was the maths test hard?)*
Ah Seng: "Aiyah, chicken feed, lah!" (Ah, it was really easy!)
2 *Ah Lian: "Wah! Ah Beng sio hoong kee can make ring ring!" (When Ah Beng smokes, he can exhale smoke rings!)*
Ah Seng: "Aiyah, damn chicken one, lah!" (Ah, there's nothing to it!)
Ah Lian: "You can, meh?" (But can you do it?)

chik ak |tchi'k a'h| A Hokkien term which has two uses: the first is an exclamation like "what a pity!" and the second is a verb that means to build bad karma, i.e. to do something that will return to haunt you.
1 *"He so smart, become scholar, then go and kill himself. Aiyoh, damn chik ak!" (He's so such a smart fellow that he became a scholar. However, he killed himself. What a pity!)*
2 *"Mr Tan whole day treat his employee like sai like that. He damn chik ak, one." (Mr Tan always treats his employees in a crappy manner. This will come back and haunt him in the future.)*

chilli padi |chilli pah-dee| Chilli padi is a small but powerful chilli pepper. A euphemism for a petite but feisty, and often sexy, woman.
▣ *"You see Sharon so small-small, but don't play-play, okay! She chilli padi one!" (Don't think that just because Sharon is so small, you can toy with her. She's tougher than she looks!)*

chin chai |ts'in ts'ai| Hokkien term meaning "unconcerned about details", i.e. easygoing, undemanding and relaxed.
▣ *"Relak, he's very chin chai about this sort of thing." (Relax, he's very laid back about such matters.)*

chin chuay tai ji |tjin tjoo-eh dtai tjee| Hokkien for "plenty of issues".
1 *"He, hor, chin chuay tai ji one." (He is full of issues.)*
2 *"Wah lau, this sort of simple-simple thing, he make until chin chuay tai ji." (How did he complicate such a simple matter?)*

chin poh / chin poh sai |chüeen bpoh sah-ee| "Chin poh" is Cantonese for "the pot is broken". Chin poh sai means "the entire pot has been broken." The equivalent of the English phrase "to let the cat out of the bag", meaning that a secret has been suddenly revealed.

1 *"Oi! Who chin poh that I kena retrench?" (Hey! Who let it slip that I was retrenched?)*

2 *"When Mr Tan took his mistress out to dinner, they met his wife's brother there. Wah, chin poh sai, man!" (When Mr Tan took his mistress out to dinner, they bumped into his wife's brother. Looks like the cat is out of the bag.)*

See also **pecah lobang**

ching-chong Another derogatory term for someone who is very "cheena". Usually used with the suffix "Chinaman". There is probably a subtle shade of difference between "ching-chong" and "cheena". "Ching-chongness" tends to be slightly more lighthearted, whereas "cheena" carries more dismissive overtones.

"You don'ch know meh? His father very ching-chong Chinaman one, always wear pyjama at home." (Didn't you know? His father is a real Chinaman, always wearing pyjamas around the house.)

See also **cheena, cheenagerk, cheenapiang**

chio |chee-oh| A somewhat impolite way of describing a woman as pretty. Not to be confused with "sio".

"Checkout that chick, man. Damn chio!" (Look at that woman. She's a real babe!)

See also **chio bu, jambu, jude, sio**

chio bu |chee-oh boo| A pretty woman. A somewhat rude term.

"Far East Plaza got a lot of chio bu." (You can find many pretty women at Far East Plaza.)

See also **chio, jambu, jude, sio**

chio kao peng |chee-oh gkao bpeng| Hokkien phrase meaning "to laugh until one falls down".

"You got see this week's TalkingCock update? I chio kao peng, man." (Did you see this week's TalkingCock update? I laughed till I fell over!)

chiong |chee-ong| Hokkien for "to rush forward". It is also used to denote creating havoc and/or having fun.

1 *"Eh, today after work, go where and chiong?" (Hey, after work today, want to go somewhere and go crazy?)*

2 *"This kind of thing, must think first. Cannot anyhow chiong!" (With such matters, you need to think carefully. You can't just rush into it.)*

cho |tzo| Hokkien for "to make" or "to do".

⊡ *"Of all people, why you go and call him? He eh sai cho, meh?" (Of all people, why did you pick him? Do you really think he can do the job?)*

cho boh |tzo boh| A Hokkien phrase meaning "idle", with some hint of restiveness too. Literally: "Doing nothing".

1 *"He kena retrench, so now whole day stay at home and cho boh." (He was retrenched, so now he spends the whole day at home doing nothing.)*

2 *"You go and sign up for Singapore Idol for what? You so cho boh, meh?" (Why did you sign up for Singapore Idol? Don't you have anything better to do?)*

See also **boh liao, cho boh lan, gatal, itchy backside, kiao kah yo lum pah, wu liao**

cho boh lan |tzo boh lahn| A ruder version of "cho boh" (above). Literally: "Does no penis".

⊡ *"You go and hire him for what? He damn cho boh lan one." (Why did you hire him? He's a useless bum!)*

See also **boh liao, cho boh, gatal, itchy backside, kiao kah yo lum pah, wu liao**

cho matrix |tzo may-triks| Literally, to "do Matrix". A term commonly used by lower-ranking National Servicemen in the Singapore Armed Forces to describe having to dodge unpleasant tasks, much like the classic slow-motion sequence in the movie "The Matrix", where Keanu Reeves' character dodges multiple bullets.

⊡ *"Wah lan eh! Chief Clerk table got helluva lot of files. Today sure whole day cho Matrix leow." (Holy cow! The Chief Clerk has a heap of files on her table. I think we'll be dodging assignments the entire day.)*

cho seng lee |tzo seng lee| Hokkien for "to do business".

1 *"You want to cho seng lee, must thick skin a bit." (If you wish to do business, you have to develop a thick skin.)*

2 *"Aiyah, relac one corner, can? Cho seng lee is like that, one." (Hey, relax! These are just the vagaries of doing business.)*

3 *"Mr Tan went Shanghai to cho seng lee." (Mr Tan went to Shanghai to engage in business.)*

chochok |cho-cho'| Derived from the Malay word "cucuk", which means "to prick" or "to poke". It is used in the sense of "disturb", "bother", "rib", or "make fun of". Like the equivalent Hokkien phrase "ji seow", it can also mean to masturbate or be a prick-tease, despite the probably innocuous source-word.

⊡ *"That guy damn joker one, always come and chochok me." (He's*

such a prankster, always coming to bother me.)
See also **ji seow**

chong sai kong |tz'ong sai gkong| The Cantonese equivalent of "ah then?" or "arbuthen?", an expression similar to "needless to say", "well, of course!" or "duh!"
⊡ *"You eat this mouldy bread, no wonder kena stomach ache! Chong sai kong!" (You ate this mouldy bread? Well, duh! No wonder you have a stomach ache!)*
See **ah then, arbuthen**

choon boh? |tzoon boh| Hokkien phrase meaning "are you accurate or not?" Used to express scepticism at a claim.
⊡ *"That goondu actually pok that chio bu? Choon boh?" (That loser actually managed to woo that pretty girl? Are you sure?)*

chop chop kali pok Onomatopoeic term denoting being in a hurry. "Kali pok" is the Singlish pronunciation of "curry puff".
⊡ *"Eh, quick leh, late oreddy. Chop chop kali pok, can?!" (Hey, we're already late! Can you hurry it up?)*

chope To reserve or hold something for somebody. Sometimes used in games to indicate having attained a "safe" position. Also sometimes uttered as an apology for deviating from a topic of conversation in order to ask a more pressing question.
1 *"If we're not at the theatre by 8, can you chope some seats for us?" (If we're not at the theatre by 8, can you reserve some seats for us?)*
2 *"Eh, cannot pasang me! I chope oreddy!" (Hey, you can't make me "it". I'm already "safe"!)*
3 *"Chope, so tonight eat what, ah?" (Just a moment, I'm very sorry about deviating from the topic of our conversation, but I really must ask what we're having for dinner tonight?)*
See also **no bilis, pasang**

chor / chor lor |chaw law| Hokkien for "rough" or "crude", and sometimes "physically rough".
1 *"You got hear Ah Lian swear, not? Damn chor lor, man!" (Have you heard the way Ah Lian swears? She's really crude!)*
2 *"Piang eh, today the other rugby team play until damn chor, man" (Whoa, the other rugby team really played rough today!)*

chuak / chuak tio |choo-a'h tee-o'h| To be shocked or stunned.
⊡ *"I went in and saw him doing donno what with the dog, and I chuak tio." (I was shocked when I went in and saw him doing god knows what with the dog.)*

chuay si |choo-ay see| Literally, "looking for death". Courting disaster.
⊡ *"Oi! Don't play near the construction site! You chuay si, is it?"*

(Hey, don't play near the construction site! Do you have a death wish or something?)

See also **ai si**

chui kana kah, kah kana lum pah |ts'ooi gkah-nah kah, kah gkah-nah lahm pah| Literally, Hokkien for "mouth like legs, legs like testicles". Used to describe someone who is extremely clumsy.

⊡ *"Ah Beng chui kana kah, kah kana lum pah, still can join the bomb disposal unit!" (Ah Beng is such a klutz, yet he still managed to get into the bomb disposal unit!)*

See also **ak kah ak chew**

chui kong lum pah song / CKLPS |ts'ooi gkong lum pah song| Hokkien phrase which translates literally as, "mouth talk, testicles feel ecstatic". Used to describe someone who mouths off only to please himself with no benefit to anyone else. Analogous to calling someone a wanker or a "NATO" (No Action, Talk Only). Often abbreviated to its initials.

⊡ *"Aiyah, you listen to the Principal for what? He whole day CKLPS only." (Ah, why are you listening to the Principal? He's full of hot air!)*

See also **NATO**

chut mia |choot mee-ah| Hokkien for "famous".

⊡ *"The beef kway teow at Lorong 9 is damn chut mia, one." (The beef kway teow at Lorong 9 is famous.)*

See also **moh tuck teng, world best**

chut pattern |choot pair-tuhn| Hybrid term which describes either someone revealing himself to be the swine he really is, or someone showing another his bad attitude. "Chut" in Hokkien means, "to come out".

⊡ *"I never thought Johnny would treat his mother like that. Chut pattern oreddy." (I never thought Johnny would treat his mother like that. He's really revealed his true colours.)*

See also **pattern**

cock Despite seemingly obscene connotations, the use of "cock" is actually benign and probably comes from the English term "cock and bull". It is probably the most popular Singlish term used to describe something or someone as being stupid, nonsensical or sub-standard; the local equivalent of "rubbish" or "crap".

1 *"Don't listen to him, he's only talking cock." (Don't listen to him, he's only talking rubbish.)*

2 *"Wah lau, you go and buy this cock thing for what?" (Hey, why on earth did you buy such a crappy item?)*

3 *"Why you so cock, go and invest in that cock dot-com?" (Why were you so stupid, investing in that lousy dot-com?)*

See also **cockanaden, kotek, talk cock**

cockanaden |kok-ker-nah-duhn| A somewhat vulgar way of describing someone as very stupid or addled. Although the word is a combination of "cock" (see above) and "naden" (a common pronunciation of the Tamil name "Nathan"), its use is not restricted to any particular race.

⊡ *Ah Beng: "Eh, where to find the Lim Peh Ka Li Kong column in the TalkingCock wepsite, ah?"* (*Hey, where can I find the Lim Peh Ka Li Kong column in TalkingCock.com?*)
Ah Seng: "Under 'Columns' lah, you cockanaden!" (*Under "Columns", you moron!*)

See also **cock, goondu, kotek, sotong**

{Name of colour} **colour** A common practice amongst Singaporeans to mention a colour, and then tag on the word "colour" after it redundantly, e.g. "blue colour" and "red colour".

[1] *"Seow leow! How come my computer all of a sudden got blue colour screen come out?"* (*What the heck? Why is my computer suddenly showing a blue screen?*)

[2] *"M&M, which colour you like? Red colour, blue colour, yellow colour?"* (*Which colour of M&M's do you like? The red, blue or yellow ones?*)

concuss An adjective used to describe the feeling of having experienced a concussion. Similar to "blur".

⊡ *"I study whole night until concuss."* (*I studied the whole night and now I'm feeling woozy.*)

See also **blur, gong gong**

condemn A Singlish adjective used to describe something as extremely horrible with no redeeming value, or a situation as totally unsalvageable.

[1] *"Ee-yurr, you go and buy that condemn statue for what?"* (*Ugh! Why did you buy that awful statue?*)

[2] *"He do until so condemn, no wonder kena sack."* (*He performed so badly, no wonder he was fired.*)

confirm / confirm and guarantee / confirm plus guarantee / confirm plus guarantee times 2, with 3 year warranty As with English, this establishes the certainty of a proposition. However, in Singlish, it is used as an adjective. Adding "and guarantee" or "plus guarantee times 2, with 3 year warranty", etc. lends greater emphasis.

[1] *"Look at her, she confirm virgin one."* (*Look at her, she is definitely a virgin.*)

[2] *Ah Beng: "Eh, you want to follow us tonight go launge, not?"*

(Hey, do you want to follow us tonight to the lounge?)
Ah Seng: "Confirm!" (Of course!)
[3] *"That guy damn hypocrite man! Got cute girl at the AGM only, he confirm and guarantee wen oppose her and stand up for his opinions." (That guy's a real hypocrite. If there's a cute girl at the AGM, he definitely won't oppose her and stand up for his opinions.)*
[4] *Ah Seng: "Oi, you returning that VCD, not?" (Hey, are you returning that VCD?)*
Ah Beng: "Aiyah, of course lah! Confirm plus guarantee times 2, with 3-year warranty!" (Of course! For sure! Definitely!)

corright The combination of "correct" and "right". Often thought erroneously to be a mispronunciation of "correct", it actually illustrates how Singlish can combine two related words to create a new word with improved potency. Often used as a response when the truth is glaringly obvious.
[·] *Ah Beng: "Your constituency kena walkover again, ah?" (Was your constituency subject to a walkover again?)*
Ah Seng: "Corright!" (Of course!)
See also **ah then / arbo / arbuthen, chong sai kong**

cosmobeng A cosmopolitan Ah Beng. Either **[1]** a man who has all the material trappings of middle-classness, yet remains a boor or **[2]** a person who retains crass, low-brow tastes despite having the requisite educational qualifications.
See **cosmopolitan**

cosmopolitan In English, to be cosmopolitan is to be free from local, provincial, or national ideas, prejudices, or attachments, i.e. someone who is at home all over the world. In Singapore, a "cosmopolitan" has a narrower definition. It is shorthand for a well-travelled and often English-educated urban sophisticate. It has become an aspirational label, and stands in contrast to being a "heartlander". See **heartlander**

counted |gkown-tet| Has the same meaning as its English counterpart, "to count", meaning worthy of consideration, inclusion or accounting. But it's just used differently.
[1] *"This exam counted, not?" (Will my results in this exam be counted towards the final computation of my grades?)*
[2] *"He got the scholarship because his father donated a swimming pool to the uni. So not counted, one." (He only received the scholarship because his father donated a swimming pool to the university. So it doesn't count.)*
See also **pakay**

cripsy The Singlish pronunciation of "crispy".
⊡ *"Wah, I like the Mehnoner french fry... outside very cripsy, inside soft-soft one." (Wow, I like McDonald's french fries... they're crispy on the outside, but soft on the inside.)*

cucuk See **chochok**

curi |choo-ree'h| Malay for "steal" or "pilfer".
⊡ *"I already chope that seat, dun curi OK?" (I've already reserved that seat, so don't take it!)*
See also **kapo**

curi ayam |choo-ree'h ah-yahm| A Malay phrase which literally means "stealing chickens", it is an expression meaning to do something surreptitiously. Exactly what the surreptitious action is depends on the doer, but it's often illicit.
1 *"My wife is out of town! Now I can curi ayam!" (Now that the wife is out of town, I can misbehave!)*
2 *"Once my boss leaves the office then I can curi ayam and talk cock with you, okay?" (Once my boss leaves the office, then I can steal away to come and chat with you.)*

Dd

da A common colloquial tag, similar to "man". Once more closely associated with Singaporeans of Indian origin, it is now used by all races.
1 *"Steady, da! I heard you kena promoted!" (Well done, man. I heard you were promoted!)*
2 *"I'm telling you, da! Take the money and cabut!" (I'm telling you, man! Take the money and run!)*

da bao The Hanyu Pinyin rendition of "tar pao". See **tar pao**

dai kor |dtai gkaw| Cantonese for "big brother", and it is used to refer to any male person more senior (and usually more powerful than you.
⊡ *"You dun bully me! Wait I call my dai kor to hantam you, then you know!" (Don't bully me, or else I'll call my big brother to beat you up!)*

dai kor dai |dtai gkaw dtai| Literally, Cantonese for "big brother big", it is also a common appellation for a triad boss. When mobile phones were first introduced, they were also referred to as "dai kor dai", presumably because they were huge in size, and anyone needing to carry one must be somebody important, like the head of a triad. This use has faded as mobile phones have become more ubiquitous, not to mention smaller.

☐ *"Dun scared, got people come and bully you, our dai kor dai sure arrow his kah kia to hantam them!"* (Don't be scared. If people bully you, the head of our triad will definitely assign his underlings to beat them up.)

See also **tua tao**

dao |dtao| Arrogant and haughty. Basically the same as "ya ya".

☐ *"After he got the scholarship, he became super dao."* (After he got the scholarship, he became very arrogant.)

See also **ya ya, sombong**

damn |damm| To sound proficient in Singlish, substitute "damn" for "very", "really" or "extremely" whenever you can.

1 *"Today damn hot, man!"* (Today is very hot!)

2 *"He kena retrench like that, damn suay, man."* (He's really unlucky to be retrenched like that.)

dey |day| An abbreviation of "adey". See **adey**

die A local exclamation similar to "damn!" but which has the additional meaning of "I'm dead!" or "I'm finished!"

☐ *"Die, lah! I forgot to bring my maths book!"* (I'm dead! I forgot to bring my mathematics text book!)

See also **mati**

die also won't die The Singlish equivalent of "what's the worst that could happen?" or "it won't kill you!", implying that even the worst that could happen isn't all that bad. Used to encourage someone to go ahead with a contemplated action, or to stop worrying about something.

1 *"Why you so worried? I tell you, die also won't die, lah..."* (Why are you so worried? It won't kill you!)

2 *"Faster go ahead with it lah! What's stopping you? At worst, die also won't die..."* (Just go ahead with it quickly! What's stopping you? What's the worst that could happen?)

See also **won't die**

die cock stand Describes one's reaction to an event of immense pleasure. Nearest English approximation: "orgasmic". One grade higher than "steam".

☐ *"Hwah, I yesterday went to Geylang to eat the beef hor fun there.*

Die cock stand, man." (Wow, yesterday I went to Geylang to eat the beef noodles. It was orgasmic, man.)

See also **orgas, steam**

die-die To go all out, with no possibility of noncompliance. The Singlish equivalent of "die trying".

☐ *"I die-die will pay you back tomorrow." (I swear upon my grave that I will pay you back tomorrow.)*

die-die must try An exhortation to sample something as a matter of urgency or necessity. Popularised by the "Makansutra" food guide and television show.

☐ *"The chicken rice at Margaret Drive, hor, you die-die must try!" (You absolutely must try the chicken rice at Margaret Drive!)*

dieded Classic example of Singlish hyperbole. Used to describe an extreme reaction, possibly of greater intensity than even dying. "Dieded", however, is never used to actually describe death.

1 *"When I saw her in her mini-skirt, I immeelly dieded." (When I saw her in her mini-skirt, I immediately dropped dead.)*

2 *"Economy so bad that his whole business within six months all dieded." (The economy was so bad that within six months, his entire business had died.)*

do business Local euphemism for taking a shit.

☐ *Teacher: "Where's Ah Seng?"*

Student: "He go do business." (He's gone to take a dump.)

See also **berak, number 2, pang sai**

do'wan |doe-wahn| Singlish contraction of "don't want".

☐ *"I told you I do'wan to do it, you still kacho me. Do'wan means do'wan, you understand, not?" (I told you I do not want to do it, yet you insist on bugging me. When I say I don't want to do it, I don't want to do it. Do you understand or not?)*

don'ch |dohnch| One of the variant Singlish pronunciations of "don't".

☐ *"I don'ch know how to do this sum." (I don't know how to do this sum.)*

See also **dun**

dong dong chiang / tong tong chiang |dtohng dtohng chee-ahng| Onomatopoeic description of a traditional Chinese funeral. Not to be confused with "dong-dong-dong chiang" (note the extra "dong") or "tok tok chiang". With Singaporeans of a certain generation, "tong tong chiang" was also a nickname for the Teachers Training College (now defunct), whose initials were "TTC".

☐ *"Boy-boy, dun go downstair and play. Today there got dong dong chiang." (Son, don't go downstairs to play, because there's a funeral*

being held there today.)
See also **dong-dong-dong chiang, tok tok chiang**

dong-dong-dong chiang |dtohng-dtohng-dtohng chee-ahng| Onomatopoeic description of noisy traditional Chinese New Year celebrations such as lion or dragon dances. Not to be confused with "dong dong chiang" (one less "dong") or "tok tok chiang".
□ *"Adooi, every Chinese New Year, our munjen neighbours got all sorts of dong-dong-dong chiang! Damn noisy, da!" (Bloody hell, every Chinese New Year, our Chinese neighbours cause a real racket with their festivities! It's really noisy, man!)*
See also **dong-dong chiang, tok tok chiang**

don't play-play / dun pray-pray A literal translation of the Hokkien phrase, "mai sng sng". A warning not to aggravate, irritate, provoke or fool with things beyond one's ability. Often deliberately mispronounced "dun pray-pray".
□ *"Ah Beng temper damn bad. Better dun play-play with him." (Ah Beng has a really bad temper. Better not provoke him.)*
See also **mai siao siao, mai sng sng**

don't care As with English, it is an exhortation to ignore or pay no heed. However, in Singlish usage, the preposition "about" is often omitted.
□ *"Aiyah, don't care him, lah!" (Ah, ignore him!)*
See also **chup seow, heck care, fuck care, juang lah**

don't say I say A very common way of prefacing a statement that could be controversial or sensitive. English equivalents include, "Don't tell anyone I said so, but..." or "This might just be my own opinion, but..." or "I'm not sure, but..." or "Don't quote me on this, but..." Virtually identical in use to "not say I say what".
□ *"Don't say I say ah, but Ah Lian's dressing is si beh obiang." (Don't tell anyone I said so, but Ah Lian's dress sense is really tacky.)*
See also **not say I say what**

do'wan |doe-wahn| Singlish pronunciation of "don't want".
□ *Ah Beng: "Eh, tonight wan' go KTV, not?" (Hey, do you want to go to the karaoke lounge tonight?)*
Ah Seng: "Do'wan." (No, I do not want to.)

do'wan done Expression of irritation or annoyance when someone turns down your offer. The English equivalent would be "fine!"
□ *Ah Seng: "I got ticket for the concert, you want, not?" (I have tickets for the concert. Do you want to come?)*
Ah Beng (in a bored tone): "Aiyah, too leceh, lah." (Ah, it's too troublesome.)

Ah Seng (disgusted): "OK lah, do'wan done!" (Alright, if you don't want it, that's just fine by me!)

drama To act in a melodramatic fashion.
⊡ *"It's only a small matter. No need to be so drama." (It's only a small matter. No need to be so melodramatic.)*

drama mama A camp or flashily effeminate personality.
⊡ *"These theatre types, hor, are all drama mamas, one." (These theatre types are such camp personalities.)*

dubdew The Singlish way of pronouncing "W".
1 *"Eh, Ah Beng bought a new bee-em-dubdew."*
2 *"The previous president of America was George Dubdew Bush."*

dun |dohn — rhymes with "own"| One of the variant Singlish pronunciations of "don't". This became the dominant spelling after the advent of SMS/text messaging.
1 *"Oi, can see, dun touch." (Hey, you can look at it, but don't touch it.)*
2 *"Dun lai dat, lah!" (Please don't be like that.)*
See also **don'ch**

dun bluff Either a warning to someone not to lie or exaggerate, or an exclamation of surprise or disbelief, similar to "you've got to be kidding me!" or "you can't be serious!"
1 *"Ah Beng kena sex change? Eh, say this kind of thing is damn serious, okay! You dun bluff!" (Ah Beng had a sex change operation? Hey, such allegations are very serious, you know! You shouldn't lie about them!)*
2 *"Ah Beng became an MP? Dun bluff!" (Ah Beng became a Member of Parliament? You must be joking!)*
See also **bluff**

dun friend |dohn fren| To cease being friends with someone.
1 *"You whole life sabo me! I dun friend you anymore!" (You're always sabotaging me! I no longer desire to be your friend.)*
2 *"You got hear, not? Ah Lian dun friend Ah Beng oreddy!" (Have you heard? Ah Lian is no longer friends with Ah Beng!)*
See also **friend, make friend**

dun mention The Singlish contraction of "don't mention it".
⊡ *Beng: "Eh, thanks for treating me to lunch."*
Seng: "Aiyah, dun mention." (Oh, don't mention it.)

dun scared |dohn sked| Singlish for "don't be scared".
⊡ *"Put some hum in your mee siam, lah! Dun scared! Try-try only. Worse come to the worst, lao sai only!" (Add some cockles to your mee siam. Don't be afraid. Just try it. At worst, you'll just get diarrhoea.)*

See also **wen die**

dun shy "Don't be shy." For emphasis, say "dun shy-shy." Probably from the Hokkien expression, "mai kek kee", meaning "don't stand on ceremony."

☐ *"Take some more, mai kek kee, dun shy, hor." (Please help yourself to more. There's no need to be shy.)*

dungu |doong-goo| Malay for stupid or feeble-minded. Often thought erroneously to be the source for the popular Singlish word "goondu", meaning a stupid person.

☐ *"Aiyah, don't ask him to help, lah. He damn dungu one." (Oh, please don't ask him to help. He's really dumb.)*

See also **goondu**

Ee

early-early dun say Singlish for "why didn't you say so earlier?" A literal translation of the Hokkien phrase "tzah tzah mai kong".

☐ *Ah Beng: "Eh, tomorrow I got reservist, so cannot go see show wif you." (Hey, I'm being called up for reservist training tomorrow, so I can't see the show with you.)*
Ah Seng: "Aiyah, why you early-early dun say! I bought the ticket oreddy." (Argh! Why didn't you say so earlier? I already bought the tickets.)

ee-yur |ee-yuhr| Uniquely Singaporean exclamation of revulsion. Can sometimes be used as an adjective.

1 *"Ee-yur! Ah Beng pick his nose and wipe the pee sai under his seat!" (Eeww! Ah Beng picked his nose and wiped the booger under his seat!)*

2 *"Ah Beng, hor, very ee-yurr one, lair! Go sheeming that time, hor, always shee shee inside the pool!" (Ah Beng is very gross. Whenever he goes swimming, he always urinates in the pool.)*

eh saba! |eh sah-bah| An exclamation similar to "well done!", "hear, hear!" or "my!" Derived from "syabas!" the Malay equivalent of "bravo!"

☐ *"Eh saba! I heard you so pandai become scholar!" (Well done! I heard you were clever enough to be awarded a scholarship!)*

eh sai / eh sai boh? Hokkien phrase meaning, "It's possible". With the "boh" added, it becomes a question, i.e. "Is it possible?", or as it's locally Anglicized, "Can or not?"
⊡ *Beng: "Eh, lend me your car, eh sai boh?" (Hey, lend me your car, won't you?)*
Seng: "Eh saaaaaiiii!" (Of couuuuurse!)
See also **can or not, mana eh sai, how can**

eng Hokkien for being free and having nothing to do. Does not necessarily connote indolence.
1 *"Wah, weekday also can go play golf. You so eng, meh?" (Wow, you're able to play golf on a weekday? Are you that free?)*
2 *"Yesterday I was damn eng, so I went Bird Park." (Yesterday, I was very free, so I went to the Bird Park.)*
See also **boh eng, chia sior eng, shake leg**

England / Engrand Deliberate mispronunciation of "English".
⊡ *"Wah, your Engrand so powderful, I catch no ball." (Wow, your facility with English is so advanced, I can't understand a word you're saying.)*

enthu |en-t'oo| Common abbreviation for "enthusiastic".
⊡ *"Eh, why you so enthu, ah? They pay you a lot, is it?" (Why are you so enthusiastic? Do they pay you a lot?)*

eskew / eskew me / skew / skew me / skews The various Singlish ways to use "excuse me". Often shortened to "eskew!" and simply, "skew!" or "skews!" when in a hurry.
1 *"Eskew me, this one how much, ah?" (Excuse me, how much is this item?)*
2 *"Skew me, ah, go to Bukit Gorblok how, ah?" (Excuse me, but how does one get to Bukit Gorblok?)*
3 *Hawker carrying hot bowl of soup, weaving through the crowd: "Skews! Sio, ah! Siam!" (Excuse me, this is very hot, so please make way!)*
See also **siam**

essciting The Singlish pronunciation for "exciting".
⊡ *"Piang eh, that tiger show was too essciting for me oreddy." (Man, that striptease performance was too exciting for me!)*

essploded The Singlish pronunciation for "exploded".
⊡ *"Ah Beng kena concuss when the nenet (grenade) essploded too close to him." (Ah Beng received a concussion when the grenade exploded too close to him.)*

every time In Singlish, "every time" is used more like "always" rather than "every single time", in that it connotes not merely the re-occurrence of a discrete incident, but rather, an eternal state of being.

[1] *"He, hor, every time like to go and ji seow the gahmen." (He always likes to provoke the government.)*

[2] *"Why you every time like that?" (Why are you always like that?")*

ex Although sometimes used to describe one's former girlfriend/boyfriend/whatever, in current Singlish, "ex" is more often short for "expensive", and is used to express incredulity, and sometimes envy.

[1] *"Wah lau, original DVD a bit the ex, leh. Better go JB and buy." (Man, original DVDs are really expensive. I think you'd better go to Johor to buy pirated copies.)*

[2] *"Julie very high-class one, you donno, meh? She always dress very ex." (Julie is very sophisticated, don't you know? She always dresses very expensively.)*

See also **gui**

expat Short for "expatriate", people who work or live in a land in which they are not natives. Lately, this term has been displaced by "foreign talent". See **foreign talent**

extra An adjective usually applied to people who do things which are unnecessary or pointless.

[1] *"Eh, Johnny! Recess already you still want to do homework! You si peh extra, you know!" (Hey, Johnny! It's recess and you're still doing your homework? You're really going overboard!)*

[2] *"This sort of simple thing don't make until so complicated, can or not? Why you so extra one?" (Why are you making such simple things so complicated? Why are you doing such unnecessary things?)*

eye power A sarcastic way to scold someone for standing by and looking on without helping, especially with manual tasks.

[·] *"Eh, come and help us move this furniture, leh! You stand there using eye power, ah?" (Hey, come over and help us move this furniture! Or perhaps you're using your eye power?)*

Ff

fail Used to describe abject failure or one's severe inadequacies.

[1] *"Wah piang, prembry 2 girl also run faster than you! Fail, lah,*

you!" (Even a primary 2 schoolgirl can run faster than you! There's something really wrong with you, man!)
2 *Radio DJ: "And what is the country immediately above Singapore on the map?"*
Caller: "Uh... India?"
Radio DJ: "Fail, lah!" (What's wrong with you?)
See also **koyak, rosak, spoi, condemn**

faster Singlish for "hurry".
1 *"Eh, this week Toto two million loler, you better faster go and buy." (Hey, this week's lottery amount is two million dollars. You'd better hurry and buy a ticket.)*
2 *"Oi, nearly eight o'clock oreddy. Faster a bit, can?" (Hey, it's almost eight o'clock already. Can you hurry up?)*

fatty bom bom |fatty bohm bohm| Used to describe a fat person, equivalent to the English "fatso" or "fatty".
· *"You eat so much lard, wait you become a fatty bom bom, then you know!" (If you continue eating so much lard, you'll become a fatso and it would serve you right!)*
See also **ah pooi, pooi, pooi eh, pooi-pooi**

fei tzai |fay tzai| Cantonese version of Ah Pooi. See **Ah Pooi**

fetch To drive someone somewhere.
1 *"You wan' me to fetch you to the MRT station?" (Do you wish me to drive you to the MRT station?)*
2 *"Eh, is someone fetching you home?" (Hey, is someone driving you home?)*

fiak |fee-ahk| A more polite local way to say "fuck".
1 *"Aiyah, this type of small-small thing... fiak it, lah!" (Oh, this kind of trivial matter... just fuck it!)*
2 *"You go and cucuk him for fiak?" (Why on earth did you go and provoke him?)*
See also **fish, for fuck, for futt**

fierce Singlish adjective describing something as "daring" or "strong".
· *"You got read that book by that opposition bugger, not? Damn fierce, boss." (Did you read that book by that opposition fellow? It was really daring, man!)*
See also **chia lat, garang, hiong, powderful, siong, terror**

fish Popular substitute for "fuck". Even milder than "fiak".
1 *"What the fish?"*
2 *"Fish you, okay!"*
See also **fiak**

fler Local pronunciation of "fellow/fella/feller".

☐ *"That fler, ah, always kena sai one." (That fellow is always getting into trouble.)*

flim The Singlish pronunciation of "film". Used for both movies and photographic film. Sometimes also pronounced "flerm".

① *"Eh, I heard Ah Kong went to see an R(A) flim yesterday." (I heard Grandpa went to see an R-rated movie yesterday.)*

② *"Nowsaday got digital camera, no need to buy flim oreddy." (With digital cameras today, I don't need to buy any film.)*

fly aeroplane Derived from the Hokkien phrase "pang puay kee", this Singlish phrase describes being stood up. Of uncertain provenance.

☐ *"Eh, tonight's function damn important, okay? Don't fly aeroplane or I make sure you die!" (Hey, tonight's event is really important. Don't stand me up, or I'll kill you!)*

See also **no sound no image, pang puay kee**

for fuck More vulgar version of "for what?" or "why on earth?"

☐ *"You go all the way there to buy newspaper for fuck?" (Why on earth did you go all the way there just to buy the newspaper?)*

See also **for what, for futt, what for**

for futt Variant of "for what?" Milder than "for fuck".

☐ *"You go and move the bookcase for futt?" (Why the heck did you move the bookcase?)*

See also **for what, for fuck**

for exampur |four air-zumper| The Singlish pronunciation of "for example". Sometimes written simply as "forazumper".

☐ *"You see this software can do many things, for exampur, you can calculate your overheads by clicking this icon…" (This software can do many things. For example, you can calculate your overheads by clicking this icon…)*

for what? Singlish for — wait for it — "what for?", i.e. a question seeking the purpose of or reason for something. You could simply ask "why?" but hey, that wouldn't be very Singaporean.

① *"Follow you go KL? For what?" (Follow you to Kuala Lumpur? Whatever for?)*

② *"You go and sign up with that MLM scheme for what?" (What on earth did you sign up with that multilevel marketing scheme for?)*

See also **for what tu donno?**

for what oso donno/for what tu donno An extrapolation of "for what" (above), meaning, "I have no idea why" or "I'm at a loss to explain why". "For what tu donno" tends to be used mostly by Peranakans and Eurasians of a certain vintage.

☐ *"She go and marry that old man, for what oso donno." (I really have no idea why she married that old man.)*

foreign talent The official term for foreigners coming to work in Singapore (displacing "expatriate"), coined by the political spin-doctors to allay the fears of the local populace that their jobs are being supplanted. Locals, however, usually seem to utter the term with a hint of sarcasm, no doubt because of the intimation that only foreigners are talented. (Note: "local talent" does not exist as an official term.)

⊡ *"All the foreign talent really got talent, meh?" (Are all expatriates necessarily talented?)*

See also **expat**

fren The popular SMS shorthand for "friend" which is creeping into everyday writing.

friend |fren| To befriend someone. Used as a verb. Sometimes repeated for emphasis.

1 *"You always disturb me. I dun friend you orreddy." (You're always bugging me. I no longer wish to be your friend.)*

2 *"Why cannot hold her hand? Friend-friend only, mah." (Why can't I hold her hand? We're only friends.)*

See also **dun friend, make friend**

frus The Singlish abbreviation of "frustrated".

⊡ *"I study so hard also kena F9. Damn frus, man!" (Despite studying so hard, I still scored only an F9. I'm really frustrated!)*

See also **bang, pek chek**

fuck care A more extreme variant of "heck care". See **heck care**

fuck spider Of uncertain origin, this term denotes either one's extreme frustration, or the act of performing a pathetic or ridiculous task. The general consensus is that it originates from the Army (the source of many creative Singlish phrases), where a "spider" was dirt in the barrel of one's rifle. If during inspection, you found a "spider" in your rifle, you'd have to strip it and clean it all over again. Hence, "fuck spider" would either be a common expletive amongst recruits, or an exhortation by an annoyed inspecting officer/NCO. Some, however, believe it dates back to an old practice amongst boys to catch spiders in the undergrowth, house them in small boxes and make them fight.

1 *"Na beh! He arrow me to do this sort of sai kang, I think I go fuck spider oreddy!" (Damn! He stuck me with this crappy task! I'm now fit to be tied!)*

2 *"Recruit! You inside the bunk fucking spider, is it?" (Recruit! What ridiculous thing are you doing inside the bunk?)*

fugly Abbreviation of "fucking ugly", used when "extremely ugly" cannot do justice.
□ *"She think she damn pretty, but acherly, she damn fugly." (She thinks she's really pretty, but she's actually really incredibly ugly.)*

function In traditional English, a "function" is a formal or official social occasion. This is generally the case in Singlish as well, though in the mid-1980s, "function" acquired a very specific meaning: an Ah Beng dance party. The strength of this association has greatly undermined the general meaning of the word.
□ *"I remember Sec 4 that time, function sure got play 'Durian Durian' and 'Careless Whisper', one." (I remember that when I was in Secondary 4, the dance parties all had Duran Duran and "Careless Whisper" on their music playlists.)*

Gg

NOTE: If you can't find certain words you think should be spelled with a "g", try looking under "k" instead. For instance, we've spelled "giam siap" as "kiam siap". This is because it's more intuitive for those unfamiliar with hanyu pinyin spelling and pronunciation. Must be considerate, mah!

gabra |gah-brah| A Malay word meaning to panic or be so nervous that you mess things up.
□ *"Acherly, she a damn solid athlete. But every track meet, hor, somehow she gabra." (She's actually a really good athlete, but somehow at every track meet, she panics and loses.)*
See also **kalang kabut / kelam kabut**

gahmen |gah-m'n| Has nothing to do with the garment industry, but is the Singlish pronunciation of "government". Origin usually attributed to incensed taxi drivers offering unsolicited political opinions.
□ *"You fight gahmen, confirm die, one." (If you choose to fight the government, you'll definitely fail.)*
See also **cheng hu**

garang |gah-rahng| Malay for "fierce" or "powerful". Can mean "impulsive", "courageous", or "foolhardy".

[1] *"The CO damn garang one, so don't ji seow him." (The Commanding Officer is very fierce, so don't provoke him.)*

[2] *"Why so garang? You not kiasi, is it?" (Why are you behaving in such a foolhardy manner? Aren't you afraid of getting killed?)*

See also **fierce, garang, hiong, powderful, siong, terror**

gasak / gasak buta |gah-sahk boo-tah| "Gasak" in Malay has two meanings: one is "to strike", and the other "to eat gluttonously". "Buta" in Malay means "blind". Thus, to "gasak buta" means to "strike blindly". In Singlish, it has three meanings: **[1]** to eat in a gluttonous manner; **[2]** to grab or swipe things in a greedy, indiscriminate manner; and **[3]** to do things in a panicky or haphazard manner.

[1] *"Alamak, look at that bugger gasak all the prawns at the buffet! Damn shyful, sial!" (My goodness, look at that guy gorging himself on all the prawns at the buffet. How embarrassing!)*

[2] *"This sort of thing must do properly, cannot anyhow gasak buta!" (You must do these things properly, and not in some haphazard manner!)*

[3] *"Wah lau! Everybody go to McDonald's and gasak all the Hello Kitty oreddy!" (Holy cow, everyone's already gone to McDonald's and grabbed all the Hello Kitty toys!)*

gatal |gah-dtahl| Malay for "itchy", with lecherous connotations. In Singlish, it describes a restive person, i.e. someone who is tempted to do something disruptive out of boredom.

[·] *Rosli: "Why you go and potong jalan Ahmad's girlfriend?" (Why did you steal Ahmad's girlfriend from him?)*
Rahman: "Aiyah, just gatal, lah." (Oh, I was just bored, that's all.)

See also **boh liao, chiak pah boh sai pang, itchy backside, wu liao**

gau mm tim |gkau mm dtim| Cantonese for "cannot manage". Often used in the sense that things are spinning out of control

[·] *"Ah Lian kena promoted to marketing manager? Wah lau, she sure gau mm tim one." (Ah Lian's been promoted to marketing manager? Huh! I bet she won't be able to handle the job!)*

gedebak gedebuk |gher-duh-ba'h gher-duh-boo| An onomatopoeic expression of Malay origin denoting a wild thumping feeling or a rough and reckless behaviour.

[1] *"Whenever I see Ah Beng in cycle shorts, hor, my heart always gedebak gedebuk, one." (Whenever I see Ah Beng in cycle shorts, my heart goes into palpitations.)*

[2] *"Eh, in the lab must careful a bit, leh! Cannot do things gedebuk*

gedebuk like that!" (Hey, when you're in the laboratory, you should be more careful! You can't do things in such a rough and reckless manner!)

gelek gelek |gay-lay'h-gay-lay'h| "Gelek" is a Malay dance, which comes from the word "menggelek", meaning to "roll over". In Singlish, it's used to describe walking in an exaggerated, hip-rolling way. It often carries effeminate connotations, but not always.

☐ *"Aiyoh, Mahmood went San Francisco to study fashion design for one year, now come back walk gelek-gelek oreddy." (Oh dear, Mahmood went to San Francisco to study fashion design for only a year, and now he's started to walk in an effeminate way.)*

geli |gher-li'h| Malay for "ticklish" or "amused". In Singlish, however, "geli" has come to mean "queasy".

☐ *"See all those maggots crawling around, I very geli." (Seeing all those maggots crawling around gives me a queasy feeling.)*

ger Common pronunciation of "girl".

☐ *"That ger quite chio, hor?" (That girl is quite pretty, isn't she?)*

See also **Ah Ger, Ger-ger**

Ger-ger Common pronunciation of "Girl-girl" See **Ah Girl, Girl-girl**

geragok |grah-goh'| "Geragau" is Malay for shrimp. Through cultural association, it has somehow evolved into "geragok" or "shrimp people", an insensitive way to address a Eurasian, i.e. a person of mixed Asian and Caucasian ancestry.

☐ *"I heard Ah Lian married some geragok, so she's now Ah Lian De Silva or Ah Lian Rodriguez or something."*

See also **serani**

geram |ger-ahm| Malay word meaning "exasperated" or "greatly annoyed".

☐ *"When I hear people do this sort of thing, ah, I get damn geram, man!" (Whenever I hear of people doing such things, I get greatly annoyed!)*

gerek |gay-ray'h| From the Peranakan expression "gereh-gereh", meaning unbecoming behaviour, which may or may not have originated from the Malay word "gerek", meaning "perforated" or "piercing". Somehow, in Singlish, it has morphed into meaning "groovy" or "cool".

☐ *"Did you see Kassim in his Marlboro leather jacket? Gerek sial!" (Did you see Kassim in his Marlboro leather jacket? Groovy, dude!)*

See also **saht, stylo**

gian |ghee-en| Hokkien for eager or enthusiastic.

☐ *"Uncle Lim damn gian to see R movies. Every week sure go*

Yangtze at least three times." (Uncle Lim is very enthusiastic about R-rated movies. Every week, he goes to Yangtze cinema at least three times.)

2 *"Hello Kitty this sort of condemn thing, how come you so gian to buy?" (What makes you so eager to buy crappy things like Hello Kitty merchandise?)*

gian png |ghee-en png| A Hokkien phrase meaning "to be eager for rice", meaning to be desperately craving something very common or pathetic.

1 *"Wah lau, Hello Kitty this sort of thing, you also go and line up. You damn gian png, man!" (You're queuing up for Hello Kitty merchandise? Man, you're pathetic!)*

2 *"Your boss treat you like that and you still por him? Why you so gian png?" (Your boss treats you so badly and you're still sucking up to him? Why are you such a wretch?)*

See also **hard up**

giah lum pah chut lai tom to'teng |giah lum pah choo' lai dtome to'h teng| A rather graphic expression which translates as "to take one's testicles out and bang them on the table". It is an act of self-flagellation, and the phrase is used when one has discovered he has done something especially idiotic or horrific.

⊡ *"Wah lau, when I found out that the char bor I was trying to buaya in the disco was actually my auntie, I giah lum pah chu lai tom to'teng!" (Oh my god, when I discovered that the woman I was trying to chat up in the disco was actually my aunt, I just wanted to crawl into a corner and die!)*

See also **tair lum pah chi saht**

gila |ghee-lah| Malay for "mad".

⊡ *"Alamak, such an ugly girl also can rabak? You gila or what?" (Oh my god, you can make out with such an ugly girl? Are you mad?)*

See also **siao**

Girl-girl More affectionate variant of "Ah Girl"

See **Ah Girl, Ger-ger**

give chance Singlish expression meaning to be fair, generous, or to give someone a break or fighting chance.

1 *"Our goalie not here yet, so give chance, can or not?" (Our goalkeeper isn't here yet. So can you give us a chance?)*

2 *"That guy always kena whack. They neh give chance to him one." (That guy is always being beaten up. He never gets a break.)*

See also **agak tarik, panchan**

glam / un-glam Short for glamorous, meaning fashionable or cool. Its antonym is "un-glam".

[1] *"Eh, that Wendy ah, so glam one! Every week also got new dress!" (Man, that Wendy is really glamorous! She has a new dress every week!)*

[2] *"Aiyah, I heard Ah Beng become insurance salesman. Damn un-glam, man!" (Oh dear, I heard that Ah Beng has become an insurance salesman. How unglamorous!)*

go fly kite Derived from the English admonition "go fly a kite!" which means "piss off", "fuck off", "buzz off", etc, depending on your level of profanity-tolerance. Of course, we economical Singaporeans have removed the extraneous indefinite article.

[·] *"He know I so busy, still ask me to do things. Ask him go fly kite, lah!" (Despite knowing how busy I was, he continued asking me to do things. So I told him to go fly a kite!)*

go head In true Singlish economy, to "go ahead."

[·] *"You go head first, later I catch up." (Please go ahead. I'll catch up later.)*

go where? Contraction of "where are you/we going?" or "where shall we go?"

[·] *"Eh, tonight go where and makan?" (Hey, where are we going to eat tonight?)*

gone case Someone or something beyond help. A lost cause.

[1] *"We tried to help, but he oreddy gone case." (We tried to help, but he was already a lost cause.)*

[2] *"You continue like this, hor, sure gone case." (If you continue like this, you'll be finished.)*

gong-gong / gong Onomatopoeic Hokkien description of being in a stunned state or daze, as if someone bashed your head like a gong. Sometimes abbreviated to just "gong".

[1] *"Wah lau, I do maths, do until gong-gong, man." (Ugh, I've been doing so many mathematics problems, I'm now in a daze.)*

[2] *"Aiyoh, that Jacques Derrida, hor, si beh cheem, leh. I read until gong-gong." (Man, that Jacques Derrida is really deep. Reading his stuff makes me giddy.)*

[3] *"Wah lau, you nearly kena langgar by that car! Why you so gong today?" (Holy cow, you nearly got hit by that car! Why are you so addled today?)*

See also **blur**

goondu |goon-doo| Idiot, twit, moron, etc. Can be both noun and adjective. There are three possible sources of the word "goondu": **[1]** the Tamil word for "fat", connoting clumsiness and awkwardness; **[2]** the Malay term for the lead marble in a game of marbles; and **[3]** a corruption of "dungu", Malay for "feeble-minded". It's very possible that somehow all three merged into a single expression.

1 *"Why are you such a goondu? This sort of simple thing also can cock up!"* (Why are you such an idiot? You're able to mess even such simple tasks up!)

2 *"Eh, why you so goondu, go and ji seow him like that?"* (Hey, why are you so stupid, provoking him like that?)

See also **bodoh, dungu, gorblok**

goose egg A big "zero". Often used as a warning to schoolchildren.

"If I catch any of you flers cheating, I will give you one big goose egg, then you know." (If I catch any of you fellows cheating, I shall award you a "zero" on the test.)

See also **jilo**

gor chiam tua kuay gu chia leng |gor tz'iahm twah gkway goo ts'iah leng| Teochew expression which literally translates as "five cents bigger than a bullock cart's wheel". Used sarcastically to criticise someone for thinking that his money is worth a lot.

"Wah, you want to buy all this for only $1 ah? You gor chiam tua kuay gu chia leng is it?" (What? You want to buy all of this for only $1? Do you think your money is that big?)

gorblok Idiot, twit, moron, etc. Can be both noun and adjective.

1 *"Wah lau, why you such a gorblok, go and put the cat in the washing machine?"* (My god, why are you such a moron, placing the cat in the washing machine?)

2 *"Wah piang, Ah Beng so gorblok, kena con into joining some pyramid scheme."* (Oh dear, Ah Beng was so stupid, he was conned into joining a pyramid scheme.)

See also **bodoh, dungu, goondu**

gostan A Malay contraction of the colonial instruction to "go astern", i.e. to reverse one's vehicle or turn it around. Can be used as a verb.

"You can gostan your car some more. Still got space behind. Come on, gostan, gostan... dun scared." (You can reverse your car further. There's still room behind. Come on, reverse... reverse... don't be afraid.)

got Denoting either **[1]** the availability of something or **[2]** the state of having done something.

1 *Beng: "Got milk or not?"* (Do you have milk?)
Seng: "Got!" (Yes, I do!)

2 *"You go buffet got eat or not?"* (Did you eat at the buffet?)

got eye see no Tarzan / got eye see no or-yee-or A brilliant example of hand-me-down Singlish wordplay, this bizarre phrase is derived from the Mandarin proverb, "you yan jian bu dao tai san": "to have eyes, but be unable to see the large mountain", meaning to be blind, ignorant or clueless. The inclusion of "Tarzan" is because Edgar Rice Burroughs' famous fictional ape man's name is transliterated as "Tai San" in Mandarin. And over time, some local wits have morphed the Tarzan reference into his trademark jungle call.

[1] *"Eh, you got eye see no Tarzan! You know who that man is or not? He's our new principal! Don't play-play, okay!" (Are you blind? Don't you know who that man is? He's our new principal! Don't play the fool around him.)*

[2] *"Wah lau, that truck so big also can langgar! You got eye see no or-yee-or, is it?" (Oh man, how could you crash into such a big truck? Don't you have eyes?)*

got licence Reflecting Singapore's highly regulated society, this is a Singlish term for "allowed to", usually employed when one is

allowed to commit a social vice, i.e. smoking or drinking.
⊡ *Seng: "Na beh, now my sister got licence from my mother to smoke!" (Damn! My sister just got permission from my mother to smoke!)*

got {...} must {...} Ubiquitous Singlish syntactic pairing. Used whenever one wishes to suggest that it is imperative to seize an opportunity.
1 *"Got food must eat, lah!" (If there is food, then you must eat it.)*
2 *"Got show must see, lah!" (If there's a show on, then you must see it.)*
3 *"Got sale, must shop!" (If a sale is on, then you must shop.)*

grandfudder road "Your grandfather's road". A belligerent expression aimed at road hogs. Similar to the English expression, "Do you own the road?"
⊡ *"Wah lau, drive so slow! Your grandfudder road, is it?" (Holy cow, you're driving really slowly! Is this your grandfather's road or something?)*

gu poon si |goo bpoon see| Hokkien phrase meaning, "Even a cow would die". Used to describe especially tough and arduous events.
1 *"Wah lau, kena do one hundred push up, gu poon si, man!" (Wow, doing one hundred push-ups is so tough, it could even kill a cow!)*
2 *"Last night we go to three launge, si beh siong. Gu poon si, man!" (We visited three lounges last night. It was very hard going. Even a cow would have been killed.)*

guanxi |gkoo-ahn see| Mandarin term meaning "relationship". In Singapore, it has come to mean the kind of building of informal relations or networks necessary to do business, mostly in China. Note: Not to be confused with the similar sounding "kuan si".
⊡ *"China do business is all about guanxi, one. Cannot anyhow go in and whack." (Doing business in China is all about building relationships. You can't just enter their markets blindly.)*
See also **kuan si**

guai / guai guai |gkwai| Cantonese and Hokkien for "well behaved" or "innocent", doubled for emphasis, and usually applied with sarcasm.
1 *"Your dog very guai, hor?" (Your dog is very obedient, isn't he?)*
2 *"Ah Beng always act like he damn tough, but when his mother call him that time, he guai guai go and do what she say." (Ah Beng always acts tough, but when his mother calls, he slinks to her obediently.)*

gui |gk'wee (Hokkien) or gkway (Mandarin)| "Expensive".
⊡ *"Wah lau, here the durian so gui, you still go and buy, ah?" (Wow, the durians here are so expensive, yet you still want to buy some?)*
See also **ex**

Hh

ha? Super contraction of "could you please repeat that again?" The equivalent of "what?"

⊡ *Ah Lian: "Eh Beng, my period two months didn't come oreddy, maybe got baby… how?" (Hey, Beng, my period hasn't come for two months. What if I'm pregnant?)*
Ah Beng: "Ha? Talk after football game, can or not?" (What did you say? Can we discuss this after the football game?)

ha ni ah pa, lum pah hor li kar |ha nee ah pa, lahm pah hor lee gkah| Vulgar Hokkien phrase used when responding to a stupid person saying "ha?" It literally means, "Ha your father, bite my balls!"

⊡ *Seng: "Just now I ask you to buy 4D, how come you neh buy?" (Earlier, I asked you to purchase a lottery ticket. Why didn't you?)*
Beng: "Ha?" (Huh?)
Seng: "Ha ni ah pa, lum pah hor li kah!"

habis |ha-base| Malay for "finished" or "the end".

1 *"Alamak, masuk two goals already! Habis lah!" (Oh god, they've scored two goals already! We're finished!)*

2 *"If the boss see you tuang like that, you sure habis, man!" (If the boss catches you skiving like that, it'll be the end of you!)*

See also **wan dan**

half past six |ha-pah-siks| Describing something or someone as being half-baked or incompetent, the term is actually a sexual reference to the angle of the dangle of the male organ. Half past six is weak, but quarter past three or 9:45 is very strong!

⊡ *"Wah piang eh, why your company so half past six one, this sort of easy thing also can cock-up." (Holy cow, why is your company so incompetent, messing up even such easy things!)*

See also **chap sar tiam**, **kucing kurap**

han na! |hahn nah| Local exclamation meaning "enough already!" or "whatever!" Often said in exasperation.

⊡ *Beng: "You know, hor, your shirt very ugly, leh…" (You know, your shirt is very ugly…)*
Seng: "Han na!!!" (Enough already!)

See also **ya lah!**

han tze |hahn tzz| Hokkien for "sweet potato". Often used to scold idiots. How this came to be used on dumb people is unclear, but it's believed that as morons often utter, "Orh", and "orh" sounds like Hokkien for "yam", so replying with a different tuber is seen as witty. Who says Hokkien is an unsophisticated language?

⊡ *Beng: "...and that's how babies are born. Understand, not?" (... and that's how babies are born. Do you understand?)*
Seng: "Orh!" (Orh!)
Beng: "'Orh'? Han tze!" ("Orh!" What a dimwit you are!)

See **orh**

hantam |hahn-tahm| From the Malay word "hentam", meaning either **[1]** to bash or beat or **[2]** to finish a task all at one go in a haphazard fashion. Sometimes pronounced "humb thumb" by cheenapiangs.

1 *"Don't go and disturb him while he so busy. He sure hantam you one." (Hey, don't disturb him while he's busy, otherwise he'll beat you up.)*

2 *"Bomb disposal must do properly, hor. Cannot anyhow hantam." (Bomb disposal is a task that must be executed properly. You can't rush and do it haphazardly.)*

See also **hoot, humb thumb, sepak, pukul**

hao lian Hokkien for arrogant, cocky or smug. Can be used as a verb.

1 *"That asshole, hor, si peh hao lian." (That miscreant is really arrogant.)*

2 *"Just because your letter got publish in the Forum page, no need to hao lian around here, okay!" (Just because your letter was published in the Forum page doesn't entitle you to act so smugly!)*

3 *"Hao lian meh?" (What's there to be arrogant about?)*

See also **atas, dao, upstairs, sombong**

happy like bird Complete euphoria.

⊡ *"You going to ORD in six days? Like that, must be happy like bird!" (You're completing your National Service in six days' time? You must be over the moon with happiness!)*

hard up In English, this term is used to denote "impoverishment" or "in great need". In Singlish, however, it describes someone who is desperate for something, not necessarily money.

1 *"Ah Beng, why you so hard up — go and buaya that girl so ugly one?" (Ah Beng, why are you desperate, going to chat up such an ugly girl?)*

2 *"Ah Seng, everybody knows you sah-kar'ing the boss because you si beh hard up for promotion." (Ah Seng, everyone knows you're sucking up to the boss because you're desperate to be promoted.)*

havoc Used to describe a wild child, or someone who's promiscuous.
▣ *"Ah Lian is damn havoc one." (Ah Lian is such a wild child.)*

hawk one or koh one? Phrase used by soya bean drink sellers to inquire if you wish your drink to be served hot or cold.

haywire all over the shop A phrase which, like many Singlish terms, originated in the Army, and describes a state of confusion and disorder throughout an organisation or place, very similar to the American "SNAFU" (Situation Normal, All Fucked Up). It is a unique Singapore fusion of the American term "haywire" (which derives from the way an old fashioned hay-baling machine would jam if a bit of wire was accidentally fed in with the hay) and the Singapore phrase "all over the shop", which describes disarray or messiness, not necessarily limited to retail stores or the main work space in a factory, the "shop floor".
▣ *"Why you all like that? Small problem only haywire all over the shop!" (Why are you all like that? A small problem crops up, and everything goes haywire!)*

heartlander In normal contexts, the heartland is an area that is politically, economically, or militarily vital to a nation, region, or culture. In Singapore, however, it refers specifically to the Housing Development Board (HDB) estates, and a "heartlander" is a label for those who stay in public housing and are therefore presumed to be of a lower socio-economic status and possess a more parochial outlook than "cosmopolitans". This is despite the fact that the vast majority of Singaporeans stay in HDB flats and are of widely differing income and educational backgrounds.
See also **cosmopolitan**

heck care An expression either used to describe someone as nonchalant or cavalier, or to exhort someone to ignore something.
1 *"This sort of serious thing, how can you be so heck care?" (How can you be so blasé about such serious things?)*
2 *"Ah Beng bothering you again? Aiyah, heck care him, lah!" (Is Ah Beng bothering you again? Ah, just ignore him!)*
See also **boh chup, don't care, fuck care, juang lah**

helicopter / Chinese helicopter An adjective used to describe a Chinese-educated person. It originated in the Army where the term Chinese-"educated" rapidly evolved through successive mispronunciation, from "educated" to "edicated" to "edicotted" to "edicotter", and eventually, "helicopter"! Often pronounced "helicotter" for added emphasis.
▣ *"My platoon is full of helicopter, one." (My platoon is full of Chi-*

nese educated people.)

heng A Hokkien word meaning "lucky" or "fortunate". Usually said after having escaped a tight spot, or avoided a near miss.

1 *"As soon as you left, the boss came out to arrow people. You damn heng, man." (As soon as you left, the boss came out to delegate work. You're really lucky to have dodged that.)*

2 *"Heng ah! The policeman didn't see me shoot the red light." (Phew! That was close! The policeman didn't see me go through the red light.)*

heng ah! bhai liam keng ah! |heng ah! bah-yee lee-ahm gkeng ah| A bit of racist doggerel recited to express one's relief at having dodged an unpleasant situation. In Hokkien, it literally means "Phew! Sikhs chanting holy scripture!" The origins of this phrase are not known.

"Lucky I siam the place before the mata come! Heng ah! Bhai liam keng ah!" (Luckily I fled the place before the police arrived. Phew!)

See also **heng**

heng kao kan |heng gkao gkahn| A Hokkien term which literally means "to be given to a dog for fucking". Used as an expression of extreme frustration.

"Na beh I buy 'SCORE!' two goals, then they go and score three. Heng kao kan, siah!" (Damn it! I bet that they would score two goals, and instead, they scored three! How frustrating!)

See also **bang, bang balls, lum pah pah lan, pek chek, giah lum pah chu lai tome to'teng**

hentak kaki |huhn-ta'h kah-kee| A Malay army drill command meaning to "march in place" and thus can refer to any form of inaction or idling. Outside of the military, it also describes someone whose career has stagnated either by choice or incompetence.

"Ah Beng used to be a high-flyer, but now he just hentak kaki." (Ah Beng used to be a high-flyer, but now he's just stuck in a rut.)

hero Has the same meaning as in English, but often connotes either a foolhardy person or someone out to grab attention.

1 *"Just pass, can oreddy. Why try and score "A"? You hero or what?" (It's sufficient just to pass. Why bother striving to score an "A"? What are you, some kind of hero?)*

2 *"It's too dangerous. Don't try to be hero." (It's too dangerous. Don't be a hero.)*

hian toh |hee-ehn dto'h| Hokkien for "flip the table". Originated from clashes between secret society members. Preludes to these fights always consisted of someone flipping over a table. Used frequently as a challenge to a fight or cheerful bantering between friends.

▣ *"Eh, you stare what? Buay song, is it? Want to hian toh, ah?" (Hey! What are you staring at? Are you dissatisfied with something? Do you wish to start a fight?)*

hiao / hiao lay lay |hee-ow| A Hokkien term describing someone as flirtatious and/or vain. The "lay lay" is added for emphasis. Can be used as a verb.

1 *"Look at Jane in her mini skirt. Si beh hiao, man." (Look at Jane in her mini-skirt. What a flirt.)*

2 *"Aiyah, she always wear jeans tight-tight. Very hiao lay lay one." (Oh, she always likes wearing very tight jeans. She's a real flirt.)*

3 *"She wear so much makeup because she wan' to go and hiao lay lay, lor." (She's wearing so much makeup because she wants to flirt.)*

See also **hiao mi, kee hiao**

hiao mi |hee-ow mi'| A combination of "hiao" (above) and "mi" (Mandarin for "honey"). Describes a flirtatious and vain girl.

▣ *"Dun be such a hiao mi, can or not?" (Can you please not be such a flirt?)*

See also **hiao**

hiong |hee-yong| Hokkien for "strong", "fierce", "aggressive" or "ruthless". Can sometimes also mean "reckless".

1 *"You go China, hor, must be careful. China people do business very hiong, one." (Be careful when you go to China. The people in China are very ruthless and aggressive when it comes to business.)*

2 *"You drive until so hiong, no wonder kena langgar go hospital." (You drive really recklessly. It's no wonder you got into an accident and wound up in hospital.)*

ho bo No, nothing to do with vagrants. This is the quintessential Hokkien greeting, meaning, "are you well?"

▣ *Beng: "Ho bo?" (Are you well?)*
Seng: "Bo ho!" (No, I'm not well!)

ho gai siao |ho kguy see-ow| Although literally meaning "good recommendation", this Hokkien phrase is always used ironically or sarcastically to express regret at having taken in bad advice.

▣ *"Ah Beng tell me go to No. 90-052 Geylang Lorong 69 look for Tiffany, say she damn jude one. Wah lan eh! Din'ch know she sooo pooi one — damn ho gai siao!" (Ah Beng told me to go to No. 90-052 Geylang Lorong 69 to look for Tiffany, saying she was really pretty. But, oh man! I didn't expect her to be so fat! What rotten advice!)*

ho mia |ho mee-ah| Literally, Hokkien for "good name", meaning "the good life".

☐ *"Stay here, everyday can go East Coast eat seafood. Ho mia, lair!" (Living here, you can go to the East Coast for seafood everyday. What a good life!)*

See also **pai mia**

ho say Hokkien exclamation denoting satisfaction, or enthusiastic endorsement.

[1] *Beng: "Eh, I blanja you makan tonight, okay?" (Hey, let me treat you to a meal tonight, alright?)*
Seng: "Ho say, ah!" (Alriiiight!)

[2] *"His company IPO oreddy, he sure ho say liao." (His company has already gone public, so he must feel really satisfied.)*

hojjiber / horrijiber / horrigible Acceptable Singlish variant pronunciations of "horrible".

[1] *"Wah lau, simple thing like this, how can do until so hojjiber one?" (Holy cow, this is such a simple task. How did he do it so horribly?)*

[2] *"I just saw that 'Star Wars Episode One' flim. Damn horrijiber one." (I just saw the film "Star Wars Episode One". It was really horrible.)*

Hokkien peng |hock-kee-en bpeng| The quintessential private soldier — salt of the earth, if not downright earthy. Forms the foundation of our armed forces, and the persons without whom this Singlish dictionary would not be possible.

☐ *"You air-lebber one, how come you kena this Hokkien peng platoon?" (You're an "A" level student. How did you wind up in this platoon full of Hokkien soldiers?)*

hong kan |hong gkahn| A very rude Hokkien phrase meaning "asking for trouble". Literally, "wanting to be fucked".

☐ *"Why you stare at me? Hong kan, is it?" (Why are you staring at me? Are you asking for trouble?)*

hoong kee Hokkien for "cigarette".

☐ *"Eh, go outside and take a hoong kee break, ai mai?" (Hey, let's go outside for a cigarette break. How about it?)*

hoot The quintessential Ah Beng term for "fight" or "beat up".

[1] *"You go and stare at the Ah Beng, sure kena hoot." (If you stare at that Ah Beng, you're sure to be beaten up.)*

[2] *"Ai tio hoot ah?" (Do you want to be beaten up?)*

See also **hantam, kiam pak**

hor Another Singlish tag. It has no real meaning, but is used in two ways: **[1]** as a sentence break similar to "you know" or **[2]** as a tag soliciting one's concurrence or response.

[1] *"He, hor, very kan cheong one." (He, y'know, is really very uptight.)*

[2] *"Ah Beng is damn kan cheong, leh. Hor?" (Ah Beng is really uptight. Don't you agree?)*

[3] *"Wah! Long long no see, man! You put on a lot of weight, hor?" (Whoa! Long time no see! You've put on a lot of weight, haven't you?)*

See also **lah, lair, leh, lor, meh**

horlan Of uncertain origin, this term is used to denote a far-off place or an unexpected situation, usually unpleasant. Some believe "horlan" is a deliberate mispronunciation of "Holland" (being a distant and unpleasant land, we suppose) while others have posited that the term may derive from the Hokkien predilection to incorporate the word "lan" into their speech, and there is some basis for this belief, as the Taiwanese reportedly use the word "horlan" to denote "bullshitting".

[1] *"Go and puay horlan, lah! I do'wan to see you anymore!" (Get lost! I don't want to see you anymore!)*

[2] *"Ah Beng reported us to the Principal? Horlan liao, lah!" (Ah Beng reported us to the Principal? We're in trouble now!)*

See also **go fly kite**

horlumpick Singlish pronunciation of "Olympics", usually by the older generation.

[·] *"Eh, you got watch the horlumpick, not?" (Hey, did you watch the Olympic Games?)*

horn To sound the horn of one's car. Used as a verb, in a way similar to the American "honk".

[·] *"Why is the car in front of us so slow? Horn the bugger!" (Why is the car in front of us so slow? Sound the horn to hurry him up!)*

horn, ah Not an exhortation to sound one's car horn, but rather, a contraction of "hold on", i.e. a request to stay on the line during a telephone call. The Singlish equivalent of "please hold".

[·] *Caller: "May I speak to Mr Tan Ah Beng, please?"*
Receptionist: "Horn, ah." (Please hold on.)

how? [1] The Singlish abbreviation of "how are you?"

[1] *"Eh, Rosli! How, man?" (Hey, Rosli! How are you?)*

[2] *"Eh, Mohan! How, da?" (Hey, Mohan! How are you?)*

[2] The Singlish equivalent of "what do we do now?"

[1] *"Ah Beng burn down the house. So how like that?" (Ah Beng burned the house down. So what do we do now?)*

[2] *"We reach Johor oreddy. So how now?" (We've already reached Johor. So what do we do now?)*

③ *"Okay, I've inserted the screw into the hole... then how?" (Okay, I've inserted the screw into the hole... now what do I do?)*

how can In true Singaporean economical style, this is a contraction of "how can this be?" or "how can this be possible?" Originates from the Malay-Hokkien hybrid phrase, "Mana eh sai?"

⊡ *"Ah Beng became a President's Scholar? How can?" (Ah Beng became a President's Scholar? How on earth did this happen?)*

See also **mana eh sai**

how many money? A common substitute for "how much is this?"

⊡ *Little girl: "Uncle, this one how many money?" (Uncle, how much is this?)*

Mamak shop owner: "$1.40."

how seow Very rude Hokkien term meaning "to talk nonsense" or "bullshit". "Seow" in Hokkien means "sperm".

⊡ *"Your watch got real diamond, meh? Don't how seow, lah!" (Does your watch have real diamonds on it? Don't bullshit me!)*

See also **kong chiao weh, talk cock**

huat sio |hoo-aht see-oh| Hokkien for "fever". In Singlish, it's used to either describe getting hot under the collar, or someone as crazy.

① *"Piang eh, every time I see Ah Lian only, I huat sio, man!" (Holy cow, every time I see Ah Lian, I get hot under the collar!)*

② *"Aiyah, that huat sio one come oreddy!" (Oh no, that crazy person has arrived!)*

See also **steam**

hum kar chan |hum gka chaan| Cantonese curse, meaning "whole family die" or "whole family bankrupt".

⊡ *"Hum kar chan, ah! You dare stab me in the back! You wait... you just wait!" (A curse upon your whole family! You dare to betray me? Just you wait!)*

hum sup loh |haam sup low| Cantonese term literally meaning, "salty and wet fellow". A lecherous man.

⊡ *"Wah lau, look at that uncle, whole day sit by the public pool looking at char bor. What a hum sup loh." (Look at that old man! He spends the whole day ogling girls at the public pool. What a dirty old man!)*

See also **chee ko pek**, **lao ter kor**

humb thumb |hahm tahm| Common mispronunciation of "hantam" by cheenapiangs. See **hantam**

humpalang |hahm'plahng| Means "everything", and may connote a lack of discrimination. The word is probably derived, at least in part, from Cantonese, due to the word "hum", which means "whole" or "entire".

[1] *Salesman: "Miss, ah, you want to buy which one, ha?" (Miss, which one do you wish to purchase?)*
Tai Tai: "I humpalang also want!" (I want the whole lot!)

See also **chapalang**

Ii

I {location} **oreddy** An abbreviated form of saying "I am already at {location}".

⊡ *Beng: "You where now?" (Where are you now?)*
Seng: "I Bishan oreddy." (I'm already in Bishan.)

I also donno |ai oh-so doh-no| The Singlish equivalent of "don't ask me" or "I'm at a complete loss". A plea of ignorance when confronted by something complicated or bewildering.

[1] *"How Ah Beng got into Harvard, I also donno." (I am at a complete loss as to how Ah Beng managed to get into Harvard.)*

[2] *"Eh, physics this sort of thing, I also donno, so please go and kacho someone else." (Don't ask me anything about physics. Please go and bug someone else.)*

See also **you ask me, I ask who?**

I also say |ai oh-so say| A phrase used to express emphatic agreement, similar to "totally" or "exactly".

⊡ *Seng: "Wah lau, weather so hot until I feel like satay liao!" (Man, the weather is so hot, I feel like a stick of satay!*
Beng: "I also say! Let's faster go aircon place!" (Me too! Let's quickly find an air-conditioned place!)

if cock can talk, chee bye can kah pager An especially rude retort used against someone who has just accused you of "talking cock". It literally means, "If the penis can talk, then the vagina can communicate through a pager". This has fallen into obsolescence along with the pager.

⊡ *Ah Beng: "Eh, Chee Soon Juan just joined the PAP!"*
Ah Seng: "Don't talk cock, lah!"
Ah Beng: "Eh, if cock can talk, chee bye can kah pager!"

immeelly |ee-mee-lee| The Singlish pronunciation of "immediately".

⊡ *"When I heard that the lottery went up to $5 million, I immeely go* *and buy." (When I heard that the lottery had gone up to $5 million, I immediately went out and bought a ticket.)*

inche |in-chay'h| Derived from the Malay word "encik" for "mister", in Singapore, this used to be way to greet or refer to a Warrant Officer in the armed forces. It has recently fallen into decline as an official term, but its use persists among reservists ("Operationally-ready NSmen" to the anal propagandists amongst you) of a certain vintage.

innards |ee-nahrds| Nothing to do with entrails, this is merely the common contraction/pronunciation of "in other words".

⊡ *"My company outsource all the jobs to India. Innards, I sure kena retrench." (My company has been outsourcing all its jobs to India. In other words, I'm sure to be retrenched.)*

iron rings A popular pronunciation of "onion rings".

⊡ *Ah Beng: "So what side dishes do you want with your chicken chop?"*

Ah Seng: "I wan' fry, salad and iron rings." (I want fries, salad and onion rings.)

is it? In Singlish, "is it" is the most common question tag, and is used regardless of the actual verb or verb to be that precedes it. It is also used on its own to express scepticism, similar to the American "yeah, right!".

1 *"You got mail, is it?" (You've received mail, have you?)*

2 *"You all going to Bali, is it?" (You're all going to Bali, are you?)*

3 *"He do this sort of thing because he pok kai, is it?" (He did this sort of thing because he's broke, did he?)*

4 *Beng: "I got accepted into Harvard." (I've been accepted into Harvard.)*

Seng: "Is it?" (Yeah, right!)

itchy backside A rather picturesque description of a restive person, i.e. someone who does something disruptive out of boredom.

⊡ *Ah Beng: "Why you go and potong jalan Ah Teck's girlfriend?" (Why did you steal Ah Teck's girlfriend from him?)*

Ah Seng: "Aiyah, just itchy backside, lor." (Oh, I was just bored, that's all.)

See also **boh liao, chiak pah boh sai pang, gatal, wu liao**

Jj

NOTE: If you can't find certain words you think should be spelled with a "j", try looking under "c" instead. For instance, we've spelled "jiak" as "chiak" and "jia lat" as "chia lat". This is because it's more intuitive for those unfamiliar with hanyu pinyin spelling and pronunciation. Must be considerate, mah!

jaga |jah-gah| Malay for "awake" or "guard", in Singlish it has come to mean "to take care of" or "look after", and is also a generic term for a caretaker or night watchman, usually of Sikh ethnicity.
1 *"Eh, I'm going to the toilet. Can you jaga my bag for me?" (I'm going to the toilet. Can you look after my bag for me?)*
2 *"Our new jaga is Mr Ujaggar Singh." (Our new caretaker is Mr Ujaggar Singh.)*

jakun |jah-koon| The Jakun are a primitive tribe of native Malays who inhabit the upper reaches of the Pahang and Johor rivers. Over the years, the term "jakun" has become a pejorative way of describing someone as unsophisticated or bumpkin-like.
1 *"This dress make me look like jakun like that." (This dress makes me look like some country bumpkin.)*
2 *"Microwave also donno how to use? Why you so jakun?" (You don't even know how to operate a microwave oven? Why are you such a country bumpkin?)*
See also **mountain tortoise, suah koo**

jambu |jahm-boo| Adjective used by Mats to describe the pulchritude of their women. Derived from the common name of a juicy, plump, pear-shaped fruit, the jambu *(Syzygium samarangense)*, known to orang putihs as the Wax Apple or Java Apple).
"Adoi, check out that minah, man. Super jambu, sial." (Whoa, check out that Malay woman, man. She's really gorgeous!)
See also **chio, jude**

jangan catastrophe Where a Mat Roker might ask one to "jangan tension", the Cambridge-educated cosmopolitan Malay of today would use this phrase to calm you down.

⊡ *"Bang, these sort of inconsequential matters, semua no problem, lah. Jangan catastrophe."* (Brother, these inconsequential matters are all not a problem. So don't panic.)

See also **ai tzai, jangan tension, lac, maintain balan, relac, steady**

jangan tension A Mat-ism, it is an exhortation to keep one's cool.

⊡ *"Aiyah, this sort of small-small thing, no problem, lah. Jangan tension."* (Oh, these small matters are no problem. There's no need to panic.)

See also **ai tzai, jangan catastrophe, lac, maintain balan, relac, steady**

jelak |jer-la'h| Malay for "satiated", and is used to express how one finds the food too rich, or that one has eaten a particular food so often that its taste has become boring or monotonous.

1 *"This curry too lemak, lah. Eat oreddy very jelak."* (This curry is too heavy in spices. I find it too rich to eat.)

2 *"Don't give me too much curry. Lately, I bit jelak, lah."* (Don't give me too much curry. Lately, I've eaten too much of it.)

jerorize |jee-roh-rize| To nullify something. Literally, to make "zero" (or as we pronounce it, "jiro" or "jilo").

⊡ *"If you don't clear your leave by the end of the year, I will jerorize them."* (If you don't clear your leave by the end of the year, I'll record it as forfeited.)

See also **jilo / jiro**

ji seow |jee see-ow| To provoke, irritate or disturb. The original Hokkien term from which this is derived means to titillate sexually.

1 *"Eh, I'm si beh busy now. Don't come and ji seow me."* (Hey, I'm really busy! So don't disturb me!)

2 *"How many times oreddy I tell him, dun ji seow the Inche. But he ngeh-ngeh go and ji seow him, so now kena sign extra."* (I've told him many times not to irritate the Warrant Officer. But he insisted on provoking him, and now he's stuck with extra guard duty.)

See also **chochok, kacau, listurb**

jibra The Singlish way of pronouncing "zebra".

⊡ *"There got jibra crossing, why you must jaywalk?"* (There's a zebra crossing over there. Why did you jaywalk?)

jilo / jero / jiro |jee-loh/jee-roh| The Singlish way to pronounce "zero".

⊡ *"Your test how come can get jilo one?"* (How on earth did you score a zero on your test?)

See also **goose egg**

juang lah Of uncertain origin, this phrase probably derives from the Malay word "juang" meaning to fight or struggle. However, in

Singlish, it has ironically come to be an expression of resignation or nonchalance, similar to "whatever" or "anything".

[1] *Ah Beng: "He every time say you, you don'ch care, meh?" (He's always talking ill of you. Don't you care?)*

Ah Seng: "Juang lah! Let him say, lah!" (Ah, forget it! Let him talk!)

[2] *Ah Chek: "Eh, what you want to eat tonight, ah?" (What do you want to eat tonight?)*

Ah Soh: "Juang lah, anything also can." (Whatever. I'm easy.)

See also **han na, heck care**

jude |joot| "Pretty." Of uncertain provenance. Hypotheses have ranged from the Beatles' song "Hey Jude" to the Catholic patron saint of the impossible.

⊡ *"Convent girls are all damn jude." (Convent girls are all very pretty.)*

See also **chio, jambu**

Kk

k Common SMS abbreviation for "OK".

KIV |kay eye vee| An acronym from colonial bureaucracy which stands for "Keep In View", i.e. items, documents or papers that should be shelved for later consideration. This label is often found on trays, cabinets and shelves in Singaporean offices. Essentially used as a verb, in the sense of "to shelve" or "put on the back-burner" or more often than not, "to procrastinate".

[1] *"I damn busy now, can I KIV it and get back to you?" (I'm very busy now. Can I hold on to this document and relay my comments later?)*

[2] *"This sort of important thing, don't rush. Better KIV and slowly-slowly think abourit." (When it comes to such important matters, it's better to put it on the backburner and think about it more carefully.)*

KLK Acronym for "kwai lan kia", Hokkien for "troublemaking child".

⊡ *"I hate going to Taka. A lot of KLKs like to go there to KLKK. (I detest going to Takashimaya. There are a lot of hoodlums walking about.)*

See also **KLKK, kwai lan**

KLKK Acronym for "kia lai kia ker" — Hokkien for "to walk about" or "stroll" with no fixed purpose in mind.

⊡ *"Eh, let's go Orchard Road and KLKK." (Hey, let's go to Orchard Road for a stroll.)*

kah si |gka see| To have the guts or gall to act in a reckless fashion.

1 *"Johnny want to challen Ah Beng to a fight? He so kah si, meh?" (Johnny's challenging Ah Beng to a fight? Since when did he have the guts?)*

2 *"He norchat find job oreddy spend so much. Damn kah si!" (He hasn't found a job yet, but he's already spent so much. What gall!)*

kacau / kachau / kachiau / kacho |kah-chao/kah-chao/kah-chee-ow/kah-choh| From the Malay word "kacau", meaning "disorderly", in Singlish, it has become a verb meaning to harass, annoy, bother, or disturb.

1 *"My exam coming, I must study! You all don't come and kachau me, okay?" (My exams are approaching and I must study for them. Please don't bother me!)*

2 *"Eh, my jigsaw puzzle I pai swee-swee, why you must go and kacho?" (Hey, I put that jigsaw puzzle together so carefully! Why did you mess it all up?)*

See also **chochok, ji seow, listurb**

kai kai |gkai gkai| Hokkien phrase literally translated as "walk-walk". Means to go out for a jaunt.

⊡ *"Come, let's go Far East and kai kai." (Come, let's go to Far East Plaza and walk around.)*

See also **KLKK**

kak pui |kahk poo-ee| Onomatopoeic term describing the act of loudly clearing one's throat and spitting out the phlegm.

⊡ *"Eh, nowsaday got SARS, you kak pui outside sure kena saman!" (Nowadays with the threat of SARS, you're sure to be fined if you spit in public.)*

kaki / kaki lang / kaki nang |kah-kee/ kah-kee lahng/ kah-kee nahng| A word of hybrid origin. "Kaki" in Malay means "legs", while "kaki" in local Hokkien means "mine" or "my own". "Lang" means persons. Somehow, the Malay and Hokkien words have blurred into a single phrase meaning "buddies" or "close companions".

1 *"Next week I'm throwing a party. Call all our usual kaki, lah." (Next week I'm throwing a party and inviting our usual gang.)*

2 *John: "Eh, Mary, my kaki lang all not free to go out tomorrow, leh. Can I go out with you or not?" (Hey, Mary, my buddies have bailed on me tomorrow. So can I still go out with you?)*

Mary: "OK, lor." (Alright.)

3 *"I every Friday go and puak kiao with my office kakis." (Every Fri-*

day night, I indulge in a little gambling with my office buddies.)

kalang kabut / kelam kabut |gkah-lang gkah-bote/gker-lahm gkah-bote| A colloquial Malay phrase which describes a chaotic panic or to rush into things in a disorganized and foolhardy manner. "Kalang" means "group" and "kelam" means murky, while "kabut" means "fog". The image is of a herd of people rushing and stumbling through a dense fog.

1 *"Eh, do this sort of thing must be careful, lah. Don't anyhow kalang kabut." (One must be careful when doing such things, and avoid rushing into it.)*

2 *"When my boss told me of the new deadline, straightaway I kelam kabut." (When my boss told me of the new deadline, I immediately went into a panic.)*

See also **gabra**

kali pok |kah-lee pok| The Singlish pronunciation of "curry puff". Can mean either the snack where curry, potatoes and (traditionally) chicken are fried in a pastry shell (similar to the Cornish pasty of England or the empanadas of Spain), or a bouffant hairstyle where the hair is piled high on the head and puffed up.

1 *"Lan eh, this kali pok all kantang no kway. Where got standard?" (Ugh! This curry puff is filled only with potatoes and no chicken! It's not up to standard!)*

2 *"You got see Ah Beng's new kali pok hairstyle, not? He go JB and do one, lair!" (Have you seen Ah Beng's new bouffant hairdo? He had it done in Johor Baru!)*

kan |gkahn| Hokkien term meaning "fuck" or "screw".

"I yesterday cock up and the company lost the contract, so I kena kan by the boss." (Thanks to my mistake, the company lost the contract and I got screwed by the boss.)

See also **lood, hong kan, kan ni na**

kan cheong |gkahn tjee-ong| A Cantonese and Hokkien term meaning nervous, harried, overanxious or uptight.

"Your exam in June, now only March, you kan cheong for what?" (The exam's in June and now it's only March. Why are you so nervous?)

kan cheong spider / kan cheong pi sai Epithet describing someone who's kan cheong, i.e. a nervous wreck. "Pi sai" is Hokkien for "nose booger". Can be abbreviated to omit the "kan".

1 *"Aiyah, ask him to do this for what? You know he's a bloody kan cheong spider." (Ah, why did you ask him to do this? You know what a nervous wreck he is!)*

2 *"Eh, relac can or not? You so kan cheong pi sai for what?" (Hey, relax, won't you? Why are you so uptight?)*

③ *"Wah lau, hurry, hurry, hurry for what? Super cheong spider." (Hey! What's the flaming hurry, you overanxious twit?)*

See also **kan cheong**

kan ni na |gkahn-nee-nah| One of the rudest phrases in the lexicon. It means either "fuck you" or "fucking" in Hokkien, depending on the context. Amongst hard core Bengs, it is used almost like a punctuation mark.

① *"Kan ni na! Today kena saman three times!" (Fuck! I got ticketed three times today!)*

② *"Look at me when I'm kan ni na talking to you!" (Look at me when I'm fucking talking to you!)*

kan ni na bu / kan ni na bu chao chee bye The rudest phrase of all. The thermonuclear weapon in the arsenal of Hokkien swearing. Use only if you wish to be beaten up or want other people to think you were raised in a longkang. Literally: "Fuck your mother/Fuck your mother's smelly cunt."

See also **tiu**

kan ti tu |gkahn dtee-dtoo| The Hokkien translation of "fuck spider".

See also **fuck spider**

kana lan eh |gkahn-ah lahn ay| Insulting Hokkien phrase meaning, "just like a penis".

⊡ *"See his face, kana lan eh, like that." (Look at his dick face!)*

kana sai |gkahn-ah sai| Hokkien phrase meaning, "like shit." Not to be confused with "kena sai".

⊡ *"You listen to him karaoke. His voice kana sai lai dat." (Listen to him karaoke: his voice is really crap!)*

See also **kena sai, sai**

kang chew |kahng tch'iu| Literally: "to hold hands". Used as a noun to describe someone else's boyfriend or girlfriend, usually at an early stage of the relationship. Might sometimes connote uncertainty about the relationship.

① *"Eh, today Ah Chee's kang chew coming or not? I want to see his taste how leh." (Hey, is Ah Chee's girlfriend coming? I want to see what his taste is like.)*

② *"Aiyah Ma, now that argly guy is only Ah Lian's kang chew. When she want to go ROM then you worry!" (Don't worry, Ma. That ugly guy is now only at the hand-holding stage with Ah Lian. When she wants to marry him, that's when you should worry!)*

kang kang / kang kang koyak |kahng kahng koh-ya'h| An expression describing one's legs being spread wide apart. The addition of "koyak", Malay for "broken", is for sarcastic emphasis.

☐1 *"Eh, can you not sit with your leg kang kang like that? Damn pai kuah." (Can you please not sit with your legs spread apart like that? It's very unbecoming.)*

☐2 *"Wah lau eh! Ah Beng just now slipped on some ice, fall down all kang-kang koyak!" (Oh my! Ah Beng slipped on some ice, and fell on the floor with his legs wide apart!)*

kang kor |kahng kohr| A Hokkien term meaning "troublesome" or "uncomfortable".

☐1 *"This kind of easy work, why you do until so kang kor like that?" (This is such easy work. Why are you doing it in a way that makes it look so troublesome?)*

☐2 *"I ask you to do this small thing, so kang kor meh?" (I'm only asking you to do this little favour. Is that so troublesome?)*

See also **leceh, ma fan**

kang tau |kahng tao| A Hokkien term which is similar to "lobang", i.e. having special connections, but may also be used in the sense of a "secret work technique".

☐ *"Don't scared, Uncle here got kang tau one. I show you how to do OK?" (Don't worry, Uncle has special connections/a secret trick. Let me show you how to do it, alright?)*

See also **lobang**

kapo / kapoh |gkah-poh| Of uncertain origin, this means to steal or pilfer.

☐ *"Eh, next time they give out coupons, can kapo one for me?" (Hey, the next time they hand out coupons, can you swipe one for me?)*

See also **curi, stun**

katek / katek ayam |gkah-te'h| Short or stunted, derived from the Malay word "katik" for "short". When paired with "ayam", Malay for "chicken", it becomes an epithet similar to "shorty".

☐1 *"Ah Seng damn katek, but his rugby still damn powderful." (Ah Seng may be short, but he plays rugby very well.)*

☐2 *"Aiyah, Ah Seng this sort of katek ayam, how to reach the top shelf?" (How is a shorty like Ah Seng supposed to reach the top shelf?)*

kau |cow| Hokkien term meaning to woo or court someone.

☐ *"Eh, she damn jude, why you dun go and kau her, leh?" (Wow, she's really pretty! Why don't you court her?)*

See also **buaya**

kau peh kau bu |kau pay kau boo| Hokkien term meaning "to make a lot of noise". Literally: "cry to the father and cry to the mother". Means either to bellyache or nag or cause a hullabaloo. Sometimes all three at the same time. Sometimes shortened to just "kau peh".

1 *"I can't tahan working with Ah Beng! He whole day kau peh kau bu one." (I can't stand working with Ah Beng! He's always griping about this and that!)*

2 *"I know I screwed up oreddy! Don't kau peh, lah!" (I have already acknowledged that it's my fault. So quit going on about it!)*

kawan |gkah-wahn| Malay for "friend" or "buddy".

• *"Ah Lian and I kawan-kawan only, lah. She's not my stead." (Ah Lian and I are only friends. She's not my steady girlfriend.)*

See also **peng yew**

kay |gkay| Hokkien for "very" or "additionally". Placed in front of any number of words for emphasis.

1 *"Wah, kay heng man, managed to escape the arrow just now!" (Whoa, that was a close call, dodging that arrow, man!)*

2 *"This fella is kay stupid!" (This fellow is extra stupid!)*

kay kiang |gkay kee-ahng| Sarcastic Hokkien phrase which translates as "faking intelligence". It usually describes someone as biting off more than one can chew or acting smarter than one actually is.

1 *"The project at first swee-swee, then Ah Beng kay kiang go and add this add that, now kana sai like that." (The project was looking just perfect, and then that "genius" Ah Beng had to add all sorts of rubbish, and now it looks like shit.)*

2 *"Eh, this sort of thing better not kay kiang. Wait you sure kena sai." (In such matters, you should be careful not to bite off more than you can chew. Otherwise, you'll be in deep shit.)*

kaypoh |kay-po| A busybody or nosey parker. Can also be used as an adjective or verb. If you're Eurasian, you can shorten it to "kayps".

1 *"Ah Beng is such a kaypoh." (Ah Beng is such a busybody.)*

2 *"Don'ch be so kaypoh, can or not?" (Can you please not be a nosey parker?)*

3 *"Why you go and kaypoh their business?" (Why did you butt into their business?)*

4 *"You know, that Cedric de Rosario is such a kayps, mane." (That Cedric de Rosario is such a busybody!)*

kayu Malay for "wood". Used to suggest stupidity in the same manner as "blockhead".

1 *"Referee kayu!" (The referee is a blockhead!)*

2 *"Swear, that Benson is such a kayu driver." (I swear, that Benson is a real idiot of a driver.)*

kebelakang pusing |ker-blah-kahng poo-seng| Malay for "turn to the rear". A military drill command that has snuck into the civilian world as the Singlish equivalent of "u-turn" or "volte face".

☐ *"The gahmen LPPL over the 'two is enough' campaign, so now boh pian kebelakang pusing." (The government's "two is enough" campaign backfired on them, so now they have no choice but to make a policy u-turn.)*

See also **gostan**

kee hiao |kee hee-ow| Hokkien for "being flirtatious".

☐ *"Auntie, why you wear until like that? Kee hiao, ah?" (Auntie, why are you dressed like that? Are you being flirtatious?)*

See also **hiao, hiao mi**

keep to yourself A request to keep something a secret. An abbreviation of the English phrase "please keep this to yourself".

☐ *"Eh, Ah Lian went to pierce her neh neh pok, you keep to yourself, okay?" (Ah Lian went to pierce her nipples. Keep this to yourself, alright?)*

kek kee |kay'k kee| Hokkien for "to stand on ceremony" or engage in formal or polite civilities.

☐ *"Aiyah, gimme present for what? We friend for so long, no need to kek kee, mah!" (Oh, why are you presenting me with a gift? We're such old friends, there's no need to engage in such civility.)*

kek sai |gkek sai| To actively control one's sphincter muscles in order to prevent defecation. Often used as a euphemism for self-censorship or self-restriction.

☐ *"Aiyah, what to do? I cannot say anything bad about him, so I just kek sai, lor." (Agh, what could I do? I'm not allowed to say anything bad about him, so I just have to hold myself back.)*

kek sim |gkek seem| Hokkien for sad, depressed or heartbroken.

☐ *"When I heard Ah Beng kena VD, hor, I damn kek sim." (When I heard that Ah Beng had contracted venereal disease, I felt really sad.)*

kelong |gkay-long| Originally, a kelong is a wooden structure built above the sea by driving wooden "piles" (made from the trunks of coconut trees, for example) into the seabed and used for commercial fishing. Colloquially, it is a term used to describe any form of cheating or corruption in any competition e.g. soccer.

1 *Heartlander version: "Wah lau, Yishun United goalie normally damn tzai, but this match perform like cock and lose 5-0! Confirm must be kelong one!" (Holy cow, the Yishun United goalie is normally very capable, yet in this game he's performed so badly and the team has lost 5-0! I'm positive there's some corruption going on!)*

2 *Atas version: "Wah lau, Queen Astrid Park Rangers normally*

damn cock, but this match somehow can win 5-0! Confirm must be kelong one!" (Holy cow, Queen Astrid Park Rangers are usually a really bad team, yet they've managed to win this match 5-0! There must be corruption afoot!)

kena |gkuh-nah| Malay term meaning "to incur" or "bring about". In Singlish, it denotes something as having happened. Closest English approximation is "to get".

[1] *"He kena scolded by the teacher."* (He was scolded by the teacher.)

[2] *"He kena whack by Ah Beng."* (He got hit by Ah Beng.)

kena {...} upside down Denotes having received especially harsh treatment. Fill in your own verb between "kena" and "upside down".

[1] *"Wah lau, today I kena screwed upside down by my boss."* (Holy cow, today I received a big telling off from my boss.)

[2] *"Piang, yesterday our football team kena thrash upside down."* (Holy cow, yesterday, our football team received a thorough thrashing.)

kena jack A term originating with the Mats, it means to be trumped, tricked or taken advantage of by someone. Possibly derived from "hijack"

⊡ *"The score is 1-0... our team all kena jack siah!"* (The score is 1-0. Our team must have been duped!)

kena qie |gkuh-nah ts'ee-eh| A rare hybrid Malay-Mandarin phrase, combining the Malay word "kena" (meaning "to have incurred") and the Mandarin word "qie" (meaning "slice"). It is used to describe undergoing something difficult or onerous, such as losing a game.

[1] *"Wah lau! Yesterday's maths exam, kena qie!"* (Oh man, I really got killed in yesterday's maths exam!)

[2] *"Yesterday, I kena qie by Ah Beng in snooker."* (Yesterday, Ah Beng really thrashed me in snooker.)

kena sai A happy marriage of Malay and Hokkien, meaning to get into trouble. Literally, "got hit by shit." Not to be confused with "kana sai".

⊡ *"He didn't pass up his homework, so kena sai from the teacher."* (He didn't hand in his homework, so he got shit from the teacher.)

keng |gkayng| Hokkien term meaning "to malinger" or feign sickness.

[1] *"He got flu, my foot! He's only keng-ing!"* (I don't believe he has influenza. He's faking it.)

[2] *"He's a big keng king!"* (He's a habitual malingerer.)

See also **chiak chua, pontang, siam, tuang**

keng chio kia |gkeng tjee-oh gkee-ah| Literally: "banana child". A Chinese person who takes on Western affectations, i.e. yellow on the outside and white on the inside.

☐ *"He go Engrand study come back oreddy act like keng chio kia." (He went to England to study, and on his return, began acting like some colonial stooge.)*
See also **chiak kantang**

ketuk |gkuh-to'h| Malay for "knock" or "strike". It is also often used to denote being taken advantage of.
1 *"Adoi! You ketuk my head for what? Pain, you know!" (Ow! Why did you hit my head? That was painful, you know!)*
2 *"You paid $300 for this piece of junk? Alamak, you really kena ketuk, man." (You paid $300 for this piece of junk? God, you really were taken for a ride!)*

kia! |gkee-ah| The local equivalent of "let's go!"
☐ *Beng: "Eh, tonight go launge, leh." (Hey, let's go to the lounge tonight.)*
Seng: "Kia!" (Let's go!)

kia lai kia ker |gkee-ah lai gkee-ah gkuh| See **KLKK**

kia si lang |gkee-ah see lahng| A Hokkien term which could be translated as either "to scare even the dead" or "to scare people to death". Either way, it is used when one has been given a fright.
1 *"Why your makeup like that one? Kia si lang!" (Why are you made up like that? It's frightful!)*
2 *"The way he drive, hor, damn kia si lang." (The way he drives is truly scary.)*

kiam |*gkee-ahm*| Hokkien for "salty", but is also used very often as a euphemism for "stingy". This has probably come about by people truncating "kiam siap", which means "tightfisted".
1 *"Eh, the soup oreddy so kiam, no need to add chiu cheng!" (Hey, the soup's already very salty. You don't have to add soy sauce!)*
2 *"Ah Chek, why you so kiam one? Give only 10 cents to charity!" (Mister, why are you so stingy, donating only 10 cents to charity?)*
See also **kiam eh, kiam siap**

kiam chye |gkee-ahm chai| Salted vegetables. A term often used to describe papers or books that are in a crumpled or messy condition.
☐ *"Why your textbook so kiam chye one?" (Why is your textbook in such a crumpled condition?)*

kiam eh |gkee-ahm ay| A generic name used to address a stingy or miserly person.
☐ *"Eh, kiam eh! Why you donate only 10 cents?"*
See also **kiam siap**

kiam pak |khee-ahm pa'h| Hokkien phrase literally meaning "owe a beating". It's used to describe someone who's asking to be beaten up.

☐ *"He behave until so yaya, damn kiam pak one, you know." (His behaviour is really arrogant. He's really asking to be beaten up.)*

kiam siap |gkee-am see-up| A Hokkien term used to describe someone as stingy and mean.

☐ *"Why you give me such a small piece of meat? So kiam siap one!" (Why did you give me such a small portion of meat? You're really stingy!)*

See also **kiam, kiam eh**

kiang |kee-ahng| Hokkien for "clever".

☐ *"Ha? Ah Beng went NUS? He so kiang, meh?" (What? Ah Beng was accepted into the National University of Singapore? Since when was he so clever?)*

See also **pandai**

kiao kah yo lum pah / KKYLP |kee-ow kah yo lahm pah| Hokkien phrase which literally means to raise one's legs and shake one's genitals. It describes being extremely idle.

1 *Sergeant: "Chao recruit! I ask you to go and do area cleaning and instead I find you here kiao kah yo lum pah!" (Smelly recruit! I told you to do area cleaning, and instead I find you skiving here!)*

2 *Ah Beng: "Ho say ah! Tomorrow got public holiday, I just want to stay at home and KKYLP." (Cool! As tomorrow's a public holiday, I intend to stay home and just relax.)*

See also **cho boh**

kiasi |gkee-ah-see| Hokkien term literally meaning, "afraid of death". Used to admonish someone for being cowardly.

☐ *"Raining only, cannot go out, meh? Why you so kiasi one?" (Just because it's raining, you can't go out? Why are you such a fraidy cat?)*

kiasu |gkee-ah-soo| Hokkien adjective literally meaning, "afraid of losing". A highly pejorative description beloved of Singaporeans. Possibly our defining national characteristic. The nearest English equivalent is "dog in a manger", though even that is pretty mild by comparison. Denotes a host of bad qualities, including greed, selfishness, acquisitiveness, rudeness, etc.

1 *"You went to get a handicapped sticker just to chope a parking space? How kiasu can you get?" (You went to get a handicapped sticker just to ensure you have a reserved parking space? What kind of mean, unscrupulous and selfish person are you?)*

2 *"See all the bleddy kiasu people lining up early in the morning to get Hello Kitty from Mehnoner!" (Look at all the greedy, avaricious and acquisitive people, queueing up so early in the morning, just so they'll be first in line to get the new Hello Kitty dolls from McDonald's!)*

kichi |gkee-chi'| Originally from "kecil", the Malay word for "small". In Singlish, it has come to mean "puny" or pathetically undersized.
☐ *"Adoi! How come this restaurant the portion all so kichi, one?" (Oh my! Why are the portions in this restaurant so tiny?)*

kilat |gkee-laht| Malay term meaning "polished", "smooth", or "shining". Used to denote someone or something that is suave or impressively refined.
☐ *"That CEO damn kilat one, no wonder he can smoke all the ang moh." (That CEO is really slick. No wonder he is able to bamboozle all the Westerners.)*

kim tang tang |gkim dtahng dtahng| Teochew and Hokkien phrase to describe someone who is very rich or opulently dressed. Literally, "dripping with gold".
☐ *"That Mrs Lee, hor, dressed like a Christmas tree, chin kim tang tang, man." (That Mrs Lee is really decked out like a Christmas tree, all dripping with gold.)*

kin kah kin chew |gkin kah gkin chew| Hokkien idiom which literally translates as, "fast hand, fast leg", and which means to be pro-active.
☐ *"Inche coming back in one hour to inspect bunk. We all better kin kah kin chew." (The Warrant Officer is returning in an hour to inspect our barracks. We'd better move fast!)*

king Someone who's an extremely good example of something. Often used together with other adjectives to describe a person who's superlative at something, usually unsavoury.
1 *"Eh, you want to contest Tanjong Pagar in the General Election, ah? You think you damn king, is it?" (What? You want to contest Tanjong Pagar in the General Election? You must think you're really great!)*
2 *"Wah piang, that guy is sotong king man... small thing also can cock up!" (Man, that guy's a real idiot — screwing up even such small matters!)*
3 *"That bobo king... target so big also he cannot kena!" (What an inept marksman — missing even such a big target!)*
4 *"Every PE lesson only, he got MC. Damn keng king!" (He's got a medical excuse for every physical education lesson. What a royal malingerer!)*

King Jame version A reference to the 1611 English translation of the Bible, and is used to signify that something is the best and most authentic in its class. Note that "Jame" is the singular of "James".

☐ *"Listen to that solid guitar solo, sial. King Jame version!" (Listen to that solid guitar solo! It's the real thing!)*

kio tio |kee-oh dtee-oh| Literally meaning "to have grabbed it", this means stumbling upon good fortune. Curiously, the opposite of "kio tio goo lan".

☐ *"Today in school I find $10 on the floor, damn kio tio man!" (I found $10 on the floor in school today! What great luck I've grabbed!)*

See also **kio tio goo lan**

kio tio goo lan |kee-oh dtee-oh goo lahn| The Hokkien equivalent of receiving the booby prize. Literally: "To grasp the bull's testicles". No doubt an act accompanied by a very angry bull.

☐ *"He din'ch know and went to buaya the dai kor dai's char bor. Talk about kio tio goo lan." (He flirted with the chief gangster's girlfriend unknowingly. Now he's in for it.)*

See also **kio tio**

kiu kiu kio |gkee-oo gkee-oo gkee-yo| Hokkien for "make a lot of noise". In Mandarin, it's "gua gua jiao".

☐ *"Aiyah, you told me how many times oreddy! I'll do it! Just don't kiu kiu kio anymore, can or not?" (Argh! How many times must you nag me? I'll do it! Just stop making so much noise!)*

knock it down A phrase employed in the Army, ordering soldiers to do push-ups.

☐ *Sergeant: "Whole lot knock it down 30!" (All of you, give me 30 push-ups!)*

kodok |gkoh-do'h| Malay for "frog". Often used in the same sense as "goondu", i.e. a moron, idiot or someone of inferior intelligence.

☐ *"Bleddy kodok, how he can flunk kindergarten also I donno." (That idiot! I can't understand how he managed to fail kindergarten!)*

See also **goondu**

kong chiao weh |gkong tjee-ow way| Hokkien phrase literally meaning "to speak bird language". Probably derived from "talk cock". It means to speak rubbish or nonsense. Although a transliteration of "talk cock", it does not share talk cock's secondary meaning of engaging in casual banter.

1 *"Ah Beng pass the exam? Kong chiao weh!" (Ah Beng managed to pass the exam? You're talking nonsense!)*

2 *"Why you go and believe Johnny? He whole life kong chiao weh only!" (Why did you believe what Johnny said? He's a big bullshitter!)*

See also **how seow, talk cock**

kong sar kong si |gkong sah gkong see| Hokkien for literally, "Talk three talk four", i.e. to engage in idle talk or gossip.

▣ *Ah Lian: "An chua, call me for what?" (Why did you call me?) Ah Soh: "Nothing lah, kong sar kong si only, lor." (Oh, nothing. Just to shoot the breeze.)*

See also **talk three talk four, talk cock**

kong si mi? |gkong see mee| Hokkien for "what are you saying?". More emphatic variants, directly proportional to the level of absurdity they address, include "kong si mi lan chiao" or "kong si mi lum pah", literally, "say what penis" or "say what testicles", meaning "what the hell are you saying?"

1 *"Wah, his report full of cheemkology, he kong si mi also I donno." (Wow, his report was so full of jargon, I had no idea what he was saying.)*

2 *"Ah Beng is buaya-ing my mother? Kong si mi lan chiao, lah, you!" (Ah Beng is trying to date my mother? What the hell are you talking about!)*

See also **talk cock**

kong tau |gkong tao| Hokkien for black magic.

1 *"I heard Ah Lian buay song Ah Beng, so she found some bomoh to do donno what kong tau on him." (I heard Ah Lian was dissatisfied with Ah Beng's behaviour, so she found a witch doctor to perform some black magic and put a hex on him.)*

2 *"Eh, I heard Ah Lian always like to cho kong tau. Better don't play-play with her." (Hey, I heard Ah Lian dabbles regularly in black magic. You'd better not mess with her.)*

kongsi |gkohng see| Hokkien for "share".

▣ *"This football, me and my brother kongsi one." (My brother and I are sharing this football.)*

koo bye |gkoo bai| A (very) marginally more polite variant of "chee bye".

See also **chee bye**

koon Hokkien for "to sleep".

1 *"I was on duty for 36 hours. I really need to koon now." (I was on duty for 36 hours. I really need to sleep now.)*

2 *"He was kooning right through the football match." (He slept right through the football match.)*

kope |gkohp. rhymes with "cope"| To steal, usually something trifling. Similar in meaning to "stun".

▣ *"Wah, where you kope all this stuff from?" (Whoa, where did you steal all this stuff from?)*

See also **curi, stun**

kopi |gkoh-bpee| Malay and Hokkien for coffee.

kopi "c" |gkoh-bpee see| Malay and Hokkien for coffee with sugar and evaporated milk.

kopi kao |gkoh-bpee gkao| Malay and Hokkien for coffee that is thicker and more strongly brewed.

kopi kosong |gkoh-bpee koh-sohng| Malay and Hokkien for coffee with no sugar and no milk.

kopi "o" |gkoh-bpee oh| Black coffee. Coffee with nothing added.

kopi peng |gkoh-bpee bpeng| Malay and Hokkien for coffee with ice.

kopi "o" peng |gkoh-bpee oh bpeng| Malay and Hokkien for black coffee with ice.

kopi siew dai |gkoh-bpee see-ew dtai| Malay and Hokkien for coffee with less condensed milk, i.e. not so sweet.

kopi susu |gkoh-bpee soo-soo| Hokkien and Malay for coffee with milk. ("Susu" is Malay for milk.)

kopi kia |gkoh-bpee gkee-ah| Hokkien for "coffee boy", meaning the waiter at a kopi tiam, dressed in the archetypal singlet (or T-shirt advertising either Guinness Stout or Tiger Beer), shorts, slippers and ABC waist pouch. Often used by Singaporean parents as a warning.

⊡ *"You don't study hard, you sure become kopi kia, one!" (If you don't study hard, you're sure to wind up as a coffee shop assistant!)*

kopi tiam |gkoh-bpee dtee-ahm| Hokkien for "coffee shop". Describes the local coffee shop with hawker stalls in it, not Starbucks.

⊡ *"Eh, come, let's go kopi tiam lim kopi." (Come on, let's go to the coffee shop for a coffee.)*

korek pantat |gkoh-ray'h pahn-taht| Literally, "dig stuff out of one's arse" in Malay. It means to gossip maliciously.

⊡ *"Ah Huay whole day long korek pantat. One day she sure damn chik ak!" (Ah Huay likes to gossip maliciously. One day she'll get her comeuppance!)*

kosh tape The Singlish pronunciation of "Scotch tape", but it refers to any kind of adhesive tape, not just the Scotch brand.

⊡ *"Eh, pass the kosh tape, can?" (Please hand me the Scotch tape.)*

kosong |gkoh-sohng| Malay for "blank" or "empty".

1 *"Eh, can order me a teh kosong, please?" (Please order a cup of plain tea without anything added for me.)*

2 *"I wan' two prata kosong, one prata telur." (I want two plain pratas and one prata with egg.)*

3 *"Ah Beng go NUS, but still come out otak kosong." (Ah Beng graduated from the National University, but he's still empty headed.)*

kotek |gkoh-te'h| Colloquial Malay for "penis", similar to "dick" or "prick". Often used to scold someone for being stupid.

☐ *"You stupid kotek! Of course go Malaysia must bring passport, what! Arbuthen!?" (You stupid prick! Of course you need to bring your passport when entering Malaysia!)*

See also **cock, cockanaden**

koyak |koh-ya'h| A Malay word meaning "spoilt" or "broken".

☐ *"The microwave is oreddy koyak. Don't use." (The microwave is already spoilt. Don't use it.)*

See also **rosak, spoi**

koyok |koh-yo'h| A Malay word meaning "quack medicine", and used to describe goods of dubious quality. The English equivalent would be "snake oil".

☐ *"Dey, dun bluff! You selling koyok, say so, lah!" (Don't try to pull a fast one on us! Just admit you're trying to sell us a load of snake oil!)*

ku ku chiao |gku gku tjee-ow| An affectionate Hokkien term for the penis, mostly used when speaking to children. Our equivalent of "little pee pee".

kua |koo-ah| Hokkien for "look".

kua lang |koo-ah lahng| Literally, "to assess a person" in Hokkien. An adjective used to describe a person who tailors his behaviour towards people depending on their relative positions in the social hierarchy or how useful they are to him.

☐ *"Many Singaporeans are very kua lang type. If you got money, they very friendly to you. If you got no money, they heck care you." (Many Singaporeans are very discriminatory. If you have money, they are very friendly to you. If you have no money, they ignore you.)*

kua chui |koo-ah tz'wee| Hokkien term that literally translates as "to watch the water", meaning to keep a lookout, usually for the authorities.

☐ *"Dun worry, you go inside. I stay here and kua chui." (Don't worry. You go inside, while I stay here and keep a lookout.)*

See also **tai sui**

kua hee Hokkien for "watch movie".

☐ *"Eh, tonight let's go and kua hee." (Let's watch a movie tonight.)*

kua meenite Hokkien/English hybrid expression meaning "to watch the midnight movie".

☐ *"Don't ask me to go and kua meenite. I sure fall asleep one." (Don't ask me to watch the midnight movie. I'm sure to fall asleep.)*

kua si mi /kua si mi kua/ kua si mi lan chiao |koo-ah see mee lahn tjee-ow| Hokkien for "what are you looking at?" or "are you staring at me?" If uttered by an Ah Beng, it's usually a prelude to a fight. "Kua si mi kua" is more belligerent than just "kua si mi", while the addition of "lan chiao" (penis) makes it ruder.

1 *"Eh, that whole bunch of people over there kua si mi, ha?" (Hey, what's that whole bunch of people over there looking at?)*

2 *"Kua si mi lan chiao? You want to kena hantam, is it?" (Are you staring at me? Do you wish to be thumped?)*

See also **an chua, see what?**

kuan si |gkuan see| Hokkien for "to be familiar with" or "make a habit of". No relation to the similar sounding Mandarin word "guanxi".

1 *"Eh, better tell me how to go. Tuas this sort of ulu place, I not kuan si." (You'd better give me directions. I'm not familiar with out of the way places like Tuas.)*

2 *"Ah Beng five year old oreddy kuan si sio hoong kee." (Smoking has been a habit with Ah Beng since he was five years old.)*

kuat |gkoo-aht| Malay for courageous or brave, in a manly sort of way. In Singlish, the meaning has been extended to include "impressive" or "powerful".

1 *"Eh, don't see him small, okay! He study very kuat one! Got six air-level, lair!" (Don't underestimate him! He's very powerful in his studies! He's secured six "A" levels!)*

See also **powderful, saht**

kucing kurap |gkoo-ching gkoo-rahp| Literally, Malay for "mangy cat", this expression means that something or someone is insignificant and half-baked, or incompetent.

"Aiyah, you think such a kucing kurap party can win the elections, meh?" (Do you really think such a crappy party can win the elections?)

See also **chap sar tiam, half past six**

kum gong Hokkien phrase meaning "stupid and blur".

"Why you so kum gong, one? He talking cock only, you go and believe!" (Why are you so stupid? He's only talking nonsense, yet you believed him!)

kum lan |gkum lahn| Hokkien for "blow job". Describes being placed in a humiliating position.

"Piang eh, ask me to come all the way here just to clean her toilet, damn kum lan, man." (Man, she called me all the way here just to clean her toilet! What a humiliating situation.)

kum pooi |gkum poo-ee| The Hokkien equivalent of "like hell!", "what for?" or "as if!"

"You think he does what I tell him to do? Kum pooi!" (You think

he does what I tell him to do? Like hell he does!)

kupoon |gkoo-bpoon| The Singlish pronunciation of "coupon", you know that thing you always request from the other fellow parking his car nearby.

"Eskew me, can I buy a one loler kupoon from you, preeease?" (Excuse me, but may I please purchase a $1 coupon from you?)

kuti |gkoo-dtee| Malay word describing the action of flicking something with one finger. Singaporeans of a certain generation associate it with the game "kuti-kuti", wherein players would use one finger to flick a pawn (usually a bottlecap or colourful plastic token in the shape of an insect or animal) towards their opponent's pawn, with the aim of flipping their pawn on top of their opponent's.

See **no bilis**

kwai lan |gkwai lahn| A Hokkien term used to describe someone who is malicious or irritating, or who deliberately stirs up trouble.

"So many times I told him not to do this sort of thing, but he's just kwai lan." (I've told him repeatedly not to do such things, but he's a real irritating creep.)

See also **sia lan**

kway |gkway| Hokkien for "chicken". Like in the West, "kway" is also used as a common term for prostitutes. It is not clear who first used the word "chicken" to describe the world's oldest profession, though the editors suspect it may have been the Westerners, since one goes to a "chicken" to get "laid"…

1 *"Eh, let's go Margaret Drive and eat kway png!" (Hey, let's go to Margaret Drive and eat chicken rice!")*

2 *"Piang eh, you every weekend go Geylang and find kway, ah?" (Goodness! You go kerb-crawling in Geylang every weekend?)*

Ll

LPPL See **lum pah pah lan**

LC / low class Meaning literally "low class". May be used either to admonish an inferior denizen, express the tawdriness of an object or venue, or even to express one's embarrassment, as if the upper crust were incapable of screwing up.

[1] *"Aiyah, why you bring me to this kind of low class KTV launge?" (Oh dear, why have you brought me to this sleazy karaoke lounge?)*

[2] *"Aiyoh, today hor, I ran for the taxi outside Hyatt Hotel and tripped on the tail of my brand new Donna Karan coat and some more, my shopping spill all over the sidewalk... soooo LC!" (Oh man, today, I ran for the taxi outside the Hyatt Hotel and tripped on the tail of my brand new Donna Karan coat and as if that wasn't enough, my shopping spilled all over the sidewalk... how vulgar I must have appeared!)*

la kopi |lah gkoh-bpee| Hokkien for "to stir coffee", i.e. to relax in a coffee shop, stirring a cup of hot coffee.

[•] *"Come, let's go kopi tiam and la kopi." (Come, let's go to the coffee shop for a cup of hot coffee.)*

lac See **relac**

lagi |lah-ghee| Malay for "additional", "again", "more", "also" or "still". In Singlish, it's often paired with an adjective to kick it up a notch.

[1] *"Wah lan, this new DVD player is lagi best." (Whoa, this new DVD player is truly the best!)*

[2] *"Piang eh, I oreddy so busy, you arrow me some more, lagi chia lat." (Hey, I'm already so busy, yet you're sticking me with more tasks. It's really sapping my strength!)*

lagi some more "Lagi" is Malay for "additionally" or "again". Paired with the seemingly redundant "some more", the hybrid phrase is equivalent to the English expression "and as if that weren't enough..." . The repetition in two languages adds emphasis to the (usually) catastrophic nature of the incident being described.

[•] *"Wah lan eh, this week damn suay, man. I kena sign extra and then lagi some more, my dog also kena langgar." (Man, this has been a really unlucky week. Firstly, I got stuck with extra military duties, and as if that weren't enough, my dog was run over by a car.)*

lah The ubiquitous Singlish tag. Used like a fullstop in a sentence. Contrary to popular belief, there is actually a specific way to use "lah". The ability to employ it is a sign you are a true Singaporean. Depending on the tone of voice, "lah" can either add a certain casualness or offhandedness to a statement, or lend a tone of exasperation. Note: "Lah" is never used with a question.

[1] *"It was just like that, lah." (Oh, It was just like that.)*

[2] *"I'm telling you it was like that, lah!" (Look, I'm telling you that's how it was!)*

[3] *"He was running all over the shop, lah." (He was simply running everywhere.)*
[4] *"Oi! Stop running all over the shop, lah!" (Hey! Stop running all over the shop, will you?)*
[5] *"Donno, lah!" (Oh, I don't know!)*
See also **hor, lair, leh, lor, meh**

lai dat "Like that". In a sentence, it is used in a way similar to how Americans pepper their sentences with "like". On its own, however, it communicates a certain resignation or capitulation.
[1] *"He look like a pig lai dat." (He, like, looks like a pig.)*
[2] *"Wah lau, I like damn tired lai dat." (Man, I'm, like, very tired.)*
[3] *Beng: "How are you?"*
Seng: "Lai dat, lor." (Oh, just like that.)
Beng: "Like what, lah!" (Like what?!)
Seng: "Lai dat, lah!" (When I said like that, I meant like that!)

lair |lare| Another Singlish tag. "Lair" is usually employed when you want to drive home a point or emphasize something. Tends to be used mostly by girls and young women, often in mock horror.
[1] *"She, hor, dress very obiang one, lair!" (She dresses really unfashionably!)*
[2] *"When they married that time, hor, she oreddy three months pregnant, lair!" (At the time of their marriage, she was already three months pregnant!)*

laling |lah-ling| The local pronunciation of "darling".
[·] *"Oh my lurf, my laling, I hunger for your tush, a long and lonely time!" (Oh my love, my darling, I've hungered for your touch, a long and lonely time!)*

lambong |lahm-bong| From the Malay word "lambung", meaning to lob or send a ball hurtling in a high arc. In Singlish it has come to mean running, falling or flailing around in a wild and aimless manner. Used mostly when playing games, it has occasionally been overheard in non-sports scenarios.
[1] *"I dunno how to shoot, but one kick and the ball went lambong, into the net." (I don't know how to shoot, but with one kick, I sent the ball hurtling into the net.)*
[2] *"The bugger was so drunk, he slip, and fell down and went lambong." (The fellow was so drunk, he slipped and fell, and then began flailing wildly.)*

lan cheow / lan chiao |lahn tjee-ow| A Hokkien term meaning "penis". Often used in a similar fashion to "like hell" or "no way!".
[·] *Recruit: "Eh, Sergeant, sign my Off Pass leh..." (Hey, Sergeant. Could you sign my Off Pass?)*

Sergeant: "Lan cheow! Knock it down 20!" (*Like hell I will! Give me 20 push-ups!*)

lan lan |lahn-lahn| A Hokkien phrase which literally translates as "penis, penis". It indicates resignation, despondency or reluctance.
1 *"Gah'men say must do, we lan lan also must do."* (*When the government says we have to do something, we have no choice but to do it, no matter how reluctant we might be.*)
2 *"I work so hard for this bleddy exam, still kena goose egg. Lan lan, man!"* (*I worked so hard for this exam, and still got a zero. How depressing!*)

lan tui |lahn tooi| Hokkien phrase literally meaning "penis split". The Hokkien version of "up yours!" or "nuts to you!".
"You want me to type 100 copies by today? Lan tui, unnerstand!" (*You want me to type 100 copies by today? Nuts to you!*)

lancing / lumsing |lahnn-sing/lahm-sing| Mispronunciations of "dancing", often deliberate.
"Eh tonight free or not? Wan' to go Zouk for lancing-lancing?!" (*Hey, are you free tonight? Want to go to Zouk for some dancing?*)

langgar |lahng-gahr| Malay for "collide" or "hit".
1 *"Did you hear about Paul's car? It kena langgar this morning."* (*Did you hear about Paul's car? It was in a collision this morning.*)
2 *"He langgar-ed me yesterday."* (*He collided with me yesterday.*)

lang loi |lang (rhymes with "gang", "fang" and "bang") loy| Cantonese for "pretty girl". Often employed by hawkers to curry favour with female customers, regardless of their age. Almost always used in an ironic or insincere way.
"Aiyoh, lang loi, dun angry leh! Uncle give you extra yew char kueh, okay?" (*Oh dear, my lovely lass, don't get angry! Let me give you a few extra crullers, alright?*)

See also **yan dao**

lao / lau Hokkien, and also Mandarin, for "old".
"He so lao also still want to go bunjee jumping." (*He's so old, yet he wants to go bunjee jumping.*)

lao cheow |lao tjee-ow| Literally, an "old bird", meaning an experienced individual. Can be used as both a noun and adjective.
1 *"Recession that time, all the lao cheow also kena retrench."* (*During the recession, even the longest serving veterans were let go.*)
2 *"If got any problem go and find him, he very lao cheow, so sure can help one."* (*If there's any problem, go and consult him. He's very experienced and is sure to be able to help you.*)

See also **old bird**

lao chio |lao chee-oh| Hokkien for "old pretty". Used to describe pretty/sexy older women. What the Americans would call a "milf". Not to be confused with "lao hiao".
⊡ *"Eh, not say I say what, ah, but I think Ah Beng's mother is a lao chio." (Hey, don't quote me on this, but I think Ah Beng's mother is a real Mrs Robinson.)*
See also **lao hiao**

lao hiao |lao hee-ow| A derisive term for a flirtatious old lady.
⊡ *"Auntie Lian Huay always wear makeup until like birfday cake lai dat! What a lao hiao!" (Auntie Lian Huay always wears so much makeup! What a flirty old lady!)*

lao kwee Hokkien term meaning to lose face. Used in the same way as "malu", denoting great embarrassment.
⊡ *"Our football team can lose to Bukit Gorblok, si beh lau kwee man!" (Our football team lost even to Bukit Gorblok. What an embarrassment!)*
See also **malu, shy, shyful**

lao lan |lao lahn| Hokkien for "gushing penis." An epithet describing bastardly behaviour.
⊡ *"You know I kena retrench, still want me to chia you lunch? Lao lan, ah!" (You know I've been retrenched, yet you still want me to treat you to lunch? What bastardly behaviour!)*
See also **lu lai lu lao lan / L-cube / L-square**

lao pee hui |lao pee hwee'h| Hokkien for nose bleed. Usually used to describe one's reaction to an arousing situation.
⊡ *"Hwah! Ah Lian's mini-skirt so short! See oreddy lao pee hui, man!" (Whoa, Ah Lian's mini-skirt is really short! Once you take a look, you'll get an immediate nose bleed.)*

lao pok |lao bpok| Hokkien adjective, describing something as crappy or lousy.
⊡ *"Your car so lao pok, who want to sit?" (Your car is so crappy, who would want to sit in it?)*
See also **lao yah**

lao sai Hokkien for "pouring shit". Naturally, it means a case of diarrhoea.
⊡ *"Ang moh png, chiak liao sure lau sai." (After eating western food, you will definitely have diarrhoea.)*

lao ter kor |lao dter gko| A dirty old man. Literally, "old pig brother" in Hokkien.
⊡ *"Wah lau, look at that uncle, whole day sit by the public pool looking at char bor. What a lao ter kor." (Look at that old man! He*

spends the whole day ogling girls at the public pool. What a dirty old man!)

See also **chee koh pek, hum sup loh, ter kor**

lao yah / lao yah pok Used to describe objects as crappy, lousy, broken or useless.

1 *"Ee-yurr, why your microwave so lao yah, one?" (Ugh, why is your microwave oven in such a lousy condition?)*

2 *"Wah lau, where you buy this car? So lao yah pok!" (Holy cow, where on earth did you buy this car? It's a piece of crap!)*

See also **lao pok**

lap lap chap chap |lahp lahp tzahp tzahp| An indiscriminate mix of everything.

"Mr Tan si sua collect art, one. His collection, hor, very the lup lup chap chap." (Mr Tan is not discerning when it comes to collecting art. His collection is composed of an indiscriminate mix of stuff.)

See also **chapalang**

lassi lomak |lah-see loh-ma'h| The Singlish pronunciation of "nasi lemak", a local culinary favourite of Malay origin, consisting of coconut rice usually accompanied by a piece of fried fish and an egg, all wrapped together in a banana leaf. "Lassi lomak", however, usually refers to the Chinese-made version, which is coconut rice served with anything ranging from sausages to fried chicken and spam.

"Let's go Fong Seng and eat lassi lomak." (Let's go to Fong Seng's restaurant and eat their version of nasi lemak.)

last time In Singlish, "last time" doesn't mean just the previous time an incident occurred, but also "before" and "in the old days".

1 *"Last time policeman all wear shorts one." (In the old days, policemen all used to wear short trousers.)*

2 *"He last time got hair like Tarzan, now totally botak. Wha'ppen?" (Before he used to have hair like Tarzan. Now he's totally bald. What happened?)*

See also **that time**

launge |lawnch| The Singaporean way of pronouncing "lounge". Usually associated with seedy karaoke/KTV bars.

"Eh, tonight want to go to Platinum Arowana 88 Launge, mai?" (Hey, do you want to go to the Platinum Arowana 88 lounge tonight?)

laylio |lay-lee-oh| The Singlish pronunciation of "radio".

"Eh, on the laylio, leh." (Hey, turn on the radio, won't you?)

lebber Singlish pronunciation of "level".

[1] *"Your training reach what lebber oreddy, ha?" (What level have you reached in the course of your training?)*

[2] *"You studying air lebber or orh lebber one, ha?" (Are you taking your "A" level or "O" level examinations?)*

leceh |lay-chay| Malay for "troublesome", and used to describe a laborious or irksome task or action.

[1] *"Aiyoh, tolong don't ask me to go and queue for 4D this sort of leceh thing again, can?" (Oh man, would you please not ask me to do annoying things like get in line for lottery tickets again?)*

[2] *"Aiyah, 15 minute also must put parking kupoon! Si beh leceh, lair!" (Argh! Having to punch parking coupons for only 15 minutes' parking is really troublesome!)*

See also **kang kor, ma fan**

leh |lay| Yet another Singlish tag, similar in usage to "lah", but which adds a slightly quizzical tone to the sentence.

[1] *"I didn't know Ah Beng was like that, leh." (Really? I honestly didn't know Ah Beng was like that.)*

[2] *"Aiyah, don't like that, leh. Wait we kena maki." (Come on, don't be like that, will you? Otherwise we're sure to be scolded.)*

See also **lah, lair, lor, hor, meh**

lelong |lay-long| Malay for "auction". In Singlish, however, it means merely to sell things off cheaply in a clearance sale, with no requirement for the goods to be sold off to the highest bidder. Definitely not a Christie's or Sotheby's scenario.

[1] *"I heard that to pay back the Ah Long, hor, he kena lelong his house." (I heard that to pay off the loan shark, he had to sell off his house.)*

[2] *"See him lelong-ing his house like that, damn poor thing, man." (It's painful to see him selling off his house. The poor thing!)*

lembik |lurm-be'h| In Malay, "lembik" means flaccid or wrinkled and hanging loose. In Singlish, it has the added meaning of limp, or physically weak and is not necessarily confined to sexual contexts, nor does it necessarily connote impotence. It could sometimes just mean "weak at the knees".

[1] *"Wah lau, I see her in her mini-skirt, I instantly lembik, man." (Oh man, I saw her in her mini-skirt and instantly went weak at the knees.)*

[2] *"I'm damn out of shape. Run 20 metres only lembik." (I'm totally out of shape. I ran 20 metres and I went all limp.)*

leow Variant spelling of "liao". See **liao**

lepak |lay-bpa'h| Malay for "to sit in a lazy way". In Singlish, it has been extended to mean "relax".

1 *"I thought you say you so busy. Then I come here see you lepak only!" (I thought you said you were very busy. But when I came here, I caught you lying about!)*

2 *"This weekend, I just want to stay home and lepak." (This weekend, I just want to stay home and relax.)*

See also **bah long long, kiao kah yo lum pah, lac, lobo, relac, shake leg**

ler / li / lu Variant pronunciations of the Hokkien word for "you".

less means hor A phrase used exclusively by Ah Lians, it translates into "that means that..." or "which means that..."

▪ *Joseffyn: "Aiyah, I cannot get the 9 o'clock show tonight, I only got the 7 o'clock show!" (Oh no, I couldn't get tickets for the 9 o'clock movie tonight! I could only get tickets for the 7 o'clock show!)*
Jazamine: "Less means hor, we must meet at the MRT station at 6.30, lah!!!" (I guess that means we have to meet at the MRT station at 6.30.)

liak boh kiew |lia'h boh gkew| Literally, Hokkien for "catch no ball". Means to completely not understand.

1 *"Wah, that movie was so cheem, I totally liak boh kiew, man!" (Wow, that movie was so deep, I completely didn't understand it.)*

2 *"His accent is so powderful, I completely liak boh kiew." (His accent is so strong, I totally didn't understand what he said.)*

See also **catch no ball**

liao |lee-ow| A Hokkien tag which depending on the context can mean either "already" or "finished".

1 *"His mother early-early si liao, loh." (His mother died very early.)*

2 *"Like that his business sure liao, lah." (In such circumstances, his business is surely finished.)*

like real The Singlish equivalent of "as if!" or "yeah, right." An expression of incredulity and disbelief.

▪ *Beng: "Eh, I just got into Mensa." (Hey, I was just accepted into Mensa.)*
Seng: "Like real!" (Yeah, right!)

lim Hokkien for "drink".

▪ *"Come, let's go kopi tiam lim kopi." (Come, let's go to the coffee shop for a cup of coffee.)*

See also **la kopi**

lim peh ka li kong |lim bpay gkah lee gkong| Hokkien phrase literally meaning, "Let your father tell you..." or "listen to your father". Used even when the speaker is not actually the addressee's father. It's a phrase which is designed to put you in your place — a subordinate position, naturally.

⊡ *"Lim peh ka li kong, if you do like that, you sure kena hantam." (Listen to one who knows better than you, if you carry on like that, you'll definitely be beaten up.)*

lippit A common pronunciation of "repeat".

⊡ *"Ha? Can lippit, please?" (Huh? Could you repeat that, please?)*

See also **again, repeat again, say again**

listurb A common pronunciation of "disturb".

⊡ *"Eh, he's sleeping, lah. Don't go and listurb him." (He's sleeping. Please don't disturb him.)*

See also **kachau, ji seow**

lizard |lee-zuhd| Common pronunciation of "dessert".

⊡ *"Lizard go where, ah?" (Where shall we go for dessert?)*

loanmai |lone-muy| A local contraction of "if you don't mind..."

⊡ *"Eh, Ah Seng, loanmai pass me the diskette with the sales file inside, can or not?" (Hey, Ah Seng, if you don't mind, could you please pass me the diskette with the sales file inside?)*

lobang |loh bahng| Malay for "hole". In Singlish, its meaning has been extended to include all the other meanings for "opening", including "tip", "connections" or "contacts".

1 *"Alamak! My pants got one major lobang, sial!" (Argh! There's a huge hole in my pants!)*

2 *"I'm looking for a job. If you got any lobang, let me know." (I'm looking for a job. If you have any openings, let me know.)*

3 *"Eh, you got any lobang to get me a cheap car or not?" (Hey, do you have any connections through which I can get a cheap car?)*

See also **kang tau**

lobo A term which originated and is still used mostly in the Army. It is used to describe someone as an idler or a job as easy to handle. It is believed to be an acronym for either "left out battle order" or "lazy old bastard".

⊡ *"Look at him, slack all day, damn lobo." (Look at him, laying about the whole day. What a lazy bum.)*

See also **bah long long, kiao kah yo lum pah, lac, lobo, shake leg, slack**

loh soh / lor sor |loh soh (Hokkien), law saw (Cantonese)| Long-winded.

⊡ *"Wah lau, this sort of simple thing also can talk so much. Why you so loh soh one?" (Holy cow, how can you talk so much even about such simple matters? Why are you so long-winded?)*

lolex The local pronunciation of "Rolex", the expensive Swiss watch preferred by Chinese businessmen.

☐ *"Mr Tan lolex damn big, man."* (*Mr Tan's Rolex watch is immense.*)

lomance / lomantic The local pronunciation of "romance" or "romantic". Can be used interchangeably.

1 *"Wah, bring me flower, ah? How come so lomance one?"* (*Wow, you brought me flowers? Why so romantic all of a sudden?*)

2 *"When chase girl that time, must be lomantic lah. Then they sure like you."* (*When courting girls, you have to be romantic. Then they're sure to like you.*)

long long no see A Singlish corruption of "long time no see"

☐ *"Wah! Long long no see, man! You put on a lot of weight, hor?"* (*Whoa! Long time no see! You've put on a lot of weight, haven't you?*)

long tio ooh siah See **meng kia, long tio ooh siah**

longkang / longkau |lohng-gkahng/lohng-gkau| From the Malay word for "drain", it is used to describe any form of man-made water passage, from small drain holes to big canals. "Longkau" is a Singapore Hokkien hybrid of "longkang" and "kau", the Hokkien word for "ditch" ("gou" in Mandarin).

☐ *"All the most tok kong makan places in Singapore are by the longkang, one."* (*All the finest eateries in Singapore are located by a drain.*)

longkau chui |lohng-gkau tz'wee| Hokkien phrase literally meaning "drain water". Used to describe an inferior brew of coffee.

☐ *"Piang eh! This Starbutts' kopi taste like longkau chui, still dare to charge so bleddy much!"* (*Holy cow, Starbutts' coffee tastes like drain water, yet they still dare to charge so much for it!*)

looksee-looksee To have a quick look around.

☐ *"Let's go to the new shopping centre and looksee-looksee, lah."* (*Let's go to the new shopping centre and have a quick look around.*)

lor |law| Yet another Singlish tag, similar in usage to "lah", but which adds a slightly weary, cynical or resigned tone to the sentence.

1 *"Aiyah, don't care him. He's always like that, lor."* (*Oh, ignore him. He's always like that.*)

2 *"I give you chance, but you still d'owan. Do'wan done, lor."* (*I gave you a chance, but you turned it down. Well, I guess if you don't want it, you don't want it.*)

See also **lah, leh, lair, hor, meh**

lost form Used to describe a lack of ability, perception and/or desirability in all aspects.

1 *"Aiyah, just now I so lost form, you know! I drop all my things all over the bus, so malu!"* (*Oh my god, I was such a klutz just now!*

I dropped my things all over the bus. How embarrassing!)

2 *"I think she very lost form lor, I mean, so fat already still wear that type of tight-tight tube!" (I think she's really clueless. She's so fat, yet she insists on wearing such a tight tube top!)*

See also **malu**

low morale Another army-inherited adjective, which is largely self-explanatory. Used to describe an unhappy and dispiriting situation, even in non-military or even non-group activities.

"That time I kena arrow go on dispatch, I was sick, then it started raining heavily. Damn low morale, man." (One time, I was put on dispatch duty. First of all, I was sick. Then it started to rain heavily. My morale felt really low.)

lu lai lu lao lan / L3L2 / L-cube L-square |loo lai loo lau lahn| Rare modification of "lao lan". Also abbreviated as "L-cube L-square" or "L3L2". Literally, "you came, and behaved like a gushing penis", i.e. "you came and you behaved like an absolute bastard".

"Wah lan eh, everything here arrange until so steady, then you come here and now everything kana sai. Lu lai lu lao lan!" (Holy cow, everything here was arranged so nicely, then you arrived and messed it all up. You came and behaved like an absolute bastard!)

See also **lao lan**

luan luan / luan luan lai |loo-ahn loo-ahn lai| From the Hokkien word for "chaotic", this means to do things recklessly, haphazardly or without a plan.

"Don't ask Ah Beng to help. He always luan luan lai one." (Don't ask Ah Beng to help. He's always doing things in a haphazard manner.)

See also **si sua lai**

lucky |lah-gkee| Singlish for "luckily".

"Lucky you neh buy that house!" (Luckily you decided not to purchase that house.)

lugi |loo-ghee| See **rugi**

lui A uniquely Singaporean word. Meaning "money", it is used only by Singaporean Hokkiens. The word is believed to have been derived from the Malay word for money, "duit".

"Eh, want to see show, not? How much lui you got?" (Hey, do you want to catch a movie? How much cash do you have?)

lum pah / lum par Hokkien for "testicles".

lum pah pah lan / lum pah pak lan A Hokkien term describing a person on whom a plan or action has backfired. Literally: "The testicles hitting the penis". The rhythm of the phrase suggests a ricocheting action, a surprisingly elegant touch in such a rude phrase. The Anglicized phrase "bang balls" probably came from this. Often abbreviated to "LPPL".

[1] *"He go and buy the puppy to impress his girlfriend, but then the puppy go and bite her. He damn lum pah pah lan now." (He went and bought a puppy to impress his girlfriend, but instead it bit her. He feels like his plan totally backfired on him.)*

[2] *"The gahmen LPPL over the "two is enough" campaign, so now boh pian kebelakang pusing." (The government's "Two is Enough" population campaign backfired on them badly, so they have no choice but to make a policy u-turn.)*

See also **bang balls**

lurf The local pronunciation of "love". Emphasized especially during karaoke sessions.

[·] *"Oh my lurf, my laling, I hunger for your tush, a long and lonely time!" (Oh my love, my darling, I've hungered for your touch, a long and lonely time!)*

Mm

MIC Acronym for 'Made-in-China'. A label for comparatively unsophisticated new immigrants or expatriates from mainland China.

[·] *"Piang! How come these MIC always talk so loud one?" (Good grief! Why do these mainland Chinese people always have to converse so loudly?)*

See also **cheena, sinkek, sua koo**

ma fan / ma huan |mah fahn/mah hu-ahn| "Ma fan" is Mandarin and Cantonese for "bother" or "bothersome" while "ma huan" is the Hokkien equivalent. Used either as a verb or adjective.

[1] *"Why you always come and mah fan me, one?" (Why do you insist on bothering me?)*

[2] *"Why they want to ask so many questions? So mah huan, one!" (Why do you want to ask so many questions? How bothersome!)*

See also **kang kor, leceh**

macam |mah-chahm| Malay term of comparison, equivalent to "like" in English. When used in Singlish, it is often used with other comparative terms and can seem redundant, but it in fact adds emphasis.

[1] *"Adoi, this kopi macam shit!" (Ugh, this coffee is like shit!)*

[2] *"Wah piang, this dessert macam taste like shit." (Holy cow, this dessert really tastes like shit.)*

[3] *"That bugger dress up until like that, macam look like come from outer space." (That fellow's get up really makes him look like an alien.)*

macnoner / mehnoner The local pronunciation of the famous American fast food chain, used especially by neighbourhood aunties and ah sohs.

[•] *"Ooi, Ah Boy. Tonight not cooking dinner, hor. Buy you happy mew at Macnoner, can?" (Hey, kiddo. I'm not cooking dinner tonight. Is it alright if I buy you a McDonald's happy meal?)*

mah si |mah see| Hokkien for "also" or "even". Used in an identical fashion to "poon".

[•] *"Why you so cheap thrill, put those Garfew in your car behind? Like that mah si song!" (Why do you engage in such cheap thrills, like placing those Garfield figurines in your car's rear window? Does that really give you satisfaction?)*

See also **poon**

mai |muy| Hokkien for "don't" or "don't want". Can also be used like "or not" at the end of questions.

[1] *"Mai like that, I warn you ah!" (Don't be like that, I'm warning you!)*

[2] *"My mee siam mai hiam." (I don't want chilli in my mee siam.)*

[3] *"Uncle, laksa mai hum." (Uncle, please don't put cockles in my laksa.)*

[4] *Beng: "Tonight want to go karaoke, mai?" (Do you want to go for karaoke tonight or not?)*
Seng: "Mai, lah." (No, I don't.)

mai hiam buay pai / mai hiam buay pai, ai hiam kana sai |muy hee-ahm bway pai, ai hee-ahm gkah-bah sai| "Mai hiam buay pai" is Hokkien for "if you're not picky, it's not bad." The phrase gets extra emphasis when tagged with "ai hiam kena sai", which literally means "if you are picky, you'll see it's actually like shit".

[1] *Samy: "The chicken rice, how?" (How's the chicken rice?)*
Seng: "Mai hiam buay pai, lah." (If you aren't picky, it's alright.)

[2] *Ah Beng: "Ah Lian's new boyfriend hamsum, not?" (Is Ah Lian's new boyfriend handsome?)*
Ah Huay: "Mai hiam buay pai, ai hiam kana sai." (If you aren't picky, he's alright. But if you are picky, he looks like shit.)

mai kei lah! |muy gkay lah| Literally from Hokkien: "Don't bluff, lah!"

☐ *Ah Beng: "You got hear? Ah Lian jip NUS, leh!" (Have you heard? Ah Lian made it into NUS!)*
Ah Seng: "Mai kei lah!" (Don't tell lies!)
See also **dun bluff**

mai siao siao |muy seow seow| Hokkien for "don't be crazy". A warning not to fool with things beyond one's ability. A variant of "mai sng sng" and "don't play-play".
☐ *"Eh, warn you, ah — mai siao siao and play with oujia board this sort of thing, ah!" (Hey, I'm warning you — don't be crazy and start playing with things like ouija boards!)*
See also **don't play-play, mai sng sng**

mai sng sng The Hokkien source of the popular Singlish phrase, "don't play-play". A warning not to aggravate, irritate, provoke or fool with things beyond one's ability.
☐ *"Skydiving is si beh dangerous, okay. Mai sng-sng, I warn you ah." (Skydiving is really dangerous. I'm warning you: don't play the fool.)*
See also **don't play-play**, **mai siao siao**

mai tu liao |muy too leow| Literally, "don't delay further" in Hokkien.
☐ *Ah Beng: "Wah seh! This weekend's Toto is 8 million dollars, leh!" (Wow! This weekend's lottery is 8 million dollars!"*
Ah Seng: "Mai tu liao! Faster go and buy!" (Don't dawdle! Hurry and buy some tickets!)

main |mah-yin| From the Malay word "main", meaning to play. In Singlish, it can also mean to manipulate a person or process for nefarious ends.
1 *"Aiyah, he main-main only, why you get so angry?" (Oh, he's only playing. Why are you getting so angry?)*
2 *"Basket, I trusted the bugger, but instead I kena main by him." (I trusted him, but he played me for a fool.)*
See also **played out**

main control |mah-yin control| Nothing to do with telepathy, the phrase is derived from the Malay word "main", meaning "to play". The phrase originally described the ability to juggle balls proficiently, but is now the Singlish equivalent of "multitasking".
☐ *"Adoi, the boss arrow me so many things, I really have to exercise main control, sial." (Whoa, the boss stuck me with so many assignments, I really have to multitask.)*

maintain balan A Mat-ism, this is an exhortation to remain calm and even tempered. Like "relac'", "balan" is the singular form of "balance".

☐ *"Aiyah, this sort of small-small thing, no problem, lah. Maintain balan." (Oh, these small matters are no problem. Kindly compose yourself and behave with some equanimity.)*
See also **lac, relac, jangan tension**

mak kau |ma'h gkau| From the Malay words "emak" (mother) and "engkau" (you), this is a colloquial Malay curse which translates as "your mother".

mak nenek |ma'h nay-nay'h| A Peranakan expression used to describe a child trying to behave like an adult. In Singlish, it is used specifically to describe a younger person who behaves like an old woman or grandmother.
☐ *"Eh? How come Ah Beng nowsaday so mak nenek, one? Whole day ask me do this, do that!" (Huh? Why is Ah Beng behaving like such an old woman nowadays, always nagging me to do things?)*

makan |mah-gkahn| Malay for "meal" or "to eat". Sometimes used to mean to swallow or trample upon someone.
1 *"Eh, let's go to Palm Beach for makan." (Hey, let's go to Palm Beach for a meal.)*
2 *"I told Johnny not to go and get involved with that gang. Now he kena makan by them." (I told Johnny not to go and get involved with that gang. Now they've swallowed him up.)*

make Short for "make money".
☐ *"Got this kind of kang tau, hor, we all can make, man!" (With these connections, we can really make money!)*

make friend Singlish for the act of befriending. "Friend" is always in the singular.
☐ *"Ah boy, go over there and make friend with Jimmy and Sally, can?" (Son, can you go over there and make friends with Jimmy and Sally?)*

make cake / make chocolate cake Singlish euphemism for having a shit. If someone doesn't get it, informing them of the cake's colouring is a hint.
☐ *Jack: "Where's Ah Beng, ah?"*
Jill: "Toilet make cake, lor." (He's taking a dump in the loo.)
Jack: "Ha? Toilet make what kind of cake?" (What kind of cake does one bake in the toilet?)
Jill: "Make chocolate cake, lor! Arbuthen?" (A "chocolate cake", of course! What else?)
See also **do business, number two, pang sai**

maki |mah-gkee| Malay for "chide", "scold" or "rebuke".
☐ *"Ah Boy went to play in the longkang and kena maki by his*

mother." (Ah Boy played in the ditch, for which he was chided by his mother.)

See also **tekan**

makkal The Indian version of a Mat, i.e. a scruffy, rough-and-tumble young man given to goofing off, loud music and motorcycles.

See also **Mat / Mat Roker**

malu |mah-loo| Malay for "shame", "embarrassment" or "loss of face".

1 *"When you talk to Jenny, don't make me malu okay?" (When you talk to Jenny, please don't paint me in an embarrassing light.)*

2 *"Our football team can lose to Macau, damn malu, man!" (Our football team lost even to Macau. What an embarrassment!)*

See also **lao kwee, pai seh, shy, shyful**

mama Racist way of addressing an Indian person who is not a Muslim. See also **mamak, thambi**

mamak |mama'h| Racist way of addressing an Indian Muslim person, stereotypically the one who makes your mee goreng, delivers newspapers, runs corner shops and changes your currency. Note: The distinction between "mama" and "mamak" is more pronounced in Malaysia. With Singaporeans, "mama" seems to be a catch-all term for anyone of Indian origin, whether Muslim or not.

See also **mama, thambi**

mama shop Corner stall selling miscellaneous sundry goods, often run by Indian Muslim shopkeepers. In the age of the 7-Eleven, these shops are now a dying breed.

mamasan handphone A cheeky description of mobile phones equipped with Multimedia Messaging Service (MMS) options.

Beng: "Wah! Seng! You got new MaMaSan handphone ah!" (Wow! Seng! You've got a new MaMaSan handphone, have you?)
Seng: "What MaMaSan? MMS, lah!!!" (MaMaSan? You mean MMS!)

mambo A phrase which originated from the retro Mambo Jambo nights at popular nightspot Zouk, it has become a generic reference to going clubbing, or enjoying 80s music like Belinda Carlisle (pronounced in Singapore as "Kah-liss-lay").

"My course damn stress lah… Wensday call people go mambo, leh!" (I'm being stressed out by this course I'm enrolled in. So on Wednesday, let's call everyone to go clubbing at Zouk!)

mana eh sai |mah-nah ay sai| A hybrid of Malay (mana — "where") and Hokkien (eh sai — "can"). A phrase expressing incredulity and outrage, loosely translatable as, "how on earth is this possible?" Anglicized as "how can?"

"I oreddy give him discount, he still bargain. Mana eh sai?" (I

already gave him a discount, yet he continued to bargain with me. How can he do such a thing?)

See also **how can?**

mana ooh eng Hybrid Malay-Hokkien phrase ("mana" is Malay for "where", and "ooh eng" is Hokkien for "having free time") used to express incredulity at being asked to do something frivolous or unimportant when one has more pressing things to do. Anglicized as "where got time?"

1 *"Go and play golf? Mana ooh eng?" (Go and play golf? Who has the time?)*

2 *"Next week got orh lebber oreddy, mana ooh eng to kuah meenite with you?" (Next week, I'll be taking the "O" level examinations. Where on earth do I have the spare time to catch the midnight movie with you?)*

See also **boh eng, chiak sior eng, chiak pah boh sai pang, eng, where got time?**

mangkuk |mahng-gko'h| A Malay word which means "bowl" or "hollow part of a tobacco pipe", "mangkuk" has come to be used to describe someone as empty-headed, i.e. stupid or brainless. Can be either a noun or adjective.

1 *"Why you so mangkuk one? Everything also cannot understand? Chih!" (Why are you so empty-headed and uncomprehending? Tsk!)*

2 *"See those two mangkuks over there, whole day sell flags." (Look at those brainless fools over there, selling flags the entire day.)*

manja |mahn-jah| Derived from the Malay word meaning "to pamper", it describes gooey, childlike and coquettish behaviour by women designed to elicit sympathy or pampering by men.

▪ *"His girlfriend is damn manja, one. Hear her speak only can kena diabetes."*

See also **tair**

manyak |mahn-ya'h| A common mispronunciation, usually by Chinese, of the Malay word "banyak", which means "a lot" or "very".

▪ *"Alamak, this place, ah, manyak Ah Beng, sial!" (Oh dear, there are a lot of hoodlums here!)*

Maseelis Mercedes — the automobile of choice for the established towkay. The bigger the model number, the better. The alphabet suffix is also important and the rank is as follows, in descending order: S, E, C, D (for the now virtually extinct diesel model). Young towkay wannabes (now also called "technoprenner") prefer to drive "bee-em-dubdew", at least till they get married and their tai-tais need to be ferried around.

Mat / Mat Roker |maht/maht roh-ker| The Mat is the Malay equivalent of the Ah Beng. Usually long-haired and scruffy, he is often in a leather or denim jacket, and sitting astride his motorcycle. A "Mat Roker" is a Mat with an unabashed devotion to heavy metal rock music. The 5Ms of the Mat Roker are: Minah, Marlboro, Motosikal, Metal and Maintain Balan.

See also **minah**

mat salleh |maht sah-lay| Malay equivalent of "ang moh". A phrase used to describe Caucasians, with a slight pejorative overtone. Some have suggested that it is a deliberate mispronunciation of "mad sailor". This conjecture cannot be confirmed, despite its obvious appeal.

▣ *"Cricket Club, hor, got manyak mat salleh." (There are many Caucasians at the Cricket Club.)*

See also **ang moh, orang putih**

mata |mah-dtah| The police. Originally from the Malay word meaning "eye", which we suppose is a reference to surveillance.

▣ *"Mata come oreddy! Faster hide the money!" (The police are here! Quickly! Hide the money!)*

See also **tua kow**

mati |mah-dtee| Malay for "die" or "dead".

1 *"You keep korek pantat about Ah Beng, wait you mati then you know!" (Be careful about gossiping maliciously about Ah Beng. You might wind up dead.)*

2 *"Alamak! I forgot to file my income tax! Mati, man!" (Oh my god! I forgot to file my income tax! I'm dead!)*

See also **die**

mati kong kah kiao A hybrid of "mati" (Malay for "dead') and "kong kah kiao" (Hokkien for "legs in the air"), meaning that one is totally, irrevocably dead.

▣ *"He sure cannot pay you back one, lah. His business mati kong kah kiao oreddy." (I'm sure he won't be able to pay you back. His business is already six feet under.)*

meenachi A very conservative young Indian girl.

meh A Singlish tag which accompanies questions. Adds a tone of incredulity or skepticism.

1 *"Ah Beng is like that, meh?" (Is Ah Beng really like that?)*

2 *"You really think you can pontang school so easy, meh?" (Do you really think you can play hooky so easily and get away with it?)*

meng kia, long tio ooh siah |meng gkee-ah, long tee-o'h ooh see-ah| Hokkien phrase literally meaning, "Don't be scared. If it hits, there'll be a sound." An exhortation to do things boldly and without fear. Sometimes accompanied by the phrase "kah-kah lai" (come forward bravely).

☐ *"Gostan some more! Meng kia, long tio ooh siah!" (You can reverse your car further. Don't worry, if it hits anything, there'll be a sound.)*

Minah / Electro Minah The feminine equivalent of the Mat, and hence the Malay equivalent of the Ah Lian. The female equivalent of a Mat Roker is the "Electro Minah."

See also **Mat / Mat Roker**

minyak |min-ya'h| Malay for "oil". Also used to describe a person as irritatingly ingratiating, slimy or sickeningly slick. Interesting historical note: In the 50s and 60s, Singapore and Malaysia were plagued by perverts known as "orang minyak" or "oily men". Their modus operandi was to wear nothing, except perhaps for underwear, and smear their bodies with oil, which made them difficult to catch during pursuit.

1 *"Adoi, that bugger, ah, manyak minyak, man!" (What an oleaginous character!)*

2 *"You don't stop it, wait I make your minyak come out!" (If you don't stop, I'll make you sorry!)*

mm chai si |mm tzai see| Hokkien admonishment meaning "ignorant of death". Used when someone is especially audacious or cavalier about consequences.

☐ *"Why you go and make fun of Ah Beng's tattoo? Mm chai si!" (Why did you make fun of Ah Beng's tattoo? You must have a death wish!)*

See also **boh bah ti, chai si**

mm sam mm say |mm sum mm say| Cantonese phrase literally meaning "not three, not four" — the equivalent of the English phrases "neither here nor there" or "neither fish nor fowl". Often used to dismiss a really stupid idea.

☐ *"Ah Beng's dot-com company really mm sam mm say, also can become technoprenner." (Ah Beng's dot-com company is neither fish nor fowl, yet he could qualify as a technopreneur.)*

See also **not three not four**

moh tau moh mei |mow tao mow may| Cantonese for "boh tau boh buay". See also **boh tau boh buay**

moh tuck keng |mow dta'h keng| Cantonese for "end of discussion." Often confused with "moh tuck teng".

☐ *Seng: "This handphone how much? Cheaper, can?" (How much is this handphone? Can you lower the price?)*

Beng: "Moh tuck keng, this one best price oreddy." (This is already

as low as I can go. End of discussion!)
See also **moh tuck teng**

moh tuck teng Cantonese for "the best" or "cannot be topped". Often confused with "moh tuck keng".
▪ *"The char kway teow at Lorong 9 is moh tuck teng one." (The char kway teow at Lorong 9 just can't be beat.)*
See also **chut mia, moh tuck keng, world best**

mong cha cha Cantonese term describing someone as being in a daze or incompetent.
▪ *"Such a simple thing also cannot do. Why you so mong cha cha?" (You can't do even this simple task? Why are you so incompetent?)*
See also **blur, gong gong, sotong**

mood Used as an adjective, to describe feeling lighthearted in anticipation of one's imminent liberation from an unpleasant situation. Originates from the phrase "ROD mood", where ROD was one's "run-out date" for leaving National Service. (In a stunningly sensible move which had a significant impact on the nation, the acronym ROD was changed several years ago to "ORD".)
1 *"Wah, his NS still got six months more, but he damn mood oreddy." (Whoa, he still has six months of National Service left, but he's already in a carefree mood.)*
2 *"Tender oreddy, so you now mood liao, lah!" (Since you've already tendered your resignation, you must be in a liberated mood.)*

more to A phrase that reflects one's leanings or preferences.
▪ *"Although you more to indie rock and I more to techno, doesn't mean we cannot be friends, what." (Although you prefer indie rock and I prefer techno, that doesn't mean we cannot be friends.)*

mountain tortoise The literal translation of the Hokkien term "sua koo", meaning a country bumpkin. Can be used as a noun or adjective.
1 *"Ah Beng is a real mountain tortoise. Come to Singapore that time, neh see washing machine before." (Ah Beng is a real country bumpkin. Before coming to Singapore, he'd never seen a washing machine.)*
2 *"You neh see airplane before? Wah lau! I din'ch know you so mountain tortoise, one!" (You've never seen an airplane before? Holy cow! I didn't realise you were such a country bumpkin!)*
See also **jakun, sua koo**

mug / mugger / chao mugger / mugger toad To "mug" in Singapore is to study by rote. A mugger is thus a hardworking student who memorises notes and regurgitates them during exams:

the very essence of a typical kiasu student. Often prefixed with the word "chao" (smelly) in front of it for emphasis. The English equivalent would be a "swot".

1 *"If I don't mug now, then later exam sure die, one!" (If I don't swot like crazy now, I'm sure to fail the exams!)*

2 *"He every time go library until it close. Damn chao mugger, siah!" (He always stays in the library until it closes. What a swot!)*

3 *"I damn buay tahan Ah Seng. He's such a bleddy mugger toad!" (I can't stand Ah Seng! He's such an awful swot.)*

muka sadin |moo-gkuh sah-deen| Malay for "to have a face like a canned sardine", i.e. where the face does not betray one's emotions, or where the placid face doesn't comport with the intense things one is saying. Equivalent of "poker face".

"He angry, meh? He one kind of muka sadin, I can't tell, sia." (Is he angry? With his impassive face, I can't tell how he's really feeling.)

mungalee Corruption of "bengali". Colloquial and often racist reference to Sikhs or Northern Indians. See also **aneh, apu neh neh, bangali, bhai, mama, mamak, thambi**

mungsat |mung-saht| A common mispronunciation amongst cheenagerks of "bangsat". See **bangsat**

munjen Tamil for "yellow", and is a racist term used for Chinese people.

"Oi! Can you tell your racist munjen friends to stop calling me an apu neh neh?"

See also **aneh, apu neh neh, bangali, bhai, cheenagerk, mat, geragok**

Nn

NATO |nay-dtoh| A local acronym standing for "No Action, Talk Only", which probably originated in the Army. Everyone is labelled this at some point in their career.

"Aiyah, don't waste time with him, he damn NATO one." (Oh, don't waste time with him. He's all talk, and no action.)

na beh / na bu / ni na beh / ni na bu |nah bay/nah boo/nee nah bay/nee nah boo| Various contractions of "kan ni na bu".

See also **kan ni na bu**

nah This single syllable is the local equivalent of "here you are" or "here, take it", used when something is given out or handed over. Possibly derived from Mandarin, where "na" means "take".
⊡ *Ah Beng: "Oi, where you put my comb?" (Where did you put my comb?) An Seng (giving it back): "Nah!" (Here you are!)*

nao hiah / ni nao hiah |nee now hee-ah| "Lao hiah" in Hokkien means "old brother" and is perfectly innocuous. When pronounced with a nasal tone, however, it becomes an expletive meaning "your old brother".
⊡ *"You potong jalan my girlfriend and now you want to borrow money? Ni nao hiah!" (You stole my girlfriend and still dare to approach me to borrow money? You bastard!)*

neh [1] |n'air| Singlish contraction of "never".
⊡ *"Eh, why you go Zouk neh call me one?" (Why did you go to Zouk without asking me along?)*

neh [2] / neh neh Hokkien for breasts. Often repeated.
1 *"Hwah, that Pamela Anderson, hor, her neh damn tua liap!" (Wow, that Pamela Anderson's breasts sure are huge!)*
2 *"Hopefully, next time my wife will be damn tua neh neh one." (Hopefully, my future wife will be extremely voluptuous.)*

neh neh pok |n'air n'air bpok| Hokkien for nipples.
⊡ *"Wah lau, his T-shirt so tight, his bloody neh neh pok can see, al." (Oh man, his T-shirt is so tight, you can see his bloody nipples!)*

neh'mine |nair-mine| A contraction of "never mind". Can be used aggressively, as a threat, similar to "just you wait!".
1 *"If you're too busy to help me, neh'mine." (It's alright if you're too busy to help me. Never mind.)*
2 *"I always help you and now you sabo me like that? Neh'mine!" (I've always helped you, and yet you've sabotaged me? Never mind, I'll get even!)*

nenet |nay-nate| The helicopter NSman's pronunciation of "grenade".
⊡ *"Wah lau, the nenet essploded too early and he concuss." (Oh my god, the grenade exploded early, and he received a concussion.)*

never die before, is it? A variant of "mm tzai si". Used to admonish someone for his or her foolhardiness. "Never" is often abbreviated to "neh".
⊡ *"You pai kah still want to go skydiving? Never die before, is it?" (Your leg is broken and you still want to go skydiving? Do you have a death wish?)*

See also **mm tzai si**

never see before, is it? A belligerent response to someone staring at you in disapproval. An expression similar to "what're you looking at?", "what's your problem?" or "what's the big deal?" Again, "never" is often abbreviated to "neh".

▫ *"I smoking, so what? Never see before is it?" (So what if I'm smoking? What's the big deal?)*

See also **kua si mi? see what?**

ngeow |nee-ow| Hokkien for "cat". Describes someone who is fastidious, nitpicky, or who deliberately finds fault.

1 *"Sergeant Tan is damn ngeow, even small-small thing also kau peh kau bu." (Sergeant Tan is a real nitpicker. He gripes even over small things.)*

2 *"Wah lan eh, you mean Madam Tan use ruler to check page margin? Why she so ngeow?" (Holy cow, you mean Madam Tan used a ruler to check the page margins? Why is she such a nitpicker?)*

ngeh-ngeh |ngair-ngair| Hokkien term describing someone who insists on proceeding with something against better advice.

▫ *"I told him don't stand near the fire, but he ngeh-ngeh go near-near, and now he no more eyebrow." (I told him not to stand near the fire, but he insisted on going very near, and now his eyebrows have been singed off.)*

no bilis A term that first originated in "Kuti-Kuti", a low budget game wherein players would use one finger to flick a pawn (usually a bottle cap or colourful plastic token in the shape of an insect or animal) towards their opponent's pawn, with the aim of flipping their pawn on top of their opponent's. The victor would then claim their opponent's pawn for his or her own. When one's pawn is in danger of being taken by one's opponent, one could shout "bilis!" and swiftly move the pawn out of striking distance. However, the counter-move would be to shout "no bilis!" before your opponent could say, "bilis" and thus deprive him of his move. In practice therefore, no one ever really got to say "bilis" as your opponent would invariably say "no bilis!" first. Out of the context of Kuti-Kuti, people used the term "no bilis" to admonish others before they could attempt dodging an unpleasant task. As Kuti-Kuti is practically extinct in today's Singapore, the term has receded into obscurity and only remembered by people of a certain generation.

no head no tail Literal translation of "boh tao boh buay", a Hokkien term which means "incomprehensible".

▫ *"Wah lau eh, that movie was damn no head no tail, one." (Man, that movie was really incomprehensible.)*

See also **boh tao boh buay**

no sound no image / no sound no picture A no-show, or an absence of response.

1 *"Eh, I thought he was supposed to be here an hour ago? You mean he still no sound no image ah?" (Huh? I thought he was supposed to be here an hour ago? You mean there's still no sign of him?)*

2 *"I sent out my CV to all these employers six weeks ago, but still no sound no picture." (I sent out my CV to all these employers six weeks ago, but have still not received any response.)*

nongsern / nongsngse |nong-sern/nong-sngs| Local variant pronunciations of "nonsense".

1 *"Why you listen to him? He whole day talk nongsern one." (Why do you listen to him? He's always talking nonsense.)*

2 *"This TalkingCock wep site, ah, is full of nongsngse one." (This TalkingCock website is full of nonsense.)*

norchat The local pronunciation of "not yet".

1 *"Oi, wait, leh! I norchat finish packing!" (Hey, wait a minute, won't you? I haven't finished packing!)*

2 *Beng: "Eh, you finish your homework, not?" (Hey, have you finished your homework or not?)*
Seng: "Norchat." (Not yet.)

not The local contraction of "or not?"

1 *"The bak kwa I give you, you got eat, not?" (Did you eat the barbecued meat I gave you, or not?)*

2 *"Ah Beng's new girlfriend jude, not?" (Is Ah Beng's new girlfriend pretty, or not?)*

not say I say what A very common way of prefacing a statement that could be controversial or sensitive. English equivalents include, "I don't mean to be critical, but..." or "this might just be my own opinion, but..." or "I'm not sure, but..." or "don't quote me on this, but..." Virtually identical in use to "don't say I say".

▪ *"Not say I say what ah, but Ah Lian's dressing is si beh obiang." (I don't mean to be critical, but Ah Lian's dress sense is really tacky.)*

See also **don't say I say**

not three not four The English transliteration of the Cantonese phrase "mm sam mm say", meaning "neither here nor there" or "neither fish nor fowl".

See also **mm sam mm say**

nowsaday Singlish mispronunciation of "nowadays", often deliberate.

1 *"Nowsaday hor, everyone play SMS leh!" (Nowadays, everyone uses text messaging on their cellphones.)*

② *"My boss nowsaday, hor, make me si beh too lan — so I heck care him lor!" (Nowadays, my boss really pisses me off, so I couldn't give two hoots about him!)*

nuah |noo-ah| From the Hokkien word for "limp" or "soft", in Singlish it has come to mean to laze about, goof off and not do anything productive.

① *"Today is my off day, I just want to stay home and nuah." (Today is my day off. I just want to stay home and laze about.)*

② *"He whole day stay at home watch TV. Si peh nuah!" (He stays at home the whole day, just watching TV. What a bum!)*

See also **bah long long, lac, relac, slack**

number one Common local euphemism for urinating.

⊡ *Teacher: "What's Ah Seng doing in the toilet?"*
Student: "Number one, lor." (He's peeing.)

See also **pang jio**

number two Common local euphemism for taking a shit.

⊡ *Teacher: "What's taking Ah Seng so long?"*
Student: "He prolly in the toilet doing number two." (He's probably taking a shit.)

See also **do business, pang sai, make cake/make chocolate cake**

Oo

OCBC Acronym standing for "Overseas Chinese, Bukan Cheena", i.e. a Chinese person who has non-Chinese, usually Western, affectations.

⊡ *"All those bananas at the Cricket Club, ah, all OCBC one." (All those Chinese European wannabes at the Cricket Club have a severe case of post-colonial hangover.)*

See also **chiak kantang, keng chio kia**

obiang |oh-bee-ahng| To be embarrassingly out of fashion.

⊡ *"Check out his bell-bottoms! Super obiang, man!" (Check out his bell-bottoms! How passé!)*

See also **orbit**

occifer Deliberate mispronunciation by Hokkien pengs of "officer".

⊡ *"Sir, not say I say what ah, but you cho occifer damn tua kee meh?" (Sir, pardon my impudence, but what's the big deal about being an officer?)*

off [1] A term normally used during National Service to denote "time-off". An "off" is a sanctioned release from duties, given on an ad hoc basis, as opposed to "leave", which is a statutory entitlement.

[1] *Beng: "Eh, where are you going?" (Hey, where are you going?) Seng: "I got one off today." (I've been allowed some time off today.)*

[2] *"I'm not on leave. I'm on off." (I'm not on leave. I've just been officially given some time off.)*

See also **off day**

[2] Economical verb meaning to turn or shut something off.

[·] *"Please off the light." (Please turn off the light.)*

See also **on**

off day Day off.

[·] *"Today is my off day." (Today is my day off.)*

See also **off**

olayavetti A racist term used amongst the Tamil community to refer to Malays, which has a meaning similar to "lazy bum".

old bird Literal translation of "lao cheow", meaning an experienced individual or veteran.

[·] *"Recession that time, all the old bird also kena retrench." (During the recession, even the longest serving veterans were let go.)*

See also **lao cheow**

oleng joo |or-layng joo| The Singlish pronunciation of "orange juice".

on [1] Economical Singlish verb meaning to turn something on.

[·] *"Please on the light." (Please turn the light on.)*

See also **off**

[2] Shares the same meaning and is used in the same way as "on the ball" and "siao on", and is probably a contraction of either.

See also **on the ball, siao on**

[3] An enthusiastic assent to participate in an agreeable activity.

[·] *"Play football tomorrow? On, man!" (Play football tomorrow? Definitely count me in!)*

on the ball Someone who's on top of things or is very hardworking and detail oriented. Perhaps excessively so. Sometimes abbreviated to just "on".

[1] *"Johnny never leaves the office until 9. He's damn on the ball, man." (Johnny never leaves the office until 9. He's really too hardworking.)*

one

2 *"Eh, Johnny! Dun stay so late, lah! This job got no overtime, you so on for what?" (Hey, Johnny. Don't stay so late! This job doesn't pay any overtime wages, so there's no point in being a workaholic.)*
See also **on, siao on**

one A Singlish tag which is derived from Chinese nominalising particles such as "de" in Mandarin and "eh" in Hokkien, and can be attached to both adjectives and verbs.
1 *"Why you so stupid one?" (Why are you so stupid?)*
2 *"Aiyah, he's like that one, lah." (Ah, he's just like that.)*
3 *"Promise you, tomorrow I do it for you swee-swee boh kay chwee one." (I promise that tomorrow, I'll do it for you beautifully.)*
4 *Beng: "Eh, which cake you bake one, ah?" (Which cake did you bake?)*
Seng: "Chocolate one, lor." (The chocolate one.)
See also **hor, lah, lair, leh, meh**

one kind Contraction of the phrase "one of a kind" — usually employed pejoratively.
· *"Ah Seng this kind of friend, damn one kind one! Every time go out he say no money, ask me pay first!" (Friends like Ah Seng are really one of a kind! Each time we go out, he says he has no money and asks me to pay first!)*

ooh Hokkien word denoting the possession of an object or quality. Thus, calling someone "boh say" means he is sufficiently "say", and "ooh chee" means he has "chee". Its antonym is "boh".
1 *"Eh, you got cigarette, not?" (Do you have any cigarettes?)*
"Ooh." (Yes, I do.)
2 *"Action movie, drama, comedy, I simi sai pun ooh." (Action movies, dramas, comedies — I have all kinds of shit.)*
See also **boh**

ooh say Hokkien phrase meaning "to have the look", usually of authority, power or coolness.
· *"He quite ooh say, hor. I think can be occifer." (He has the right look, so I think he might make a suitable officer.)*
See also **boh say**

ooh yia boh? |oo yee-ah boh| Hokkien phrase meaning, "is it for real?" or "are you sure?" or "are you kidding me?"
· *Ah Lian: "Eh, I heard Ah Seng pass his orh lebber..." (Hey, I heard Ah Seng passed his "O" levels...)*
Ah Beng: "Ooh yia boh?" (For real?)
See also **yau mo gau chor?**

open coffee shop The local euphemism for the fly/zipper on one's trousers being down or undone.

☐ *"Wah lau! When I went up to receive the prize from Minister that time, why you neh tell me I open coffee shop?! So malu!" (Holy cow, when I went up on stage to receive the prize from the Minister, why didn't you tell me my fly was open?! How embarrassing!)*

See also **tzao kng**

oppit The local pronunciation of "office".

☐ *"Your oppit where ah? Shenton Way there, ah?" (Where's your office? In Shenton Way?)*

or kong |or gkawng| A fine, or to be fined. Can be used both as a verb and a noun. Thought to be from Hokkien, but this has not been confirmed.

1 *"Nao hiah, that day speeding kena caught on camera, then tio $300 or kong! Si beh suay!" (Oh brother! I was caught speeding on camera and got slapped with a $300 fine! How unfortunate!)*

2 *"Don't anyhow spit, hor, wait kena or kong then you know." (Don't spit indiscriminately. You might be fined.)*

or kwee |or gkwee| Literally, "turtle" in Hokkien. But it's somehow evolved to be a euphemism for "pimp".

or kwee keng |or gkwee gkeng| The Hokkien term for "brothel", it literally means "black turtle house".

or kwee tau / or gkwee tau Hokkien for "head pimp", it literally means "the turtle's head".

or-bi-good Not the name of a Singaporean Jedi Knight, this is a Singlish expression which is used to convey one's belief that someone deserves his current predicament. Often said while making an action like a chicken flapping its wing, with arm curled, and the elbow hitting one's side. Of unknown derivation. The English equivalent would be "serves him right!"

☐ *"Ah Seng is such a ya-ya papaya. Now he fail his 'N' level, or-bi-good!" (Ah Seng is such an arrogant twit. Well, now he's failed his "N" level exams. Serves him right!)*

or cos Common pronunciation of "of course".

☐ *"I got pass my driving test? Or cos, lah! Arbuthen?" (Did I pass my driving test? Of course! What did you think?)*

orang putih |oh-rahng bpoo-tay| Malay term literally meaning, "white people". Describes Caucasians.

See also **ang moh, ang moh gao, ang moh kwee, chao ang moh, mat salleh**

orbit A term of uncertain provenance, meaning "extremely obiang". Possibly a deliberate mispronunciation of "off-beat". May also connote being "out of this world".

☐ *"Are those spandex tights he's wearing? Orbit or what?" (Are those spandex tights he's wearing? How unbelievably tacky!)*
See also **obiang**

oreddy The Singlish pronunciation of "already". This has also become the de facto spelling in the SMS age.
☐ *"I rush to buy ticket, but oreddy sold out." (I rushed to buy tickets, but they were already sold out.)*

orgas The local abbreviation for "to have an orgasm". Describes experiencing intense pleasure. Can be both verb and adjective.
1 *"Every time I hear her sing, I immeelly orgas, man." (Every time I hear her sing, I immediately have an orgasm.)*
2 *"Her laksa is damn orgas, man." (Her laksa is orgasmic.)*
See also **die cock stand, steam**

orh Popular singlish expression of realization or revelation, similar to "oh, I see!" or "now I get it!"
1 *"Orh…. so it's behind your house, is it?" (Oh, I see, so it's behind your house!)*
2 *"So you see, Ah Beng is like that because his father and mother are actually brother and sister!"*
"Orh!" (Oh, that explains everything!)
See also **han tze**

orh lebber The local, and deliberately sarcastic, pronunciation of "O" level, the Cambridge-administered examinations taken by secondary school students in their final year. Can be used as both noun and adjective.
1 *"Wah lau, I only got orh lebber, how to find job?" (Darn, with only "O" level qualifications, how am I to find a job?)*
2 *"Eh, you orh lebber only, don't ya ya, okay!" (You only have "O" level qualifications, so don't be arrogant!)*
See also **air lebber**

orh pee sai Hokkien for "picking one's nose".
☐ *"Ah Wai always got nothing better to do, forever orh pee sai." (Ah Wai is so idle, all he does is pick his own nose.)*

oso |oh-so| The local pronunciation of "also".
1 *"This kind of shit job he oso want." (He also wants even this kind of crappy job.)*
2 *"If you all going Sentosa, I oso come along, can?" (If you're all going to Sentosa, can I also tag along?)*

oso can |ohso-can| A common pronunciation of the words "also can", and is usually found at the end of sentences. Means "this is okay with me", or "this can also be done". The norm is to stretch out the vowels according to how accommodating the speaker is willing to be.

1 *"This one you want to pay by instalment, oso can." (If you wish to pay by instalments for this, that's also fine.)*

2 *"You only owe me $5. But if you want to give me $10, ooooosso caaaan." (You only owe me $5. But if you want to give me $10, that's fine by me!)*

otak |oh-dta'h| Malay for "brain", as well as a popular Malay dish consisting of spicy ground fish wrapped in banana leaves and grilled.

▫ *"Alamak! Simple thing like this also can cock up! Your otak go where?" (Oh my god! How did you mess up a simple matter like this? Where are your brains?)*

otak udang |oh-dta'h oo-dahng| "Prawn brain" in Malay. A popular epithet.

▫ *"Please don't ask him to join our team. He's a real otak udang."*

outstation In traditional English, an "outstation" is a remote outpost or station. In Singlish, "outstation" is a generic term applied to anyone going overseas for business, whether under an assigned posting or not.

1 *"Next week I outstation, so cannot attend your birthday." (Next week, I am going overseas on business, so I will be unable to attend your birthday celebrations.)*

2 *"Mr Tan not in. He go outstation China two months." (Mr Tan is not in. He's been posted to China for two months.)*

ow bway kong Variant spelling of "aw buay kong". See **aw buay kong**

own time own target / OTOT Another Army-inherited term, meaning to perform a task at one's leisure, or using one's discretion.

1 *Private: "Eh, Sergeant! Give how long to sio hoong kee?" (Sergeant, how long is our cigarette break?)*
Sergeant: "OTOT." (At your own discretion.)

2 *"This assignment not very urgent. You own time own target can oreddy." (This assignment is not very urgent. You can take your time to finish it.)*

ownself A term which denotes that a task has been performed through one's effort alone.

1 *"This painting you ownself do, ah?" (Did you paint this painting by yourself?)*

2 *"Can you ownself buy the drinks? My hands already full, lah." (Can you buy the drinks yourself? My hands are already full.)*

[3] *"Eh! Can you ownself do your homework instead of copying from others?" (Hey, can you please do your homework by yourself, instead of copying from others?)*

Pp

pai kia |pai gkee-ah| Hokkien phrase which literally means "bad kid" or "bad boy". Describes a young ruffian.

⊡ *"You go and mix with all those pai kia, one day sure kena sai." (If you continue fraternizing with ruffians, you will surely get into trouble.")*

pai kua |pai kwah| Literally, "awful to see" in Hokkien, it describes unbecoming behaviour.

⊡ *"Eh, you wear skirt can not so short, can? Si beh pai kua!" (Hey, can you please not wear such short skirts? It's really very unbecoming!)*

pai mia |pai mee-ah| Literally, Hokkien for "bad life", meaning someone is unlucky.

⊡ *"Wah lan eh, everyday kena work so hard for so little pay… Pai mia, man." (Damn, I work so hard everyday for so little pay. My life must be cursed.)*

See also **ho mia**

pai seh |pai say| Hokkien for "shy" or "to have a sense of shame". Can be used to express humility or embarrassment.

[1] *"When it comes to asking favours, Ah Beng is damn buay pai seh one." (Johnny has no qualms about asking for favours.)*

[2] *"This is the third time I'm borrowing money from you. Damn pai seh, man." (This is the third time I'm borrowing money from you. I feel really ashamed.)*

pain |bpayn| In true Singlish economy, "painful".

[1] *"Ow! Why you step on my foot? Damn pain, you know!" (Ow! Why did you step on my foot? That was really painful, you know!)*

[2] *"Why you so gu niang? Hit you with pillow also say pain!" (Why are you such a wimp? Crying out in pain from being hit by a pillow!)*

pak |pa'h| Hokkien for "hit" or "beat".

⊡ *"Ah Beng kena pak until he gong-gong." (Ah Beng was hit until he became dizzy.)*

pak bang |pa'h bahng| Hokkien for "to swat mosquitoes", meaning that one's business is extremely slow.

☐ *"See Ah Beng pak bang inside his mobile shop, damn sad. But who ask him to open in such an ulu place?" (It's really sad seeing Ah Beng sitting idly in his mobile phone shop, with no customers. But it's his fault for choosing such an out-of-the-way location.)*

pak buay si |pa'h bway see| Hokkien phrase meaning "indomitable", "indefatigable" or "unfaltering". Literally "beat but won't die".

1 *"That bloody cockroach! Pak buay si one!" (That bloody cockroach! It refuses to die even after a beating!)*

2 *"Wah lau, that Bruce Willis in Die Hard, pak buay si eh!" (Holy cow, Bruce Willis's character in Die Hard was really unwavering in his determination.)*

pak chew cheng |pa'h chew cheng| Literally, to hit the hand gun. The Hokkien euphemism for masturbation. The Mandarin equivalent is "da shou qiang".

pak chiao |pa'h tjee-ow| A Hokkien term which literally translates as "beat bird". It either describes someone with a squint, a lazy eye or who is "cockeyed", or is used to scold someone for his or her inability to see properly. One wonders whether the term was derived from an activity that is often said to cause its practitioners to go blind.

1 *"Why Kate Moss so popular? She a bit pak chiao one." (Why is Kate Moss such a popular model? She's got a lazy eye.)*

2 *"The statue is so bleddy big, why you cannot see? You pak chiao, is it?" (The statue is so huge, yet you couldn't see it? Are you cockeyed or something?)*

See also **bak chew tak stamp**

pak kiu |pa'h kew| Hokkien phrase literally meaning "hit ball". Covers all sports involving a ball, from soccer to snooker.

☐ *"Eh, tonight you wanna go to Kim Seng to pak kiu or not?" (Hey, do you want to go to Kim Seng tonight to play some ball?)*

pak puay kee |pa'h pway gkee| Hokkien for "beat aeroplane", yet another euphemism for masturbation. To be distinguished from "pang puay kee".

See also **pak chew cheng, pang puay kee**

pak tor |pa'h taw| To go on a date.

☐ *"Eh, hurry up leh! I got to go pak tor with my char bor." (Hey, hurry up, won't you? I have a date with my woman!)*

pakat |pah-gkaht| Malay for "to conspire" or gang up against someone.

☐ *"Now all the high-tech companies want to pakat against Microsoft." (Now all the high-tech companies are colluding against Microsoft.)*

pakay / boh pakay / no pakai / tak pakai |bpah-gkay| Derived from the Malay word "pakai" which means to wear (clothes), or to use or apply. Somehow, in Singlish, it's morphed to mean "genuine" or "true". Its English equivalent would be "to count (as legitimate)". It's often used in the negative form, e.g. "boh pakay" or "tak pakai", meaning "inapplicable", "unusable", "ersatz", or "it doesn't count", depending on the context.

1 *"This Lolex watch boh pakay one, made in China!" (This Rolex watch is not genuine, because it's made in China.)*

2 *Ah Beng: "My joker got pakay or not?" (Does my joker count or not?) Ah Seng: "Wah lau, you got play cards before or not? Since when joker got pakay? Joker boh pakay, lah!" (Holy cow, have you played cards before? Since when have Jokers been counted? Jokers are never counted!)*

See also **sorry boh pakay**

paktology |pahk-tor-lor-jee| The study and practice of "pak tor", i.e. dating.

☐ *"You so fast got another girlfriend? You studying for PhD in paktology is it?" (You've found another girlfriend so quickly? Are you studying for a PhD in dating?)*

palalalogram |pair-ler-lair-lo-gram| The Singaporean Chinese-educated person's pronunciation of "parallelogram". Often heard in classrooms.

☐ *"Eh, the area of this palalalogram how to find, ha?" (Hey, how do you find the area of this parallelogram?)*

panchan |pahn-chahn| To give someone a chance, or to forgive someone. Of possibly Malay origin.

☐ *"Alamak, you so poor thing, this time I panchan you, lah." (Oh, since you're so pitiful, this time I'll let you off the hook.)*

See also **agak tarik, give chance**

pandai |bpahn-die; sometimes bpahn-day| Malay for "clever".

☐ *"Talk cock, lah, you! Since when Ah Beng so pandai can become scholar?" (You're talking nonsense! Since when was Ah Beng clever enough to win a scholarship?)*

See also **kiang**

pang chui lao |bpahng tzooi lao| Hokkien for "let the water flow", meaning "forget about it". The equivalent of "water under the bridge".

☐ *"Okay lah, today you cannot make it, neh'mine. Pang chui lao, lah." (Alright, if you can't make it today, never mind. It's water under the bridge.)*

pang jio / pang lio |pahng jee-oh/lee-oh| Hokkien for "urinate".
☐ *"In the jungle, if you need to pang jio against a tree, must say sorry to it first." (In the jungle, please apologise to the trees before urinating against them.)*

See also **number one, shee-shee**

pang puay kee |pahng poo-ay gkee| Hokkien for "fly aeroplane", a phrase of unknown derivation that describes being stood up by somebody.
☐ *"Wah lau, I kena pang puay kee! Wait for him one hour, never come!" (Damn, I've been stood up! I waited for him for an hour, but he didn't turn up!)*

See also **fly aeroplane, no sound no image**

pang sai |bpahng sai| Hokkien for "defecate".
☐ *"Eh, you wait a while, can? I need to pang sai." (Hey, can you wait a while? I need to take a dump.)*

See also **berak, do business, make cake, number two**

pantang |bpahn-dtahng| Malay for "abstain" or "refrain", in Singlish it has come to mean "superstitious".
☐ *"He very pantang one. Got 4D that day, he wen eat chicken rice in case his bets all 'tzao gai' (literally, Cantonese for running chicken, which means to wind up with nothing)." (He's very superstitious. On days with lottery draws, he won't eat chicken rice in case his bets all come to nought.)*

pao bak chang |bpao ba'h tzahng| Literally, Hokkien for "wrapping meat dumplings". Used to describe girls who lack flattering figures, but who insist on wearing figure-hugging clothes.
☐ *"Piang eh, Ah Lian so fat still want to wear tight-tight clothes! Macam pao bak chang like that, man!" (Holy cow, Ah Lian is so fat, yet she still wears such tight clothes! She looks like a dumpling!)*

pao niu |pao new| One of the rare Singlish terms of Mandarin origin, it means to go on the prowl for women.
☐ *"Eh, this Saturday, let's go East Coast and pao niu." (Hey, this Saturday, let's go prowling for women along East Coast.)*

See also **buaya, pok**

pasal |bpah-sahl| Believed to be of Malay derivation, this means "matter", "affair" or "business", as in "that's my business, not yours" rather than a commercial enterprise.
☐ *"Eh, I tell you, ah, this thing is my pasal, so don't come and kachau, okay?" (I'm telling you, this is a personal affair, so don't meddle!)*

2 *"I warn you oreddy he what kind of person. Wait he hantam you, that one not my pasal, okay?"* (I've already warned you about what kind of person he is. If he beats you up, that's none of my business.)

pasang |bpah-sahng| Malay for either "to pair off", "to rise" or "to fix in position". In Singlish, however, it is the equivalent of becoming "it" in a game of tag. It's used mostly in the context of games, but can also be used for general purposes to denote being assigned a task or position. Note: To avoid being pasang, it is common to make a V-sign with both hands and yell, "chope!"

1 *"Why I always pasang when we play catching?"* (Why am I always "it" when we play tag?)

2 *"Eh, cannot pasang me! I chope oreddy!"* (Hey, you can't make me "it". I'm already "safe"!)

3 *"Aiyah, I kena pasang be the goalie in today's game!"* (Oh shucks, I've been assigned to be the goalkeeper in today's game!)

See also **arrow, chope, no bilis**

pattern One's unique habits, mannerisms or ways. Singlish for "modus operandi".

· *"I see his pattern oreddy, I know he sure try to sabo us, one."* (After observing his mannerisms, I knew that he would definitely try to sabotage our operations.)

See also **chut pattern, pattern tzuay kuay badminton**

pattern tzuay kuay badminton |bpeh-tuhn tzoo-eh koo-eh badminton| Literally: more patterns than badminton. Phrase describing someone as extraordinarily complicated, or even devious. Can also be used to allege that someone is full of excuses.

· *"Wah lau, dun do business with him. He pattern tzuay kuay badminton."* (Don't do business with him. He's such a wily character.)

pax Shorthand for "persons" or "participants" in the hospitality industry, "pax" has become increasingly common in everyday usage.

1 *"Mr Tan, I just want to confirm, hor, your reservation tonight how many pax, ah?"* (Mr Tan, may I just confirm the number of people under your reservation tonight?)

2 *"Our restaurant today got special offer: 10 pax only $88."* (Our restaurant is having a special offer today: only $88 for 10 people.)

pecah |bper-cha| Malay for "broken" or "to break". Often mispronounced "pee-chia" by Bengs.

· *"Once you pay for the goods, if pecah already, that's your problem."* (Once you pay for the goods and it breaks, that's your problem.)

pecah lobang |bper-cha loh-bahng| A Malay phrase which literally means to break a hole. It's used in the same way as the English phrase "to let the cat out of the bag."

⊡ *"Dun tell him anything secret. He like the BBC like that, sure pecah lobang." (Don't tell him anything confidential. He's like the BBC — sure to broadcast it.)*

See also **chin poh**

pek chek |bpek chek| Hokkien term denoting intense exasperation or frustration.

⊡ *"Wah lau, whole life kena arrow this kind of job, si beh pek chek, man!" (Darn! I'm always getting stuck with this kind of job. It's really frustrating!)*

See also **bang**

peng san |bpeng sahn| Hokkien for "to faint".

⊡ *"The stock market so hojjiber, I want to peng san." (The stock market is so bad, I feel like fainting.)*

peng yew Hokkien for "friend".

⊡ *"Ah Lian and I peng yew-peng yew only, lah. She not my stead." (Ah Lian and I are only friends. She's not my steady girlfriend.)*

See also **kawan**

pia chui |bpee-ah tsooi| Hokkien phrase meaning to get into unruly fights with gangsters.

⊡ *"Wah lau, you for nothing go and stare at that Ah Beng with tattoos. Later sure pia chui one!" (Oh my goodness! You stared at that tattooed gangster for no reason. You're sure to get embroiled in a gang fight later!)*

See also **hoot**

piak! |pee-ahk| Singaporean sound effect for being slapped or whipped, or being snapped into pieces. Can be used onomatopoeically.

1 *"And then, hor, his wife gave him one tight slap — piak!" (Then, his wife slapped him — slap!)*

2 *"Ah Beng this morning kena rotan — piak!" (Ah Beng was caned this morning — piak!)*

3 *"I think so I put too many clothes on the teck koh, because it suddenly piak." (I think I must have put too many clothes on the pole, because it snapped suddenly.)*

pian chiak |pee-ehn tsia'h| Hokkien term which literally translates as "cheat to eat". As opposed to "tan chiak", it means doing something which may seem impressive to others but is actually quite easily done. Usually used when a person wants to show that he or she is humble.

☐ *Beng: "Wah, your computer very good leh!" (Wow, your computer skills are very good!)*
Seng: "No, lah, pian chiak, pian chiak, only mah..." (Oh no, there's really nothing to it...)

piang! |pee-ahng| Singaporean sound effect with two distinct applications, depending on the tone. If a high pitched tone is used, it denotes glass shattering. If a lower tone is used, it denotes something collapsing or being dropped. (No relation to the cry, "wah piang!")
[1] *"My mother dropped her glass — piang!" (My mother dropped her glass, which shattered loudly.)*
[2] *"And then, hor, the Hotel New World came down — piang!" (Then, the Hotel New World collapsed with a loud crash!)*

piang Abbreviation of "wah piang". See **wah piang**

ping pair lang kio |bping bpair lahng gkyo| Onomatopoeic description of a ruckus, usually employed by exasperated parents or elders against noisy, hyperactive kids.
☐ *"Oi! How to read newspaper when you si gin nah upstair ping pair lang kio?" (Hey! How is one supposed to read the newspapers when you kids are causing such a racket upstairs?)*

pinkerton A pejorative term originating from Puccini's opera Madama Butterfly, describing local girls who will only go out with Caucasians. Now out of vogue. Probably more suited to addressing Caucasian men who have an Asian female fetish.
See also **sarong party girl**

play cheat Inexplicably, to cheat.
☐ *"I warn you, ah, don't play cheat or I tell teacher then you know!" (I'm warning you: don't cheat or I'll report you to the teacher!)*
See also **bangsat, cheaterbug**

play punk |play pahng| To provoke, irritate or aggravate.
☐ *"I told you not to do it, you still go and do. Don't come and play punk with me, ah, I tell you first!" (Despite my telling you not to do it, you went ahead. Don't play the fool with me, I'm warning you!)*

play out / played out To be conned, manipulated, or played for a fool. Note: The Singlish version of "play out" does not share the same meaning as its traditional English counterpart, which means to use up or exhaust.
[1] *"You oreday promise to go to the concert with me. I warn you, ah, don't play me out, okay!" (You've already promised to go to the concert with me. I warn you: don't back out and play me for a fool!)*
[2] *"Wah lau, I kena played out by Johnny, man!" (Holy cow, Johnny*

played me for a fool!)
See also **main, play punk**

pok |bpok| Derived from the Hokkien word for "attempting a go" at something, in Singlish it has come to be a very impolite way of describing a man pursuing the affections of a woman.
⊡ *"Eh, she damn jude. You think I should go and pok her?" (She's really pretty. Do you think I should go and court her?)*
See also **buaya, chee hong, pao niu**

pok kai |pok gkai| Cantonese for "go die in the street". In Hong Kong, it is a general purpose swearword, but in Singapore it seems to mean that you're either broke, have gone out of business or declared bankruptcy. Sometimes, the Hokkien word "liao", meaning "finished", is added for extra emphasis, as in "pok kai liao". If you want to sound even more Hokkien, just drop the "kai", i.e. "pok liao".
1 *"Of course he pok kai liao. He was playing contra shares, mah." (Of course, he went broke. He was engaging in margin trading.)*
2 *"Lend you money? Lim peh pok liao, lah!" (Lend you money? I'm broke, darn it!)*

pondan |bpone-dahn| Malay for "transvestite", but in Singlish, it also means "effeminate" or "gay". Can be used as both noun and adjective.
1 *"Last time Desker Road there can see many pondan, one." (Before, you could see many transvestites along Desker Road.)*
2 *"These arty-farty types a lot are pondan, one." (Many of these arty farty types are effeminate.)*
See also **ah quah, bapok**

pontang / ponteng |bpon-dtehng| From the Malay word "ponteng", meaning to skive, play truant or swindle. In Singlish, it's restricted to skiving or playing truant.
⊡ *"I know it's a school day, but I decided to pontang." (I know it's a school day, but I decided to play hooky.)*
See also **siam, tuang**

pooi |bpoo-ee| Hokkien for "fat".
⊡ *"Wah lau, last time he so skinny, now how come so pooi?" (Wow, he used to be so thin. How did he get so fat?)*
See also **Ah Pooi, fatty bom bom, fei tzai, pooi eh, pooi-pooi**

pooi eh Variant form of "Ah Pooi", meaning "Fatty".
⊡ *"Eh, pooi eh! Don't eat so much, leh!" (Hey, Fatty! Don't eat so much!)*
See also **Ah Pooi, fatty bom bom, fei tzai, pooi, pooi eh, pooi-pooi**

pooi-pooi Chubby, as opposed to fat.

⊡ *"Aiyoh, your dog so pooi-pooi, so cute, one!" (Oh, your dog is such a cute, chubby fellow!)*
See also **Ah Pooi, fatty bom bom, pooi, pooi eh**

poon |bpoon| From the Malay word, "pun", meaning "also". In Singlish it is closer in meaning to "even", like the Hokkien equivalent, "mah si".
⊡ *"Why you so cheap thrill, put those Garfew in your car behind? Like that poon song!" (Why do you engage in such cheap thrills, like placing those Garfield figurines in your car's rear window? Even that gives you satisfaction?)*
See also **mah si**

por |paw| Hokkien term literally meaning "to carry". An act of sycophancy. Buttering someone up, or brown-nosing. Possibly derived from "angkat bodek", the colloquial Malay equivalent, which means to carry someone's testicles.
⊡ *"Eh, I know you want good marks, but don't por the teacher until so obvious, can or not?" (I know you want good grades, but please don't butter the teacher up in such an obvious fashion!)*
See also **angkat, sah kah**

por ma |paw mah| Cantonese for "dilly-dally" or "slow coach".
⊡ *"Aiyoh, Ah Beng is very por ma, one. Every morning take one hour to comb his hair before he can leave the house!" (Good grief, Ah Beng's a real slow coach. Every day, before leaving the house, he must spend an hour combing his hair.)*

potong |pboh-dtohng| Malay for "cut off" or "amputate", in Singlish it is more specifically used to describe castration or being emasculated.
⊡ *"Wah lau, his girlfriend dumped him for another woman, like that might as well potong, man!" (Oh dear! His girlfriend dumped him for another woman? If I were him, I'd castrate myself!)*

potong jalan |pboh-dtong jah-lahn| A Malay term that means "cutting a (new) road". In Singlish, it is used to describe the act of being overtaken on the road by another vehicle, or generally being bypassed, intercepted or cut off, but is also commonly used to describe stealing another's boyfriend/girlfriend. Sometimes it is shortened to just "potong", but very rarely.
[1] *"Oi! Must line up, you know! Cannot anyhow potong jalan!" (Hey, you've got to get in line! You can't just jump queue!)*
[2] *"Rahim was supposed to get the job, but suddenly kena potong jalan by some foreign talent." (Rahim was supposed to get the job, but an expatriate swooped in and he was passed over.)*
[3] *"Ah Beng was buaya-ing Jenny, but then Johnson came and potong jalan him." (Ah Beng was wooing Jenny, but Johnson entered the*

picture and cut him off.)

④ *"Oi! Who say you can potong jalan my girlfriend?" (Hey! Who said you could steal my girlfriend?)*

pow ka leow |bpao gkah lee-ow| Comprehensive; all-encompassing. Literally, Hokkien for "bag everything".

⊡ *"Wah lau, the Coxford Singlish Dictionary is damn pow ka leow. Everything also got." (Holy cow, the Coxford Singlish Dictionary is really comprehensive. It's got everything!)*

powderful Deliberate mispronunciation of "powerful", for emphasis.

⊡ *"His body odour was damn powderful." (His body odour was really overpowering.)*

See also **chia lat, fierce, garang, hiong, siong, terror**

power A contraction of "powerful", which, depending on the context, can mean, variously, "strong", "overpowering", "unbelievable", etc. and can be either praise or denigration.

① *"His music, ah, damn power, sial." (His music is really powerful.)*

② *"Damn power lah you, your own mother also can sabo." (Sabotaging your own mother like that — you're really too damned much!)*

prembry Common pronunciation of "primary".

⊡ *"I remember prembry school that time, hor, I was a class monitor." (I remember that I was a class monitor in primary school.)*

prolly A common contraction of "probably".

⊡ *"Ah Beng go where? Prolly go toilet, lor." (Where did Ah Beng go? Probably to the toilet.)*

puas |bpoo-ahss| Malay for "satisfied" or "content".

① *"After my stingy boss gave me that kind of bonus, I went to scratch the bastard's car until puas." (After my stingy boss gave me such a low bonus, I went to scratch the bastard's car until I was satisfied.)*

② *"Rahima now got new job, new car, even new suami. Like that, she sure puas, oreddy." (Rahima has a new job, a new car, and even a new husband. She must be really contented.)*

③ *"Yesterday, we whack durian until we damn puas, man." (Yesterday, we ate durians till we reached a state of blissful satisfaction.)*

See also **song**

pui chao nuah |pwee chow noo-ah| Literally, Hokkien for "to spit smelly spittle". Describes being extremely fed up, dissatisfied or disgruntled.

① *"Wah lan, I for nothing kena extra from my PC. Make me want to pui chao nuah, man!" (Damn! I was assigned extra duties by my platoon commander for no good reason! It makes me want to spit!)*

② *"That Singapore Idol reject, every time he starts to sing, everyone pui chao nuah at him." (Everyone gets really annoyed each time that Singapore Idol reject starts to sing.)*

puki |bpoo-gkee| Malay expletive which is the equivalent of "chee bye" (vagina), it is derived from the Malay word "pukang", or crotch. See also **chee bye**

puki mak |bpoo-gkee ma'h| The nuclear weapon of Malay swearing. The equivalent of "motherfucker" or "your mother's vagina". Not to be used lightly. See also **kan ni na bu chao chee bye**

pukul |bpoo-gkole| Malay for beat or hit repeatedly.

⊡ *"Ah Beng went to disturb those Mat Rokers and kena pukul until he peng san." (Ah Beng annoyed a group of Mat Rokers and was beaten till he became unconscious.)*

See also **hantam, sepak**

pumchek |pahm-tche'h| Derived from a colloquial Malay pronunciation of "puncture", it is now the default Singlish term for having a flat tire.

⊡ *"Yesterday my car pumchek on the AYE, damn leceh, man!" (Yesterday, I had a flat tire on the Ayer Rajah Expressway. It was really troublesome.)*

Qq

THERE are no entries under "q" because in Singlish, the hard "q" sound can be replaced by "k", as in "kway" or "kua si mi", while the Mandarin use of "q" as in words like "qing", can be substituted by "ch", as in "ching".

Rr

rabak rabak |rah-ba'h rah-ba'h| Malay for "petting" or "making

out". In Singlish, the continuous tense is "rabaking".
1 *"Alamak, such an ugly girl also can rabak rabak! You gila or what?" (Oh my god, you can make out with such an ugly girl? Are you mad?)*
2 *"Eh, check out behind the bushes, lah. Ah Beng and Ah Lian are rabaking there." (Hey, if you check behind those bushes, you'll find Ah Beng and Ah Lian petting away.)*

ready oreddy |reddy awreddy| A commonly-used redundancy to indicate a state of readiness.
· *"Can we go now? I'm ready oreddy." (Can we go now? I'm ready.)*
See also **oreddy**

relac / relac one corner / lac A Mat-ism, exhorting one to relax. "Relac" is ostensibly even more laid back than "relax", as it is in the singular. Now, this has been shortened even further to "lac".
1 *"Eh, Joe! Exam so far away. Relac one corner, lah." (Hey, Joe! The exams are so far away, so just relax, will you?)*
2 *"Lac, man! You so kan cheong for what?" (Relax, dude! Why are you so uptight?)*
See also **jangan tension, lac, maintain balan**

repeat again A commonly-used redundancy asking someone to repeat what they've said.
· *"I can't hear you. Can you repeat again?" (I can't hear you. Can you repeat it for me, please?)*
See also **again, balik, lippit, say again**

rojak |roh-ja'h| A salad of mixed vegetables and miscellaneous items, tossed with sauce. Of Malay origin, it has been adapted by all races. In Singlish, it is used as an adjective, to describe something as being either eclectic, or just plain messy.
1 *"This sort of multicultural event, ah, don't plan properly will come out all rojak." (If one doesn't plan these multicultural events properly, they could easily become a mess.)*
2 *"Piang, your wep site use so many fonts, looks damn rojak, man!" (Holy cow, you've used so many different fonts in your website that it looks really messy, man!)*
See also **chap chye**

rosak |roh-sa'h| Malay for "damaged" or "spoilt".
1 *"Your TV rosak oreddy, why you still keep?" (Your TV set is already broken, why are you still keeping it?)*
2 *"Adoi, Ramli, why you anyhow go and rabak my sister? You damn rosak, sial!" (Ramli, why did you make out with my sister? There's something wrong with you, man!)*

See also **koyak, spoi**

rotan |roh-dtahn| Malay for "cane". It has two meanings in Singlish. The first is to receive a caning. It can also be used to describe a young girl as a "lolita" or "jailbait", as caning is often the sentence for engaging in or soliciting underage sex.

1 *"I told Ah Seng dun employ that illegal Bangla. Wait he kena rotan, then he know!" (I told Ah Seng not to employ that illegal Bangladeshi worker. I guess he'll learn his lesson when he gets sentenced to caning!)*

2 *"These convent girls, ah, all damn rotan one." (These convent girls are all lolitas.)*

rugi |roo-ghee| Malay for "to suffer a loss." In Singlish, it is usually applied in situations where one has missed an opportunity or lost an advantage (often financial), rather than anything really catastrophic. Hardcore Bengs pronounce it "loogi".

"I bought US loler when it was so high, now drop oreddy, I rugi big time, man." (I bought the US dollar when it was high, and now that it's dropped, I've lost a lot of money.)

Ss

SBC Acronym for "simply boh chup", meaning extremely cavalier or inconsiderate.

"Wah lau! Parking lot so big, you still park until like that! Damn bloody SBC, sial." (Holy cow! The parking lot is so big, yet you still park in such a manner! You're truly inconsiderate!)

See also **boh chup**

SBS An acronym for "si beh sian", or "very bored".

"I everyday also kena take the same crowded bus to school. SBS, man." (Everyday, I'm forced to take the same crowded bus to school. How tedious!)

See also **sian**

sabo Singlish contraction of "sabotage". Used to cover instances of everything from practical jokes and tricks to outright betrayal.

1 *"You don'ch sabo me, I warn you, ah!" (I'm warning you: don't you dare sabotage my plans!)*

2 *"He was hoping to take over as chief, but then his predecessor*

sabo him by spreading all sorts of rumours." (He was hoping to take over as chief, but then his predecessor sabotaged his succession by spreading all sorts of rumours.)

sabo king A supreme saboteur.

⊡ *"He's a damn sabo king. I told him I do'wan to go for the meeting, and he still arrow me to go!" (He's a real saboteur. I told him I didn't want to go for the meeting, but he still nominated me to go!)*

sadden Multipurpose term used to describe feeling upset or annoyed by any unfortunate state of affairs, whether irritatingly trivial or actually tragic.

1 *"His off day also kena recall to office to zap things. Sadden, sial." (Even on his day off, he was recalled to the office to do photocopying. How annoying!)*

2 *"He save for so long to buy that Maseelis, then driving out of the showroom that time, suay-suay kena langgar. So of course he now damn sadden, lah." (He saved for so long to buy that Mercedes, then, when he was driving out of the dealership, he unfortunately got into a collision with another vehicle. So of course he's really upset.)*

sah-kah Literally, "three legs" in Hokkien. Meaning sycophancy or buttering someone up, the phrase comes from a rude hand action whereby three fingers are held up to denote supporting someone's genitalia.

⊡ *"If you don't sah-kah the boss, you won't get your bonus." (If you don't curry favour with the boss, you won't get your bonus.)*

See also **angkat bola, por, sah-kah chua**

sah-kah chua |sah kah tzoo-ah| A sycophant. Literally, "three-legged snake" in Hokkien.

⊡ *"Look at the bloody sah-kah chua, giving the boss's wife a birthday present!" (What a sycophant! Giving the boss's wife a birthday present!)*

See also **sah-kah**

saht Of uncertain provenance, it's the local equivalent of "cool" or "groovy".

1 *"You got tickets to the sold out concert? How come you so saht one?" (You got tickets for the sold out concert? How did you get to be so cool?)*

2 *"That Alfian Sa'at's plays, hor, all damn saht one." (Alfian Sa'at's plays are all really cool.)*

See also **saht saht boh chio**

saht saht boh chio The ultimate in coolness or grooviness — literally: so cool that there is no smile. This comes from those "cool" models you see in magazine ads or fashion spreads who always look frosty, grouchy or dazed.

⊡ *"Eh, Ah Lian, how come your photo your face always so saht saht boh chio, one? You think you Kate Moss, is it?" (Hey, Ah Lian! Why are you always adopting such frosty, blank expressions in your photographs? Do you think you're Kate Moss or something?)*

See also **saht**

sai Hokkien for "shit".

1 *"His shirt is like sai like that." (His shirt looks like shit.)*

2 *"Sai lai leow." (Here comes shit — the local equivalent of "the shit just hit the fan".)*

See also **berak, kana sai, make cake, number two, pang sai**

sai kang |sai gkahng| Literally, Hokkien for "shit work", i.e. an unpleasant and often demeaning job or task.

⊡ *"I chao recruit only, mah, that's why boh pian kena do this type of sai kang." (I'm only a lowly recruit, that's why I have no choice but to do these really unpleasant duties.)*

sala |sah-lah| Malay for "wrong" and "incorrect".

⊡ *"His house is over there, not here. You go sala oreddy, lah." (His house is over there, not here. You have come to the wrong place.)*

saman |sah-mahn| The Malay word for "summons". Singaporeans use it as a verb, meaning "to be fined" or "summonsed to attend court".

1 *"You better not litter, udderwise sure kena saman one!" (You better not litter, because you're sure to get fined!)*

2 *"Na beh, I ran back to my car to change kupoon, but the fler oreddy saman me!" (Damn! I ran back to my car to change my parking coupon, but the fellow had already issued me a parking summons.)*

samseng |sahm-seng| Local Hokkien for "gangster" or "thug".

⊡ *"He's a real samseng, always want to whack people." (He's a real thug, always spoiling for a fight.)*

sapu |sah-bpoo| Malay for "sweep". Commonly used in the sense of "grab" or "snatch".

⊡ *"Eh, don't be greedy and sapu all the free gifts, lah!" (Hey, don't be greedy and grab all the free gifts!)*

See also **gasak**

sarong party girl / SPG A pejorative term describing local girls who will only go out with Caucasians. Often abbreviated to just "SPG". (Entered popular usage after the publication of the bestselling book, Sarong Party Girl).

say again A request for someone to repeat something.

☐ *"I didn't hear what you just said. Say again?" (I didn't hear what you just said. Could you say it again?)*

See also **again, lippit, repeat again**

say first Used as an expression to lay down one's ideas/thoughts/feelings/intentions before doing/saying something. Can also be used as a question concerning the order or priority of things to be done.

1 *"OK, say first, today after work go where and chiong?" (Okay, let me jump in first and ask where we want to play after work today?)*

2 *"Eh, say first leh, you still lurf me or not?" (Go on, do you still love me or not?)*

say me {or him, her, etc.} Essentially an unparticularized accusation or criticism about one's behaviour.

1 *"Dun say her already, lah… always late one lah, she!" (Oh, quit griping about her. She's always late!)*

2 *Beng: "Can you be more punctual, not?" (Can you be more punctual, please?)*
Seng: "Why you always say me, ha?" (Why are you always criticising me?)

say so Singlish contraction for "why didn't you say so?" or "you should have told me so".

☐ *Jenny: "The magazine you borrow — where ah?" (That magazine you borrowed — where is it?)*
Fanny: "Put back already. Inside your drawer." (I've replaced it. It's inside your drawer.)
Jenny: "Aiyah, say so, lah!" (Oh, why didn't you say so!)

say some more Sarcastic warning to another person not to continue their abuse, perhaps even after the argument has ended.

1 *Ah Beng: "You damn cock up, ah you!" (You're really incompetent, aren't you!)*
Ah Seng: "Still say some more! Whack you then you know!" (If you insist on continuing your spurious accusations, I shall be forced to hit you!)

2 *Mother: "I tol' you you play all the time sure cannot pass exam!" (I warned you that if you played all the time, you would be unable to pass your examinations!)*
Son: "Say some more, lah! Like I care!" (Go on, keep criticizing me! See if I care!)

sayang |sah-yahng| Malay for "love" or "darling". In Singlish, it has an additional meaning, akin to "what a pity".

1 *"Your mother very sayang her pet cat, hor?" (Your mother really loves her pet cat, doesn't she?)*

2 *"Sayang, marry me, leh!" (Darling, won't you marry me?)*

[3] *"I see them throw away so much food, I always feel damn sayang like that." (I always think it's such a pity whenever I see them throw away so much food.)*
See also **sim tiah**

scared what An expression of bravado.
[·] *"Go to jail, go to jail, lor. Scared what?" (Who's afraid of going to jail?)*

scuse |skews| Short for "excuse me". Used in place of the phrase "get out of my way!" in a vague (and insincere) attempt to be polite.
See also **eskew me, skew**

se lang |suh lahng| Mandarin for "coloured wolf", i.e. a lecher or pervert.
[·] *"Girl-girl, when you go out that time, hor, must careful se lang, okay?" (Little girl, whenever you go out, you must beware of lechers.)*
See also **bian tai, chee ko pek, ter koh**

sedap Malay for "delicious".
[1] *"Wah, her laksa is damn sedap, man!" (Wow, her laksa is really delicious!)*
[2] *"Try adding some hum to your mee siam, lah. Even more sedap. I neh bluff you." (Try adding some cockles to your mee siam. It'll make it even more delicious, I'm not kidding.)*
See also **shiok**

see how To leave the matter alone and watch how it develops. Often repeated for emphasis.
[·] *"I oreddy submitted the application form. So now just see how, see how, lor." (I've already submitted the application form. So now I'm just waiting for the response.)*

see me no up To be looked down upon or underestimated by someone. Can also be used to accuse someone of being condescending.
[1] *"You know me for so long and still treat me like that? You see me no up, is it?" (You've known me for so long, yet you're treating me in this manner? Are you looking down on me?)*
[2] *"Dun see me no up, okay! You see me small-small, but I can do 60 push-up!" (Don't look down on me! I may appear small, but I can do 60 push-ups!)*

see what? A belligerent contraction of "what are you looking at?". The English transliteration of "kua si mi?", which is the Ah Beng prelude to a fight.
[·] *"See what? I break my nose, damn funny to look at, meh?" (What are you looking at? Is my broken nose so funny to look at?)*
See also **an chua, kua si mi, never see before is it?**

see you small A statement of condescending magnanimity, equivalent to, "I'm letting you off this time out of the generosity of my heart, because you're inconsequential."

☐ *"Today I panchan you, neh call my kakis come to hantam you. See you small only." (I'm letting you off the hook by not calling my gang to beat you up. That's because you're only a small fry and not worth the effort.)*

sell backside A classic example of Singlish hyperbole. While it alludes to prostituting oneself, it is used in conjunction with any instance when one has to do something unsavoury in order to make ends meet.

1 *"Die, today I kena fired. Tomorrow got no choice, must go Desker Road and sell backside oreddy." (Oh god, I was fired today. I guess I have no choice but to go to Desker Road tomorrow and prostitute myself.)*

2 *"Heng ah! I today touch 4D. No need to sell backside anymore." (Phew! I won the lottery today! I don't have to take up anymore demeaning work in order to make ends meet.)*

semen A very unfortunate local pronunciation of "cement".

semen mixture A very unfortunate local pronunciation of "cement mixer".

senang |suh-nahng| Malay for "cushy", i.e. a pleasant and easy task or posting.

☐ *"Ah Beng kena sent to HQ. Damn senang, man." (Ah Beng was posted to the headquarters. That's a really cushy posting.)*

See also **switch off**

send Local shorthand for "to give someone a ride" or "drop someone off".

☐ *"Can you send me to the bus stop?" (Could you drop me off at the bus stop?)*

See also **fetch**

seng lee cho tua |seng lee tzoh dtwah| Hokkien term which literally translates as "business do big". Used (with a bit of sarcasm) to comment on someone who appears to be a show-off or very busy, giving others the impression that he/she is doing very well in his/her job.

☐ *"Wah, now you carry two handphone ah? Seng lee cho tua liao, hor?" (Wow, you're now carrying two handphones? Looks like you've hit the big time, eh?)*

senget |say-ngay'h| Malay for "listing to one side", as with a ship. In Singlish, it has been expanded to mean "slanted" or "crooked".

☐ *"Wah lau, how you can pass driving test when your parking so senget one?" (Holy cow! How do you expect to pass your driving test when your parking is so crooked?)*

seow |see-ow| Hokkien for "crazy". Variant spelling of "siao".

[1] *"You want to go and talk at Speakers Corner? You seow or what?" (You want to go and speak at Speakers Corner? Are you mad?)*

[2] *"Look at that seow char bor!" (Look at that crazy woman!)*

See also **gila, siao**

sepak |suh-pa'h| Malay for slap or kick.

☐ *"If you don't faster give me the remote control, I sepak you then you know!" (If you don't hand me the remote control quickly, I'm going to whack you!)*

See also **hantam, pukul**

sepet |say-pe'h| Malay for "single eyelid" or "slanted eyes". A pejorative term used to describe Chinese people and their behaviour or tastes.

☐ *"Adoi, Rosli! How come you got this Jay Chou CD? Since when you listen to sepet music?" (Holy cow, Rosli! Why do you have a Jay Chou CD in your collection? Since when did you start listening to chinky music?)*

See also **cheena, cheenagerk, cheenapiang**

serani Another Malay term to describe Eurasians. Derived from the Arab word "nasrani", meaning Nazarene, or Christian. Considered less demeaning than "geragok".

See also **geragok**

set! Probably an abbreviation of "that's settled", it functions as the local equivalent of "agreed!"

☐ *Beng: "So, tomorrow go eat chilli crab, ah?" (So, shall we eat chilli crab tomorrow?)*
Seng: "Set!" (Agreed!)

See also **on [3]**

settle |sair-tur| To bring a dispute or matter to an end. With Ah Bengs, this invariably involves physical violence.

[1] *"Eh, this thing drag on for damn long oreddy. Can you faster go and settle?" (Hey, this thing has dragged on for far too long. Can you hurry up and settle it?)*

[2] *"You not satisfied, is it? Okay! Let's go aw buay and settle!" (Are you unhappy about something? Very well, let's go outside and bring this matter to a close!)*

See also **aw buay kong**

seven morning eight morning cry father cry mother A

literal translation of a hybrid phrase — "qi zao ba zao" (Mandarin for "early in the morning", literally: "seven early, eight early") and "kau peh kau bu" (Hokkien for "to bellyache"). It means to complain loudly first thing in the morning.

⊡ *"You ah, lost 10 dollars only what! Don't seven morning, eight morning, cry father, cry mother and wake up the whole neighbourhood!" (You only lost 10 dollars! Don't wake up the entire neighbourhood so early in the morning with your bellyaching!)*

See also **kau peh kau bu**

sewer serpent Deliberate mispronunciation of "civil servant". See also **cheng hu kang**

shack To be extremely tired. Not to be confused with "shag" (the British colloquialism for having sex) even though it's often misspelled that way in Singapore.

⊡ *"I shagged so much last weekend, so now I'm damn shack, man." (I had so much sex last weekend, so I'm now totally exhausted.)*

shaddup |shah-dup| Common Singlish pronunciation of "shut up".

shag See **shack**

shake leg To be idle.

⊡ *"Eh, you got homework, hurry up go and do! Don't just sit here and shake leg!" (Hey, if you have any homework, you'd better hurry up and complete it! Don't just sit here, idling about!)*

See also **chiak sior eng, eng**

shake leg company (SLC) To amble about idly. Similar to "KLKK" See also **KLKK**

shee shee Onomatopoeic Hokkien term for urinating. Mainly used with kids.

⊡ *"Boy-boy, you better go shee shee before we drive to Malaysia." (Son, you'd better have a pee before we drive to Malaysia.)*

sheeming Common Singaporean pronunciation of "swimming".

⊡ *"Today damn hot, man. Let's go sheeming!" (Today is really hot. Let's go swimming.)*

shiok |shee-oke| Originally a Malay exclamation, but now a universal Singaporean expression denoting extreme pleasure or the highest quality.

1 *"This char kway teow is damn shiok, man!" (This char kway teow is superb!)*

2 *"I ate the char kway teow until damn shiok." (I ate the char kway teow, which was an extremely pleasurable experience.)*

show half ball To describe a girl who is revealing substantial cleavage.

☐ *"Check out Ah Lian today, man. Her dress is so low cut, she show half ball." (Check out Ah Lian today. Her dress is so low cut, she's showing too much cleavage.)*

shy In English, "shy" means to be timid, reserved or diffident. In Singlish, "shy" has the added meaning of "embarrassed" or "embarrassing".

☐ *Our football team, even Bukit Pantat FC also can lose! Damn shy, man!" (Our football team lost even to Bukit Pantat FC. How embarrassing!)*

See also **lao kwee, malu, shyful**

shyful |shy-foo| A unique Singaporean conflation of "shy" and "painful", meaning "painfully shy". "Shy", however, carries the Singlish meaning of "embarrassing" rather than the traditional English meaning of diffidence or reserve, so "shyful" can also mean "painfully embarrassing".

☐ *"When he went up to shake hand with the VIP, he accidentally let out this big-big fart. So shyful, you know!" (When he went up to shake hands with the VIP, he accidentally let out this huge fart. What a painful embarrassment!)*

See also **lao kwee, malu, shy**

si beh / si peh |see bay/see bpay| Hokkien term meaning "very" or "extremely".

1 *"This curry is si peh hiam man!" (This curry is very spicy!)*

2 *"Professor Lau's class was si beh cheem." (Professor Lau's class was completely incomprehensible.)*

si gin nah |see gheen nah| In Hokkien, "si" means "to die", while "gin nah" is "children". A Hokkien term which can roughly be translated as "bloody kid". Used in exasperation. See also "si noong kia", which has the same meaning.

☐ *"Si gin nah! Your own father also dare to disturb?!" (Bloody kid! You dare to annoy even your own father?!)*

See also **si noong kia**

si mi / si mi lan / si mi lan chiao |see mee lahn chee-ow| "Si mi" is Hokkien for "what?". With "lan" or "lan chiao" (penis) tagged on, it becomes much more belligerent, not to mention rude, and often contains a veiled warning not to complicate matters. The closest English approximation would be "what the fuck?"

1 *"Sergeant say you want to find me. Si mi lan?" (The sergeant said you were looking for me. What the fuck for?)*

2 *"I ask you to make me a Hello Kitty birthday cake, and you gimme this. This is si mi lan chiao?" (I asked you to make me a Hello Kitty cake for my birthday, and instead, you gave me this. What the fuck*

is this?)
See also **si mi tai chi**

si mi tai chi |see mee tai tjee| Hokkien for "what's the matter?" Often used belligerently.
⊡ *"You call me out here so early. Si mi tai chi?" (You've called me out here so early. What's the matter?)*
See also **si mi lan chiao**

si noong kia |see noong gkia| Teochew version of "si gin nah".
See also **si gin nah**

si sua lai |see soo-ah lai| Hokkien and Teochew expression that literally means "anyhow come". To do something in an indifferent or disorganised manner.
⊡ *"This meeting is very important, don't si sua lai OK?" (This is a very important meeting. Please don't do anything in a haphazard fashion.)*
See also **luan luan / luan luan lai**

sia lan |see-ah lahn| Hokkien term describing someone as arrogant, haughty and contemptuous.
⊡ *"Ah Leong got a really sia lan face. People see only want to hantam him." (Ah Leong has a really arrogant demeanour. The moment people see him, they want to beat him up.)*
See also **kwai lan**

sia suay |see-ah sway| Hokkien for "to embarrass" or "let down".
⊡ *"I warn you, you better get good grades. Don't sia suay, okay!" (I warn you, you better get good grades! Don't embarrass me!)*

sial / sia |see-ahl/see-ah| "Sial" in Malay means "unfortunate" or "futile". However, since being co-opted by the other races, it is tagged onto sentences as an expression of emphasis, sympathy, or even of admiration. It is not limited to disastrous situations. Ah Bengs often omit the "l" when uttering it.
1 *"That girl damn jude, sial!" (That girl is really pretty, man!)*
2 *"Wah, your guitar damn good, sia…" (Whoa, your guitar skills are really good, dude…)*
3 *"Ah Beng in his Armani suit look damn stylo, sia!" (Ah Beng looks very stylish in his Armani suit!)*
4 *"John kena langgar? Sadden, sial…" (John was involved in a vehicular accident? Oh dear!)*

siam |see-ahm| Hokkien term for "get out of the way". Can either be used to shoo people away, or in the sense of making oneself scarce or dodging a task.
1 *"Siam ah! Sio ah!" (Get out of the way! This [bowl of soup] is hot!)*

2 *"I saw the boss coming, so I thought I better faster siam." (I saw the boss coming, so I thought I'd better make myself scarce.)*

See also **eskew, scuse, skew, siam one corner / SOC**

siam one corner / SOC A hybrid Mat and Beng-ism, exhorting one to make oneself scarce in order to dodge work.

1 *"Fwah, later boss looking for people to do stock check, better go siam one corner first." (Damn, the boss is looking for people to conduct an inventory audit. I'd best make myself scarce.)*

2 *"Recruit Tan was charged for SOCing when he was supposed to do his SOC." (Recruit Tan was charged for shirking his duties, when he was supposed to be running the Standard Obstacle Course.)*

See also **take cover**

sian |see-en| Hokkien for "sleepy", but in practice, it also connotes conveys boredom, weariness, frustration and emptiness. Possible English equivalents would be "ennui" or "malaise".

1 *"My job is damn sian, man." (My job is really tedious and boring, man.)*

2 *"Wah lau eh, I do A-maths, do until sian oreddy." (Damn! I'm totally bored stiff of doing Additional Mathematics problems!)*

sian ji pua |see-en tjee bpoo-ah| "Sian" describes something as boring or tedious. "Ji pua" is Hokkien for "half". Put together, the phrase can be loosely translated as "too boring by half", meaning it is extremely boring. Can be used to express one's lack of enthusiasm even before the tedious event has actually taken place.

1 *"Sian ji pua, man! This disco is damn boring!" (This disco is too boring by half.)*

2 *"My mudder want to arrow me go shopping with her. Haven't go oreddy I sian ji pua." (My mother wants me to accompany her shopping. I'm really not looking forward to it.)*

sian tao Hokkien term meaning "bullshitter".

· *"Wah lau, let's get out of here. Sian tao come oreddy." (Holy cow, let's get out of here. Here comes that bullshitter.)*

sian tao ong Hokkien phrase meaning "king of the bullshitters".

· *"He whole day talk cock — damn sian tao ong, one." (He talks rubbish the whole day. He's the king of the bullshitters.)*

See also **talk cock king, tua pao sian, tua pian sian**

siang kah pager Hokkien for "who paged/beeped me?" To be said very loudly in public places, such as cinemas or during performances. Has fallen out of fashion along with pagers.

siao |see-ow| Hokkien for "mad" or "crazy". Variant spelling of "seow".

1 *"You want to go and talk at Speakers Corner? You siao or what?"*

(You want to go and speak at Speakers Corner? Are you mad?)
2 *"Look at that siao char bor!" (Look at that crazy woman!)*
See also **gila, seow**

siao liao |see-ow lee-ow| A Hokkien exclamation which literally means "already gone crazy". Used whenever a situation has gone badly wrong, or when someone is going into a frenzy.
1 *"Alamak! I fax my application to the wrong company! Siao liao! Siao liao!" (Oh my god! I faxed my application to the wrong company! I'm doomed. Doomed!)*
2 *"Wah lau eh, today the stock market go up 300 points, then come down 400 points! Siao liao!" (Oh my god, today the stock market went up by 300 points, then fell by 400 points. It was madness!)*

siao on Same meaning as "on the ball".
· *"Oh no! We're competing against Ah Seng! He always damn siao on, one." (Oh no! We're competing against Ah Seng! He's always on the ball.)*
See also **on, on the ball**

siao ting tong |see-ow dting dtong| Onomatopoeic Hokkien term for a dumbbell or crazy person.
· *"Why you go and put the cat in the microwave? Siao ting tong!" (Why did you put the cat in the microwave? You lunatic!)*

sim tiah A Hokkien phrase which literally means, "heart pain". The Singlish equivalent of "it's such a pity."
· *"Look at them throw all that food away. Damn sim tiah, man." (It makes my heart ache to see them throw all that food away.)*
See also **sayang**

sinkek |sing-kay'h| Condescending term, used by Malays or Peranakans to describe someone who is very traditionally Chinese, or old-fashioned. No doubt it derives from the Hokkien term "sin kek" which means "new guests". The Malays and Peranakans probably thought the new arrivals were unsophisticated arrivistes. The term is going out of fashion, and is being replaced by "cheena" or "sua koo", and with the increasing immigration of mainland Chinese, "MIC".
See also **cheena, MIC, sua koo**

sio |see-oh| Hokkien for "hot". As with English, it can also describe people as sexy.
1 *"This soup is sio, boy." (This soup is very hot.)*
2 *"That chick is damn sio, man." (That woman is really sexy!)*
See also **chio, steam**

siong |see-ong| Hokkien for "tough", "fierce" or "difficult".

[1] *"BMT nowsaday not so siong like last time." (Basic Military Training is not as tough as it used to be.)*
[2] *"Na beh, these maths sums are si beh siong, man." (Damn, these mathematical problems are really difficult.)*
See also **chia lat, fierce, garang, hiong, powderful, terror**

siu ye |siew yeh| Cantonese for "supper", i.e. a late night meal. An extremely popular pastime amongst Singaporeans. Can be used both as a noun and verb.
[1] *"Come! Let's go siu ye in Geylang!" (Come! Let us go for supper in Geylang!)*
[2] *"Go where for siu ye, ah?" (Where shall we go for supper?)*

skali / skarly |skah-lee| Adapted from the Malay word "sekali", meaning "once" or "on one occasion", denoting a one time occurrence. However, in Singlish, it is commonly used to convey a warning. "Skali" loosely means any one of the following, depending on the context: **[1]** "If you're not careful, you may find out that..." **[2]** "What would happen if..." **[3]** "Unexpectedly, it turns out that..." **[4]** "All of a sudden..."
[1] *"You better don't anyhow go clubbing and disturb girls. Skali kena hantam by her boyfriend, then you know." (You'd better not go clubbing or chatting girls up indiscriminately. If you're not careful, you might be beaten up by their boyfriends.)*
[2] *"You everyday go to work damn late and leave so early. Skarly your boss find out, how?" (Everyday, you leave for work so late and come back so early. What will happen if your boss catches you?)*
[3] *"We early already say we want to go Zouk with them. Skali last minute they go and cancel." (Early on, we said we wanted to go to Zouk with them. But unexpectedly, they cancelled on us.)*
[4] *"I was driving and then skarly this idiot runs in front of me!" (I was driving along this road, when all of a sudden, this idiot runs in front of me.)*
[5] *"You don't go and read so many porno magazines, skarly you go blind!" (Don't read so many pornographic magazines. If you're not careful, you'll go blind!)*

skew / skews / skius Variants of "excuse me".
See also **eskew, scuse, siam**

slack Describes someone as lackadaisical or sloppy in one's work.
[·] *"His work is damn slack. Better don't hire him." (His work is really sloppy. Better not to hire him.)*
See also **bah long long, nuah**

slaykay Derived from the Malay word "selekeh", meaning sloppy or slovenly.

⊡ *"Wah lau, this sort of high-class function, how can you dress so slaykay one?" (Holy cow! This is a very classy event. How could you turn up dressed like a slob?)*

small air Literal translation of the Mandarin term "xiao qi", meaning petty and unduly sensitive.

⊡ *"Eh, better dun say him so much in your blog. This kind of small air person, hor, skarly go and sue you for defamation." (You'd better not criticize him so much in your blog. You never know with such petty people. He might sue you for defamation.)*

smoke / throw smoke A term derived from the Army, where smoke is used to conceal tactical operations. Means to bluff, cause a diversion, confuse someone, or bullshit. It's used commonly during examinations, when someone has no idea how to answer the question and has to bullshit all the way.

1 *"I know you and Ah Huay are going pak tor. Don't try and smoke me." (I know you and Ah Huay are going on a date. Don't try and lie to me.)*

2 *"Wah lau, the essay question so cheem, donno what to write. So I just smoke all the way, lah." (Holy cow, the essay question was so difficult, so I just bluffed my way through it.)*

3 *"So many years neh say anything, then suddenly election time kau peh kau bu. I think he throw smoke only, lah." (He's kept quiet about it for so many years, then all of a sudden, just when the elections come around, he starts complaining loudly. I think it's all a diversion.)*

sng seow Idiomatic Hokkien for "to settle a score" or "avenge an injustice".

⊡ *"You sabo me like this? Nehmine. One day I find you to sng seow, then you tzai si." (So you've sabotaged my plans. Never mind. The time will come when I'll seek you out to settle the score, then you'll know what death means.)*

so how? Economical Singlish term, essentially an abbreviation of "so what now?" or "what do we do now?"

⊡ *"The show oreddy sold out. So how?" (The show has been completely sold out. What do we do now?)*

solid An adjective describing something or someone as being very impressive.

1 *"Did you see her performance? Solid, man!" (Did you see her performance? It was excellent!)*

2 *"Pam Anderson is damn solid, man!" (Pamela Anderson is really impressive!)*

sombong |sohm-bohng| Malay for arrogant and haughty. Basically the same as "ya ya".
⊡ *"Piang eh, Ah Lian is si beh sombong one. I saw her in school and she never say hello." (Holy cow, Ah Lian is really haughty! I saw her in school, but she didn't even say hello.)*
See also **atas, cheng, dao, upstair, ya ya**

some more The Singlish equivalent of "furthermore..." or "in addition to..."
1 *"He so fat, some more like to wear tight-tight T-shirt, how to find girlfriend?" (He's so fat, and furthermore, he likes to wear very tight T-shirts. How on earth does he expect to find a girlfriend?)*
2 *"You just ate three plates of char kway teow, and then some more you go and eat two durians all by yourself. Tomorrow sure lao sai." (You ate three plates of char kway teow. Additionally, you ate two durians all by yourself. You're sure to have diarrhoea tomorrow.)*

something wrong A Singlish adjective used to describe something as being defective.
1 *"Eh, I think your car, hor, something wrong, lair!" (Hey, I think something is wrong with your car.)*
2 *"Ha? You join an opposition party? You something wrong or what?!" (Huh? You joined an opposition party? Is there something wrong with you?)*

song / song-song A Hokkien term which is a combination of "satisfied" and "at peace", denoting a sense of bliss. Sometimes repeated for effect.
1 *"Wah, your estate got good food, got good view, you must be damn song, lah." (Wow, your estate has good food and a good view. You must be really contented.)*
2 *"We ate the chilli crabs, eat until song-song." (We ate the chilli crabs, which put us in a state of bliss.)*

song-song kau Joo-long A riff on "song-song", i.e. blissful satisfaction. A state of bliss that extends all the way to even distant locations like Jurong.
See also **song, song-song kau Geelong**

song-song kau Geelong A riff on "song-song kau joo-long" (above), this time composed by Singaporean students studying in Melbourne. Geelong is a suburb in the boondocks, like Jurong is in Singapore. See also **song, song-song kau Joo-long**

sorry boh pakay |sorry boh bpah-gkay| Hybrid English/Hokkien/Malay phrase meaning that saying sorry just isn't good enough.
⊡ *Ah Kok: "Why you potong jalan my girlfriend?" (Why did you*

steal my girlfriend?)
Ah Beng: "Aiyah, sorry lah!" (Oh, I'm sorry!)
Ah Kok: "Sorry boh pakay! Ai tio hoot?" (Sorry's not good enough! Are you looking for a beating?)
See also **boh pakay, sorry no cure**

sorry no cure A (slightly) more Anglophile variant of "sorry boh pakay". See **sorry boh pakay**

sotong Malay for "squid". Used to describe someone as inept, dazed or in a world of his own. Presumably, it comes from the squid's emission of a cloud of ink, hence the popular phrase, "blur like sotong." May be used as both noun and adjective.
[1] *"Aiyah, why you ask him to go and do things? He damn sotong one!" (Oh, why did you assign him tasks? He's always in a world of his own!)*
[2] *"Why are you such a sotong?" (Why are you always in such a daze?)*
See also **blur like sotong, blur like fuck, blur toad**

spend To treat.
[1] *"Eh, today is my first pay day, so I spend you all lunch, lah!" (Hey, as today is my first pay day, I'm treating everyone to lunch!)*
[2] *"Wah, you want to spend me? You touch 4D or what?" (Wow, you wish to give me a treat? Did you win the lottery or something?)*
See also **blanja**

spiak **[1]** A local and deliberate corruption of "speak".
[•] *"Eh, gahmen say Singlish no good, so we must learn how to spiak good English!" (The government says Singlish is not good and that we must learn how to speak good English.)*

[2] Of uncertain derivation, "spiak" is used to describe someone who is behaving in an extravagant or indulgent manner, and hint to him that he is being ostentatious or pretentious.
[1] *"Wah, today you wear so spiak for what? Pak tor, ah?" (Wow, why are you decked out so extravagantly today? Do you have a date?)*
[2] *"Wah, your sandwich got put caviar, so spiak, ah?" (Whoa, you're spreading caviar on your sandwich? My, how indulgent!)*

spoi |spoy| Deliberate mispronunciation of "spoil", used to convey regrets or disappointment over unfortunate events or behaviour. Can also be used simply to describe physical damage.
[1] *"Eh, your handphone spoi oreddy, faster buy a new one, lah!" (Hey, your mobile phone is already damaged. You should quickly get a new one.)*
[2] *"Wah piang, sec 2 girl also go and buaya! Damn spoi, lah, you!"*

(You're trying to pick up even 14-year-old girls? There's something really wrong with you, man!)

3 *Radio DJ: "And what is the country immediately above Singapore on the map?"*
Caller: "Uh... China?"
Radio DJ: "Spoi ah!" (What's wrong with you?)

See also **fail, koyak, rosak**

spoil market |spoi mah-gkate| A term used to describe someone who does his work so well, he makes his colleagues look bad.

· *"Check out Ah Seng's report! Got leather binding and colour transparencies all! He damn spoil market one." (Check out how Ah Seng's report has leather binding and colour transparencies! He's really making the rest of us look bad.)*

standard Up to standard. Used to denote quality or skill.

1 *"Chin Mee Chin kaya is damn standard, man. Die-die must try!" (The kaya from Chin Mee Chin Confectionery is really excellent. You absolutely have to try it!)*

2 *"Wah lan, this prata so cold, damn no standard. Eat oreddy also not shiok." (Holy cow, this prata was served cold. It's really substandard. Eating it was really unsatisfying.)*

stayback A term used to describe being retained an extra year in school, or prevented from moving up a grade.

1 *"Play computer game some more, lah! Skarly you fail exam and kena stayback, then you know!" (If you carry on playing more computer games, you might fail your exams and be prevented from moving up a grade!)*

2 *"Of course Bukit Gorblok Primary always win the football championship, lah! Their team all stayback donno how many years one, mah!" (Of course Bukit Gorblok Primary always wins the soccer championship. Their team is composed entirely of students who've been retained.)*

stayber pah marber |stay-ber pah mah-ber| A deliberately sloppy pronunciation of the words "stable" and "marble", the phrase literally means to play marbles in a stable fashion. It is used to describe someone who has shown exceptionally steady behaviour under stress. May also be used as an exhortation to keep cool.

1 *"Wah piang, Recruit Phua kena from OC stand in the rain whole day. He si beh stayber pah marber!" (Wow, the Officer-in-Charge made Recruit Phua stand in the rain all day, and he's still okay. He's very cool.)*

2 *"Ah Beng today pah billiard si beh chun, sia. Every cue damn stayber pah marber one, boss!" (Ah Beng's billiard playing today is*

very accurate. Every shot is very steady.)

③ *"Eh, this sort of thing don'ch stress! Must stayber pah marber!" (Don't get stressed over these things. You have to stay calm.)*

See also **ai tzai, lac, maintain balan, relac, tzai**

stead |stehd| To be one's steady boyfriend or girlfriend.

⊡ *"Ah Lian, be my stead, leh!" (Ah Lian, won't you go steady with me!)*

steady Used either as a compliment or as an exhortation to calm down. Super Bengs may pronounce it "stay-lee".

① *"You managed to pok Ah Lian? You damn steady lah!" (You managed to woo Ah Lian successfully? You're really cool!)*

② *"So you became a prefect? Steady, da!" (So you became a prefect? That's cool!)*

③ *"Fail 'O' level, scared what? Steady!" (So what if you failed your "O" level exams? Stay cool!)*

See also **ai tzai, maintain balan, relac one corner, tzai**

steady pom pee pee |steady bpom bpee bpee| An extension of "steady", this is an adjective describing someone's prowess or sangfroid, i.e. ability to remain cool under pressure. This phrase actually began as "steady poon pee pee", i.e. "so steady that one is compelled to whistle in appreciation". Somehow, the whistling association has faded away.

⊡ *"Wah! Matthew's MCQ is steady pom pee pee one, leh! He no need to study also can get full marks." (Wow, Matthew was really cool and performed really well in the multiple choice section. He didn't study, but yet he scored full marks.)*

See also **steady**

steam To be "turned on" by or wildly enthusiastic about something.

① *"Wah, Ah Lian wear mini skirt so short, I damn steam her." (Wow, Ah Lian's wearing such a short skirt, it's turning me on.)*

② *"Such a solid jacket, sell so cheap. I see only steam oreddy, must buy." (Such a beautiful jacket going for such a cheap price? When I saw it, I was overcome with desire. I simply had to buy it!)*

See also **die cock stand, huat sio, orgas**

–ster An army suffix, attached to verbs to describe their perpetrators, e.g. someone who "kengs" (malingers) is a "kengster", while someone who "tuangs" (skives) is a "tuangster". A lesser form than "king" as in "tuang king" or "keng king".

⊡ *"Eh, all you kengsters! Don't pretend-pretend you sick so you can stay back and tuang, ah!" (Hey, you malingerers! Don't pretend to be sick so you can remain behind and skive!)*

See also **king, keng, tuang**

stone An adjective/verb conveying either a lack of any activity, a state of stupor or stunned bewilderment. While it may owe its origins to hallucinogenic drug use, the Singlish use of the term seems to have lost all connection with it.

1 *"The guy never do anything, one. So stone!" (He didn't do anything. He's like a block of wood!)*

2 *"Eh, let's go Orchard, man. Stop stoning!" (Hey, let's stop sitting around in this vegetative state and go to Orchard Road instead.)*

3 *"Wah lau, the maths exam question so cheem one. I see only I stone." (Holy cow, the maths exam questions were really difficult. I was stunned when I saw them.)*

See also **blur, sotong, stoner**

stoner Someone who's guilty of "stoning", i.e. someone who's either very stupid, lazy or constantly in a stupor, or sometimes all three at the same time.

"Why you go and ask him to organize the party? He's a bloody stoner!" (Why on earth did you ask him to organize the party? He's such a lazy idiot!)

See also **blur, sotong, stone**

stun To pilfer or shoplift. Of uncertain origin.

1 *"Ah Beng got caught at Centerpoint stunning some CDs." (Ah Beng was caught shoplifting CDs at Centerpoint.)*

2 *"Wah lau eh, Ah Seng is so rich, still go Metro and stun this sort of small, small thing." (Holy cow, Ah Seng is so rich, yet he still shoplifted such trifling items from Metro.)*

stylo / stylo milo Stylish, fashionable.

"Wah, check out Ah Beng's Versace jeans! Since when he so stylo milo one?" (Whoa, check out Ah Beng's Versace jeans! Since when did he become so stylish?)

See also **gerek**

sua |soo-a'h| A Hokkien word meaning "to be over with" or "settled".

"I Thursday pay you, then we sua oreddy, ah?" (Once I pay you on Thursday, I'll take it that things are settled between us?)

See also **ai lai mai sua**

sua koo |swah-koo| A Hokkien term which literally translates as "mountain tortoise". Used to describe or suggest that someone is unsophisticated and ignorant. The Singlish equivalent of a "country bumpkin" or a "hick".

"You donno how to use a microwave oven? Why you so sua koo one?" (You don't know how to use a microwave oven? Why are you such a country bumpkin?)

See also **jakun, mountain tortoise**

suan |swahn| To ridicule or insult someone.
① *"Why you go and suan him like that? What has he ever done to you?" (Why did you insult him like that? What has he ever done to you?)*
② *"Wah lau, did you see? He kena suan in TalkingCock.com!" (Holy cow! Did you see that? He was ridiculed in TalkingCock.com!)*
See also **tua**

suay / suay-suay |sway| Hokkien for "calamity" or "extremely unlucky". When repeated, it becomes "unfortunately", "sadly" or "tragically".
① *"The same day his father die, his wife cabut with his bookie. He si peh suay, man." (The same day his father died, his wife ran off with his bookie. He's really very unlucky, man.)*
② *"He just come out of the hospital that time, suay-suay kena langgar by a bus." (He had just been discharged from the hospital when unfortunately, he was run over by a bus.)*

suda |soo-dah| Malay for "completed" or "already finished". Can sometimes be an expression of moving on after misfortune or injustice, if not amounting to forgiveness.
① *"I early-early go McDonald's but the Hello Kitty all suda sold out." (I went very early to the McDonald's but the Hello Kitty toys were already sold out.)*
② *"Aiyah, I know you very too lan him, but suda, lah. Later on, he sure kena, one." (I know you're really angry with him, but let it go — it's over. He's bound to get his just desserts later on.)*

suka |soo-gkah| Malay for "like".
⊡ *"I really suka that girl, can introduce or not?" (I really like that girl. Can you introduce us?)*

suka-suka Derived from the Malay term "suka", meaning "like", this means to do as one likes, without regard for what is appropriate.
⊡ *"Eh, you can't just suka-suka shee-shee inside the lift, okay!" (Hey! You can't just urinate inside the elevator whenever you feel like it!)*
See also **suka**

sumpah |soom-bpah| Malay for "to swear an oath". In Singlish, "sumpah" does not have the secondary meanings of "curse" or "call down spirits" as it does in Malay.
① *"I sumpah on the lives of my Ah Kong, Ah Ma, Lau Peh, Lau Bu — I neh steal your money!" (I swear on the lives of my grandparents and parents that I did not steal your money!)*

[2] *"Can you faster go to the Notary Public and sumpah this affidavit?" (Can you quickly swear this affidavit before a Notary Public?)*

sup sup soi Cantonese term used to describe something as small and/or unimportant.

[1] *"Don't bother me, lah. All this is sup sup soi one." (Don't bother me. All this is inconsequential to me.)*

[2] *Beng: "Thanks for treating me to dinner."*
Seng: "Aiyah, sup sup soi, lah." (Oh, it was nothing.)

sure The Singlish abbreviation of "sure to". The equivalent of "definitely".

[1] *"If I tio beh pio, I sure treat you to lunch, one." (If I strike the lottery, I'll be sure to treat you to lunch.)*

[2] *"Ah Beng sure fail his 'N' lebber, one." (Ah Beng is sure to fail his "N" level exams.)*

sure can one Phrase used to bolster one's/someone else's confidence that something can be achieved. "Sure to be able to".

[•] *"This thing so easy to do, sure can one." (This thing is so easy to do. It's totally achievable.)*

surface |sur-furs| Singapore Civil Service-speak for bringing a matter to the attention of one's superiors, through the hierarchy of decision making.

[•] *"Send me your report, lah, and I'll surface it to the Board at the next meeting." (Send me your report, and I'll bring it to the Board's attention at the next meeting.)*

susa |soo-sah| From the Malay word "susah", meaning "difficult to bear", or "misery". In Singlish, it has the additional lesser meaning of "extremely troublesome".

[•] *"On this rainy day, ask me to go all the way to Tuas, damn susa, man." (Having to travel all the way to Tuas on such a rainy day is a really miserable experience.)*

See also **suay**

suspender Not braces, i.e. the adjustable straps or bands worn over the shoulders with the ends buttoned or clipped to the waistband of a pair of trousers to support it. Rather, in Singapore, especially during the 1960s and 1970s, "suspender" (always in the singular, and often pronounced "sospender') referred specifically to men's briefs, i.e. close-fitting, legless underpants with an elastic waistband. Now defunct except amongst old-timers.

suspect Singlish for "suspicion". You save one syllable!

[•] *"I got a suspect, hor, that Ah Beng kena arrested." (I have a suspicion that Ah Beng was arrested.)*

swee / swee-swee Hokkien for "pretty" or "beautiful". Also used to describe something as properly or correctly done.

[1] *"Wah, Ah Lian today wear until very swee, hor! Tonight go pak tor, ah?" (Wow, Ah Lian is dressed very beautifully today! Does she have a date tonight?)*

[2] *"My best friend's girlfriend is damn swee, man. I also want to kau. How?" (My best friend's girlfriend is very pretty. I want to woo her too... but how?)*

[3] *"Wah lau! Your best friend's girlfriend also want to buaya? Damn buay swee, man!" (What? You want to woo your best friend's girlfriend? That's not done!)*

[4] *"Eh, since you volunteer to do this, dun cock-up, okay? Better do swee-swee little bit..." (Since you volunteered to do this, don't screw it up. You'd better do it properly.)*

swee swee boh kay chwee |swee swee boh gkay tzui| Hokkien phrase which literally translates as "beautiful and not diluted with water", meaning something is already perfect.

▪ *"Don't kachau! Everything is swee swee boh kay chwee." (Don't mess with it! Everything is just perfect!)*

switch off To be idle or lazy. Mostly used as an adjective but sometimes as a noun.

[1] *"Ah Beng got posted to HQ? Wah lau, that job damn switch off one!" (Ah Beng was posted to the headquarters? Wow, that is a really easy posting!)*

[2] *"Aiyah, don't be so switch off, try and help can or not?" (Can you please be more helpful?)*

[3] *"Don't bother to ask Ah Seng to do it, he damn switch off, one!" (Don't bother asking Ah Seng to do it; he's a total bum!)*

See also **senang**

Tt

tackle |tair-kerr| To court a girl, perhaps aggressively. Uncertain derivation, possibly from football or even fishing.

▪ *"Lisa got expensive taste, you sure you still want to tackle her?" (Lisa has really expensive tastes. Are you sure you still wish to court her?)*

See also **buaya, kau, pok**

tactical |tair-ti-kur| Another term from the Army, Singapore's most prolific Singlish contributor. It means to think quickly and strategically, usually in the context of avoiding notice or being stuck with an unpleasant task. Oddly enough, it's also used as a verb.

⊡ *"Eh, if you do'wan to kena arrow, then you better tactical and take cover a bit, skarly the ossifer catch you then you kena." (If you wish to avoid getting an unpleasant assignment, you'd best make yourself scarce, before the officer catches you.)*

tahan Malay term meaning to endure, withstand or tolerate.

1 *"Waiter, where is my duck rice? Cannot tahan already, faster leh!" (Waiter, where is my duck rice? I can't stand it any longer! Please hurry up!)*

2 *"I think we tahan his nonsense too long oreddy." (I think we've tolerated his nonsense for too long.)*

See also **buay tah han**

tai chi |tai chee| Singlish for deflecting an unpleasant task to others. Comes from the passing hand motions in the Chinese martial art of tai qi quan.

1 *"If your boss arrow you, just tai chi it to others, lor." (If your boss assigns you an unpleasant task, simply pass it on to others.)*

2 *"Wah lau! This sort of sai kang, why you tai chi to me?" (Holy cow! Why did you pass this crappy assignment onto me?)*

tai ji |dtai tjee| Hokkien for "matters" or "issues".

1 *"You si mi tai ji, also can come and find me." (If you have any outstanding matters, feel free to look me up.)*

2 *"He, hor, got a lot of tai ji, one." (He is full of issues, i.e. he's a very complicated person.)*

See also **boh tai ji, chin chuay tai ji**

tai soi |tai soi| Cantonese equivalent of "kua chui". See **kua chui**

tair |dt'air — rhymes with "hair'| A Cantonese term used to describe gooey, childlike and coquettish behaviour.

⊡ *"Whenever Ah Lian wants Ah Beng to do something for her, she becomes si beh tair." (Whenever Ah Lian wants Ah Beng to do something for her, she gets all cutesy-pie.)*

See also **manja, tair pao**

tair lum pah chi saht |dtair lahm pah tjee saht| One of the most graphic expressions in this dictionary, it is also one of the most inspired. Literally, it is Hokkien for "commit suicide by squeezing your testicles". The Hokkien equivalent of hara-kiri, it expresses profound regret and frustration, and is often said after having confessed to doing something monumentally stupid.

⊡ *"Ah Beng accidentally threw his winning 4D ticket into the incinerator? Wah lau, like that he might as well tair lum pah chi saht." (Ah Beng accidentally threw his winning 4D ticket into the incinerator? Holy cow, he might as well kill himself by squeezing his testicles!)*

tair pao |dt'air bpow| Someone, invariably a young lady, who behaves very "tair", i.e. coquettish.

⊡ *"Have you met Ah Beng's new girlfriend? When she got a paper cut only, she will go over and ask him to kiss-kiss. Damn tair pao, man!" (Have you met Ah Beng's new girlfriend? Whenever she gets a paper cut, she asks him to kiss her boo-boo. How cloying!)*

See also **tair**

tak apa |ta'h ah-pah| A contraction of "tidak apa", Malay for "never mind". In Singlish, however, there has come to be a distinction in use between "tak apa" and "tidak apa". "Tak apa" is used as the equivalent of "never mind" or "don't worry about it", while "tidak apa" has come to mean uncaring, apathetic or cavalier.

⊡ *Raman: "Eh, sorry, man. I can't make it for your wedding." (Sorry, but I can't make it for your wedding.)*

Ah Seng: "Tak apa, lah. You can come for the next one." (Oh, never mind. You can come for the next one.)

See also **tidak apa**

tak jadi |ta'h jah-dee| A colloquial Malay expression meaning "it did not work out", or "it did not come into being".

1 *"Ah Beng and Ah Lian pak tor since prembry school, but in the end they tak jadi." (Ah Beng and Ah Lian have been dating since primary school. But in the end, it didn't work out between them.)*

2 *Mohan: "Oi, Ah Beng! Your new job, how?" (Hey, Ah Beng! How's the new job?)*

Beng: "Aiyah, tak jadi, lor." (It didn't work out.)

See also **buay kia**

take cover Can mean either to be wary, to hide from someone, to dodge responsibility, or sometimes, to skive. From (where else?) the military.

1 *"Ah Beng found out you were trying to potong Jenny, so you better take cover." (Ah Beng found out you were trying to steal Jenny from him, so you'd better go into hiding.)*

2 *"Mr Tan is going to arrow someone to write his speech — better take cover and go for lunch." (Mr Tan is about to delegate the writing of his speech to someone. We'd better make ourselves scarce by going for lunch.)*

See also **siam**

take you go market and sell The classic Singapore threat to children. Works like a charm every time.

☐ *"If you don'ch stop making noise, ah, I tomorrow take you go market and sell!" (If you don't stop making noise, I'll sell you off at the market tomorrow!)*

talent Used to describe someone who is attractive or sexy, or has assets to admire.

1 *"Eh, let's go Arts Canteen and look at the talent." (Hey, let's go to the Arts Canteen and check out the pretty girls.)*

2 *"Wah lau, Ah Lian dress like that, got talent." (Whoa, when Ah Lian dresses like that, she's really sexy.)*

See also **jude, chio, foreign talent**

talk cock / talk cock sing song / talk cock sing song play guitar To speak rubbish or nonsense. Probably originates from the English phrase "cock and bull", i.e. bullshit. "Sing song" and "play guitar" are added for emphasis. "Talk cock" by itself also has the more benign meaning of "casual banter", "idle gossip" or "chatting". The American equivalent would be "shooting the breeze".

1 *"Ah Beng managed to pass the exam? Don't talk cock!" (Ah Beng managed to pass the exam? Don't talk nonsense!)*

2 *"The Minister is just talking cock." (The Minister is talking rubbish.)*

3 *"I met Johnny at the kopi tiam just now, and we were talking cock for a while." (I met Johnny at the coffee shop just now, and we engaged in a spot of idle banter.)*

See also **how seow, kong chiao weh, kong sar kong si, talk three talk four**

talk cock king Someone who is extremely adept at bullshitting.

☐ *"He such a talk cock king, no wonder can cho lawyer." (He's such an expert bullshitter. No wonder he became a lawyer.)*

See also **sian tao ong, tua pian sian**

talk cock session Self-explanatory: a session in which people talk cock.

1 *"Aiyah, the conference was one long talk cock session!" (Ah, the conference was just one long bullshit session!)*

2 *"What are we doing here at the kopi tiam? Nothing, lah. Talk cock session only." (What are we doing here at the kopi tiam? Oh, nothing. We're just shooting the breeze.)*

talk rot / talk rots A more subdued variant of "talk cock". See also **talk cock**

talk three talk four / talk 3 talk 4 The English transliteration of the Hokkien "kong sar kong si", i.e. to chitchat or indulge in idle talk.

▣ *Ah Lian: "An chua, call me for what?" (What the heck did you call me for?)*
Ah Soh: "Nothing lah, talk 3 talk 4, lor." (Oh, nothing. Just want to chat.)

See also **kong sar kong si, talk cock**

tan [1] |dtahn| Hokkien for "wait".

▣ *"Tan, okay, I go buy 4D, very fast come back, one." (Wait here while I purchase some lottery tickets. I'll be back in a jiffy.)*

[2] |tahn| Hokkien word describing a successful business or lucrative trade.

[1] *"He sell those imported chestnuts, tan kao seow, man." (He's making money hand over fist by selling those imported chestnuts of his.)*

[2] *"I din'ch expect that sell chok also can tan, man." (I really didn't expect that porridge could be so lucrative.)*

tan boh chiak / tan boh lui |tahn bo tzee-a'h/tahn bo looi| Hokkien for literally "earn no food" and "earn no money". Used to describe something that is useless or not worth your while.

▣ *"Why you want to go study Arts? Tan boh chiak one lah!" (Why do you wish to study the Arts? You can't earn a living from it.)*

tan chiak |tahn tjee-a'h| Hokkien term meaning "earn to eat". It describes a hardworking act in order to survive or excel in whatever someone is doing (usually in the context of a career).

[1] *"Wah lau, you si peh tan chiak, leh! Boots kiwi until so shing!" (Wow, you're really putting your nose to the grindstone, polishing your boots till they shine!)*

[2] *"Why I sell Kleenex? Have to tan chiak, what!" (Why am I selling tissue paper? I have to earn a living, don't I!)*

[3] *"His workmanship cannot make it. I think he is just the tan chiak type." (His workmanship isn't very good. I think he's just in this line to make a living, not because he has any passion for it.)*

See also **pian chiak**

tan chiak peng |tahn tjee-a'h bpeng| Literally: "the soldiers who have to do onerous tasks to earn their food". A derogatory term used to describe regular soldiers in the Army. It is always used somewhat smugly by National Servicemen, whose service period runs out after only two years.

tan ku ku |dtahn gkoo gkoo| Literally: "wait long-long". Hokkien phrase meaning "forget it, it won't happen."

☐ *"You want to buaya her? Tan ku ku, lah!" (You want to date her? Forget it, it'll never happen!)*

See also **wait long-long**

tan lui |tahn looi| Hokkien for "make money".

1 *"Sell this sort of condemn thing, how to tan lui?" (How do you expect to make any money selling such rubbish?)*

2 *"You see Ah Beng gong-gong lai dat, but acherly he damn kiang to tan lui." (Ah Beng may appear to be a dullard, but in fact, he's really clever at making money.)*

See also **tan chiak**

tao / tau Hokkien for "head".

☐ *"You dun shaddup, I kok your tao, then you know!" (If you don't keep quiet, I will give you a knock on the head!)*

tao hong Hokkien for "air in the head", meaning "to go mad".

☐ *"Don't think of the girl so much. Wait you tau hong then you know." (Don't think of the girl so much. You'll go mad.)*

tao kah chew |dtao kah chee-oo| Literally, Hokkien for "lend a hand and a leg", i.e. to help. (By requiring an additional leg, the Hokkiens are either more generous in providing aid, or more needy.)

☐ *"Wah lan eh, this box is si beh heavy! Oi! Tao kah chew, leh!" (Holy cow, this box is really heavy! Hey! Lend a hand, won't you?)*

tao tiah |tao tee-ah| Hokkien for "headache". In Singlish, it can also mean troublesome.

1 *"Ask me to do this sort of thing, wah lau eh, damn tao tiah, lair!" (It really gives me a headache when you ask me to do such things.)*

2 *"Doing this sort of thing, damn tao tiah man." (This task is very troublesome.)*

tao yan Mandarin for "detestable", "nasty" or "hate". In Singlish, it is often uttered coquettishly by Ah Lians as a sort of feigned protest.

1 *"Alamak, so much homework, really tao yan man!" (Oh god, there's so much homework. I really hate it!)*

2 *"I damn tao yan his kiam siap ways!" (I really detest his stingy ways.)*

3 *Ah Beng: "Eh, you quite jude, hor." (Hey, you're quite pretty, you know.)*

Ah Lian: "Ee, tao yan!" (Oh, you're so despicable!)

tapi |dtah-bpee| Hokkien contraction of the Malay word "tetapi", meaning "but" or "however".

☐ *"Frankie wants a new Marseelis, tapi he boh lui." (Frankie wants a new Mercedes, but he has no money.)*

tar pao / tar pow |dtah bpow| Hokkien term meaning "takeaway" (UK) or "takeout" (US) food. To order food from a restaurant that is to be taken home for eating.

☐ *"Can you go and tar pao some char kway teow on your way home?" (Can you buy a packet of char kway teow on your way home?)*

See also **bungkus, da bao**

tar por |dtah bpor| Hokkien for "man" or "male". See also **char bor**

tarik harga |tah-ray' har-gah| Literally, Malay for "pulling on the value", i.e. haggle. In Singlish, it's used mostly to describe playing hard to get during the courtship process.

1 *"Alamak, I give up on dating, lah. All the char bor in Singapore all tarik harga only." (Oh, I give up on dating. All the women in Singapore like to play hard to get.)*

2 *"Aiyah, 50 sen only you want to tarik harga! Damn cheapskate, lah, you!" (You're haggling over 50 Malaysian cents? What a cheapskate you are!)*

teck koh |dtek gkoh| Hokkien for "wooden pole". Often used to describe a very skinny person.

1 *"Eh, can you hurry up put the clothes on the teck koh?" (Please hurry and place the clothes on the pole.)*

2 *"Wah lau, Ah Lian went to the slimming centre and now she become a teck koh oreddy!" (My goodness! After going to the slimming centre, Ah Lian now looks as thin as a clothes pole!)*

tecnoprenner The local pronunciation of "technopreneur", i.e. an entrepreneur in the field of technology. The term seems to be popular mainly in Singapore and Malaysia.

☐ *"Ah Beng sell pirated DVD, considered tecnoprenner, meh?" (As a DVD pirate, can Ah Beng be considered a technopreneur?)*

teh |dtay| Malay and Hokkien for "tea".

☐ *"Go and buy me a teh, can or not?" (Could you please buy me a cup of tea, please?)*

teh "o" |dtay oh| Tea with nothing in it.

teh susu |dtay soo-soo| Tea with milk ("susu" is Malay for milk).

teh tarik |dtay dtah-ray'h| The local version of cappuccino, where milky tea is aerated by repeatedly pouring the tea between two containers, an increasingly rare skill.

tekan |dtuh-gkahn| Malay for "to press down". In Singlish, it has been expanded to mean being abused or scolded.

1 *"Uh-oh, the sergeant is off to tekan the recruits again." (Uh-oh, the sergeant is off to scold the recruits again.)*

[2] *"Why you so cham, always kena tekan by your boss one?" (Why are you so unlucky, always being yelled at by your boss?)*
See also **maki**

tekan session Self-explanatory: a session in which people get tekan-ed, i.e. scolded or yelled at.
[·] *"We screwed up the deal, so go back HQ sure kena one long tekan session." (We messed up the deal, so we're sure to get yelled at when we return to the headquarters.)*

tempolary |dtem-bper-larry| A common pronunciation of "temporary".
[·] *"Dun scared. Your condition only tempolary, one." (Please don't be afraid. Your condition is only a temporary one.)*

tepi sikit |dtuh-bpee see-gkit| Malay term meaning "move aside a little" or "shift to one side". An ego-bursting term usually preceded by invoking the name of someone more impressive than the person you're addressing.
[·] *(Said to someone who's playing golf very badly): "Oi, Tiger Woods, tepi sikit."*

ter |dtuhr| Hokkien for "pig".

ter bak |dtuhr ba'h| Hokkien for "pork".

ter bak chek |dtur ba'h tchek| Generic name for a pork butcher.

ter kor |dtur gkor| Literally, Hokkien for "piggy brother" and used to describe a lecherous man.
[·] *"Mr Lim next door is a real lao ter kor. Every week go Desker!" (Our next door neighbour Mr Lim is a real dirty old man. He goes to Desker Road every week!)*
See also **bian tai, chee ko pek, se lang, lao ter kor**

terbalik |dtur-bah-lay'h| A colloquial Malay word meaning "upside down" or "inside out". Sometimes used to mean a reversal. Common Beng mispronunciations include "tombalik" and "tombaling".
[1] *"Eh, you wore your shirt terbalik today. The label's on the outside." (You've worn your shirt inside out today. The label's on the outside.)*
[2] *"You always sabo people, one day terbalik then you chai si." (You're always getting people into trouble. One day, the situation will be reversed, then you'll know what it feels like.)*

terror |dtair-rur| Singlish for "terrifying", "powerful" or "outrageous". Not necessarily derogatory.
[1] *"Tonight you sure got date with Ah Lian, one. See you dress so terror." (You must have a date with Ah Lian tonight. You're really dressed to impress.)*
[2] *"Did you see Paramjeet run the 2.4? Wah lau, damn terror, man."*

(Did you see Paramjeet run the 2.4 kilometre race? Wow, he was really impressive.)

3 *"Wah lau! How come your perfume smell like kiam her, one? Damn terror, man!" (Holy cow! Why does your perfume smell like salted fish? It's horrible!)*

See also **chia lat, fierce, garang, hiong, powderful, siong**

teruk |dtuh-ro'h| Malay for "severe", or "tough".

"The exam was damn teruk, man." (The exam was really tough.)

See also **siong**

thambi |dtahm-bee| Yet another racist manner of addressing a Tamil person. "Thambi" itself is innocuous, but when used as a generic appellation for Southern Indians, it is clearly racist.

that time A common redundancy that is used to denote time or a discrete event.

1 *"When he 10 year old that time, hor, he oreddy got moustache." (When he was 10 years old, he already had a moustache.)*

2 *"Four o'clock that time, I was at the kopi tiam." (At four o'clock, I was at the coffee shop.)*

3 *"Wah lau, he in charge that time, hor, waste a lot of money, lair." (Man, when he was in charge, he wasted a lot of money.)*

See also **last time**

thick skin The Singlish version of "thick-skinned", meaning resistant or impervious to criticism or reproach.

"Yah, we all know Ah Beng sing like toad like that, but tell him oso no use. He damn thick skin, one." (Yes, we all know Ah Beng sings like a toad, but there's no point in criticising him. He's very thick-skinned.)

tiam |dtee-ahm| From the Malay word "diam", meaning "quiet" or "silence", and now co-opted into Hokkien and Singlish.

"Tiam lah, I dowan to hear any more kau peh kau bu." (Oh, be quiet, will you? I don't want to hear any more of your bellyaching.)

See also **shaddup**

tidak apa |dtee-da'h ah-pah| Malay for "never mind". In Singlish, it has come to mean uncaring, apathetic or cavalier. Note: In Singlish, "tidak apa" has come to have a different use than its contraction "tak apa".

1 *"With this kind of tidak apa attitude, how you expect to be promoted?" (With your apathetic attitude, how do you expect to be promoted?)*

2 *"He always do things very tidak apa, one. Better dun hire him." (He always does things in a cavalier fashion. Better not to hire him.)*

See also **tak apa, heck care**

tikam / tikam-tikam |dtee-gkahm| In Malay, "tikam" means to bet or choose randomly. Commonly used by secondary school kids who need to answer multiple choice questions, or impatient people in the 4D queue.

1 *"Aiyah, the MCQ is si beh difficult, man. All donno how to do, so I just tikam all the way, lor." (Oh no, the multiple choice questions are really difficult. I didn't know how to do any of them, so I just guessed randomly.)*

2 *Beng: "Eh, what number to play for 4D, ah?" (Hey, what number should I buy for the lottery?)*

Seng: "Aiyah, tikam-tikam can oreddy, lah." (Oh, just choose any old number.)

tin teh |dtin dtay| Hokkien term describing either a cluttered state or unnecessary objects taking up space or getting in the way.

1 *"Piang, why you keep so many old newspapers in your house? Tin teh, only!" (Holy cow, why are you cluttering your place by keeping so many old newspapers?)*

2 *"He go and put that gold fountain in the middle of his living room, damn tin teh, man!" (That gold fountain he placed in the middle of his living room really takes up a lot of space.)*

tio |dtee-oh| Hokkien exclamation whose closest English approximation is "got it!" or "correct!" Suggests hitting the target or achieving something, usually but not necessarily pleasant.

1 *"Eh! I heard Ah Beng tio 4D, man!" (Hey, I heard Ah Beng struck the lottery!)*

2 *Beng: "You wan' your flat to get upgraded, then you must vote gahmen, lah. Tio bo?" (To get your flat upgraded, you must vote in the government. Isn't that correct?)*

Seng: "Tio!" (Correct!)

3 *"Wah, Ah Beng yesterday tio from his OC, man!" (Yesterday, Ah Beng got it from his officer-in-charge.)*

See also **kena, kio tio goo lan**

tiu / tiu lei lo mo / tiu lei lo mo chao hai "Tiu" is the Cantonese equivalent of the Hokkien "kan", meaning "fuck". And "tiu lei lo mo" is "fuck your old mother", and the ultimate is "tiu lei lo mo chao hai", which has the same meaning as that thermonuclear weapon of Hokkien swearing "kan ni na bu chao chee bye". If you want to be discreet, with the right intonation "tiu lei lo mo chao lo hai" can also mean "throw your mother's smelly old shoes away".

See also **kan ni na bu chao chee bye**

toad Contraction of "blur toad".

☐ *"Tsk! Right in front of you also cannot see! Why you so toad, one?" (You can't see it, even though it's right in front of you? Why are you such a dope?)*

See also **blur toad, sotong**

togo |dtoh-goh| A term derived from "togok", colloquial Malay for "guzzling drinks", e.g. "Ali togok segelas air", meaning "Ali gulped down a glass of water". However, in Singlish, "togo" has come to mean embarking on a heavy drinking binge (only of alcoholic beverages).

1 *"Eh, tomorrow is public holiday, so tonight, let's all go pub and togo, leh!" (As tomorrow is a public holiday, let's all go to the pub tonight and get drunk.)*

2 *"The night before his wedding, his buddies all take him go togo until he peng san." (The night before his wedding, his buddies got him so drunk that he passed out.)*

toh |dtoh| A Hokkien word meaning "to collapse" or "fall". Used to describe failure.

☐ *"He set up a bak kut teh stall in the Malay Village? Business sure toh!" (He set up a pork rib soup stall in the Malay Village? His business is sure to fail.)*

tok chai tao |dtok tsai tao| Hokkien phrase literally translated as "cut cabbage head". It means to swindle or bamboozle.

☐ *"Wah, you pay so much for this fake Lolex? Kena tok chai tao oreddy, lah!" (What? You paid so much for this fake Rolex? You've been swindled!)*

tok kong |dtok gkong| Hokkien term meaning "superb" or "top of the line".

1 *"Check out his DVD player. Tok kong, man!" (Check out his DVD player. It's the top of the line.)*

2 *"Wah lau eh, Ah Lian's body is si beh tok kong." (Holy cow, Ah Lian has a really superb physique.)*

tok tok chiang |dtock dtock chee-ahng| Onomatopoeic description of a wayang, i.e. a traditional Chinese opera, often staged out in the open. Not to be confused with "dong dong chiang" or "dong-dong-dong chiang".

☐ *"Hungry Ghost that time, hor, got a lot of tok tok chiang one." (During the Hungry Ghost Festival, many traditional Chinese operas are staged.)*

See also **dong-dong chiang, dong-dong-dong chiang**

tolak |dtoh-la'h| Malay for deduct, refuse or push, depending on the context. In Singlish, it usually means to divert an unpleasant task to someone else.

☐ *"Eh, this kind of sai kang, you dun tolak to me, I tell you first, ah!" (Don't you dare pass me all your crap assignments!)*

See also **tai chi**

tolong |dtoh-lohng — some Ah Bengs pronounce it "dtor-long"| Malay for "help". Can sometimes be used in the sense of "give me a break".

1 *"Eh, this thing is damn heavy. Tolong, can or not?" (Whoa, this thing is really heavy. Could you lend me a hand?)*

2 *"You want me to go with you to watch the NDP? Tolong, lah." (You want me to watch the National Day Parade with you? Give me a break!)*

tombalik / tombaling |dtome-bah-lek/dtome-bare-ling| Common mispronunciations of the Malay word "terbalik" by Chinese educated Singaporeans.

See also **terbalik**

too lan |dtoo lahn| Rather rude Hokkien term meaning "disgruntled" or "pissed off".

☐ *"I lend him so much money, now he treat me like that, I damn too lan, one." (I've loaned him so much money, yet he's now mistreating me. That really pisses me off.)*

toot |dtood| Used to describe stupidity or uncoolness. Can be both noun and adjective.

1 *"Why is he such a toot? Whole year study and can still fail PSLE!" (Why is he such a dumbbell? He studied the entire year and still managed to fail the Primary School Leaving Examinations!)*

2 *"Eh, your bag, ah, is damn toot! You NUS oreddy and still use Powerpuff Girls bag!" (Your bag is really uncool! You're in the university and still carrying a Powerpuff Girls bag!)*

See also **tuh**

tor hwee Literally meaning "vomit blood", this is a Hokkien phrase which denotes experiencing extreme difficulty, intense suffering, or great irritation.

☐ *"Yesterday, hor, I teach my son maths, teach until tor hwee." (Yesterday, I taught my son mathematics and it made me want to vomit blood.)*

See also **vomit blood**

tua [1] |dtwah| Hokkien for "big".

☐ *"Donno what he feed his fish, but they're all si beh tua chiak now." (I don't know what he feeds his fish, but they're all really big-sized now.)*

[2] |dtwah| A Hokkien term which is the equivalent of the African-American term "diss". A word which describes showing or being shown a lack of respect.

1 *"Eh, I waited one hour for you but you neh turn up! Tua me, is it?" (Hey, I waited an hour for you, but you didn't turn up. Are you showing me disrespect?)*

2 *"I neh do anything to you, why you go and tua me like that?" (I never did anything to you, so why did you show me such disrespect?)*

See also **suan**

tua chiak |dtwah tjee-a'h| Literally, "big-sized" in Hokkien. Usually applied to living creatures.

1 *"Wah, Ah Beng! I six month only never see you, how come you suddenly so tua chiak?" (Whoa, Ah Beng! I didn't see you for only six months. How did you grow so big during that time?)*

2 *"Ah Lian's dog is damn tua chiak. It nearly reach her armpit!" (Ah Lian's dog is really huge. It's almost as tall as her armpits!)*

tua kang |dtwah kahng| Hokkien phrase literally meaning "big hole". Used to describe someone telling an exaggerated story about his prowess.

⊡ *"Wah, he always talk until so tua kang. Donno whether real, not." (He's always telling these fantastic, boastful stories. I wonder if there's any truth in them.)*

tua kee |dtwah gkee| Hokkien for "big shot". Literally, "big stick".

⊡ *"You lan copler only, what! Why you act so tua kee?" (You're only a lance corporal. How dare you act like such a big shot?)*

tua kow |dtwah gkao| The police. Literally in Hokkien: "big dog".

⊡ *"Tua kow come oreddy! Faster hide the money!" (The police are here! Quickly! Hide the money!)*

See also **mata**

tua liap |dtwah lee-up| Hokkien for "big round ones", and can be used to describe breasts, testicles, eyes, or anything that is big and round.

⊡ *"Piang eh, those watermelons all mutant one, ah? How come so tua liap?" (Holy cow, are those mutant watermelons? Why are they so large?)*

See also **tua kee**

tua pao sian |dtwah pao see-en| Literally, Hokkien for "god of the big cannon", i.e. a bullshitter and braggart. Similar to "tua pian sian" (below).

⊡ *"Listen to him talk, confirm he's a tua pao sian." (Just listening to him talk, you know he's a bullshitter.)*

See also **sian tao ong, talk cock king, tua pian sian**

tua pian sian |dtwah pee-en see-en| Hokkien phrase literally meaning "big bluff god". Describes someone who's extremely proficient in bullshitting or conning people.

1 *"Tua pian sian come oreddy, be careful your money." (Here comes the big con man. Be careful with your money.)*

2 *"Here comes the tua pian sian. Let's hear what cock he wants to talk today." (Here comes the big bullshitter. Let's hear what rubbish he wants to talk about today.)*

See also **sian tao ong, talk cock king, tua pao sian**

tua tao |dtwah tau| Literally, Hokkien for "big head". A term for a gang leader. Is also the local name for the pacific green-lipped mussel.

"Eh, just now at the hawker centre, hor, I saw my tua tao eating tua tao." (Hey, just now I saw my gang leader at the hawker centre eating mussels.)

See also **dai kor dai**

tuang |twahng| To skive or dodge responsibilities.

"I'm supposed to be in class, but I've decided to tuang." (I'm supposed to be in class, but I've decided to skip it.)

See also **chiak chua, keng, pontang, siam, chao, tuang king**

tuang king An accomplished skiver. An artful dodger.

"When it comes to work, he always disappears. Super tuang king, that one." (When it comes to work, he always disappears. He's a real artful dodger.)

See also **tuang**

tuh Used to describe someone as geeky, uncool or lacking in common sense. Unlike "toot", "tuh" is restricted to people.

"Why you tuck your shirt in your underwear? You damn tuh, man!" (Why did you tuck your shirt in your underwear? That's really uncool!)

See also **bodoh, goondu, gorblok, toad, toot**

tution |dtew-shen| The Singlish pronunciation of "tuition" (tew-wee-shen). Probably a conflation of "tutor" and "tuition". Refers to additional after-school tutoring, usually provided at home. One of Singapore's largest cottage industries.

"I cannot go Vivo with you today. I got tution." (I can't go to Vivo City with you today. I have a tuition session.)

tution teacher |dtew-shen titcher| A home tutor.

"Not say I say what, but my tution teacher, hor, is quite chio." (I hate to say this, but I find my home tutor quite hot.)

tulukkan A racist term for Indian Muslims used by non-Muslim Indians. Comes from the word "turk" as Indian Muslims once pledged allegiance to the Ottoman Caliphate.

tum sim |tahm seem| Hokkien for "greedy".

☐ *"He oreddy got one girlfriend, now want a second one. So tum sim, one!" (He already has one girlfriend, but now wants a second one. How greedy!)*

tumpang |dtome-pahng| A Malay word meaning "to hitch a ride" or "piggyback". Can also mean asking someone to do a favour for you while they are doing something else. Note: If you're a serious Ah Beng, you'll pronounce this "lompang".

1 *"Eh, my wife took my car today. Can I tumpang your car to work?" (My wife took my car today. Can I hitch a ride to work in your car?)*

2 *"Eh, since you're going to the post office, can I tumpang you to buy some stamps?" (Since you're going to the post office, can I trouble you to buy some stamps for me?)*

tup pai |dtahp bpai| Hokkien for "every time" or "always".

1 *"Aiyah... he tup pai like that one lah." (Sigh... He's always like that.)*

2 *"He tup pai go Sim Lim to buy pirated DVDs." (He's always going to Sim Lim Square to buy pirated DVDs.)*

See also **every time**

tzai |tzah-yee| Hokkien for "steady": a compliment about one's coolness or sangfroid.

☐ *"Ah Lian agreed to pak tor with him? Since when he so tzai one?" (Ah Lian agreed to go on a date with him? Since when did he become so cool?)*

See also **can, steady, ai tzai**

tzai chiu |tzai chee-ew| Hokkien for "steady hand". Means to be good at keeping cool under stressful conditions.

☐ *"Eh, this sort of thing better go and ask Ah Beng to handle. He NS that time in the Bomb Disposal Unit, sure damn tzai chiu one." (You better ask Ah Beng to handle these matters. He served his National Service in the Bomb Disposal Unit, so he's bound to be very cool-headed.)*

tzai si |tzai see| Hokkien for "to know death". Used as an admonishment. The equivalent of "now you know!" or "serves you right!"

☐ *"You whole day go Geylang, wait you kena VD then you tzai si!" (You're always going to Geylang. If you get a venereal disease one day, it will serve you right!)*

See also **mm tzai si**

tzao gai |tzao gkai| Literally, Cantonese for "running chicken", which means to wind up with nothing.

⊡ *"He very pantang one. Got 4D that day, he wen eat chicken rice in case his bets all tzao gai." (He's very superstitious. On days with lottery draws, he won't eat chicken rice in case his bets all come to nought.)*

tzao kng |tzao gk'ng| Hokkien term meaning to expose one's underwear unintentionally.

⊡ *"Don't look! Jane tzao kng again." (Don't look! Jane has accidentally exposed her underwear again!)*

See also **open coffee shop**

tzao kor |tzao gkaw| Hokkien for "take care of" or "look after".

1 *"When he young that time, got no one tzao kor, so that's why he become samseng." (When he was young, no one looked after him. That's how he became a gangster.)*

2 *"Eh, this sort of important thing, how can you go and ask a gorblok like him to tzao kor?" (How could you ask a moron like him to take care of such an important matter?)*

Uu

udderwise / ungderwise Singlish pronunciations of "otherwise".

⊡ *"You better pass your PSLE, ungderwise next year I take you go market and sell!" (You better pass your Primary School Leaving Examinations, otherwise next year I'll sell you off at the market!)*

ulu |ooh-loo| Malay term used to denote the remoteness of a place, with connotations of backwardness.

⊡ *"Why you take me to Jurong this sort of ulu place?" (Why did you take me to a place as out of the way as Jurong?)*

uncle |ung-gker| Not just your father's brother, in Singapore, this term of respect can be used to address any male person old enough to actually be your uncle. See also **auntie**

unglam The opposite of "glam". See **glam**

untahantable Unbearable. Derived from the Malay word "tahan" meaning to "endure" or "bear".

▣ *"Adoi, the weather nowadays so damn hot, it's bloody untahantable, man." (Oh, the weather nowadays is so hot, it's really unbearable.)*
See also **buay tahan**

until In English, "until" is used to denote the reaching of a specified time or occurrence, e.g. "He worked until it was 6 o'clock", or "He read until his guests arrived". In Singlish, the use of "until" is not limited to instances of time or events, but can include destinations and even states of being.
1 *"You go until where oreddy?" (Where have you reached?)*
2 *"He walk until the jetty then he stop." (He walked till he reached the jetty, then he stopped.)*
3 *"He sleep until so song, don't kachau him, lah." (He's sleeping so soundly. Don't disturb him.)*

up the lorry A phrase to describe a very bad outcome. Derived from the scene at funerals where the coffin is being placed onto the lorry to be transported to the burial grounds. Also possible to be used in the case of a gang fight scene when the leader shouts to the members to retreat.
▣ *"Today got test, you neh study, ah? Like that, up the lorry, lor!" (You didn't study for today's test? You're up the creek without a paddle!)*

upstair / upstairs Used to suggest someone's snobbishness or arrogance. Possibly a literal translation of "atas", though it's not clear which came first.
▣ *"Nowsaday, Ah Beng very upstair, one. Wen drink kopi tiam kopi, only drink Starbucks." (Ah Beng has become very snobbish recently. He won't drink coffee from the coffee shop, only from Starbucks.)*
See also **atas, dao, sombong, ya ya**

Vv

vanstine day A popular Singlish pronunciation of "Valentine's Day".
▣ *"If I dun give my girlfriend a present for Vanstine Day, she sure hantam me, one." (If I don't give my girlfriend a Valentine's Day gift, she'll beat me up for sure.)*

vengayam Tamil for "onion". Used frequently to describe stupid people.

▣ *"Dey, can you not whole day long hang out with these vengayam?" (Dude, can you please refrain from associating with these idiots?)*

very the Singlish phrase meaning, inexplicably, "very". Usually employed with a sarcastic tone.

① *"Wah lau eh, he ah, his armpit very the smelly, you know!" (Holy cow! His armpit is very smelly!)*

② *"Piang eh, your skirt very the short, hor?" (Holy cow! Your skirt's very short, isn't it?)*

See also **a bit the**

very what one An indefinable, elusive quality about something or someone. The Singlish equivalent of the French phrase "je ne sais quoi", but almost always negative.

▣ *"She, hor, very what one, you know!" (She has a certain annoying quality that I can't quite describe.)*

vomit blood Literal translation from the Hokkien phrase "tor hwee", which is used to describe undergoing extreme difficulty, intense suffering or great irritation. "Vomit" is often pronounced "womit".

▣ *"Yesterday, hor, I teach my son maths, teach until vomit blood." (Yesterday, I taught my son mathematics until I wanted to burst a blood vessel.)*

See also **tor hwee**

Ww

wah lan / wah lan eh / lan eh |wah lahn| Hokkien term which can be loosely translated as "oh penis". Probably the most common Singlish ejaculation of all, it is used in a similar manner to "oh my goodness", "wow", "damn!" or "holy cow!", depending on the tone employed, and the context. More polite variants include "wah lau" and "wah piang".

① *"Wah lan eh! How can you do this sort of thing to me?" (Damn it! How can you do such a thing to me?)*

② *"My first thought when I saw her was 'wah lan eh'." (My first thought when I saw her was, "Oh my god!")*

③ *"Lan eh, I ask you to do this sort of simple-simple thing, you can also cock up!" (Holy cow, how could you screw even such a simple*

thing up?)
See also **wah lau**, **wah piang**

wah lau / wah lau eh / lau eh The most common polite variation of "wah lan". See also **wah lan**

wah piang / piang / piang eh |wah bpee-ahng| Another polite variation of "wah lan". Can be abbreviated to just "piang".
1 *"Wah piang! Check out his Johor Baru perm! Like bird's nest, siai!" (Holy cow! Check out his Johor Baru perm! It's like a bird's nest!)*
2 *"Piang, you go and paint your car pink for what?" (Goodness, why did you paint your car pink?)*
3 *"Piang eh, how come you can fail primary school maths one?" (Holy cow! How on earth could you fail primary school mathematics?)*
See also **wah lan**

wah seh |wah say| An exclamation similar to "wow", usually employed when one is impressed about something.
• *"Wah seh! Check out that chio bu, man!" (Wow! Check out that pretty girl, man!)*

wait A popular threat or warning in Singlish. The equivalent of "if you're not careful..." How "wait" came to be used in this manner is probably via the Malay word "nanti", meaning "wait", which is used in an identical fashion.
1 *"Don't listurb those Ah Bengs. Wait they hoot you then you know." (Don't annoy those Ah Bengs. If you're not careful, they'll beat you up.)*
2 *"You don't study hard, wait you become road sweeper." (If you don't study hard, you might wind up as a road sweeper.)*
3 *"Nao hiah, you want to potong jalan my girlfriend, is it? Wait I hantam you then you know!" (Bloody hell! So you wish to steal my girlfriend away, do you? Keep this up and I'll give you a real thrashing!)*
See also **skali**

wait long-long The Anglicized version of the Hokkien phrase "tan ku ku", which means "forget it" or "it'll never happen".
• *"You want raise from this boss? Wait long-long ah!" (You want to get a raise from this boss? It'll never happen!)*
See also **tan ku ku**

wake up your idea(s) Singlish phrase that's especially popular in the army, meaning "get a clue" or "stop daydreaming".
• *Sergeant: "Who say you can tuang like that, recruit? You better wake up your idea!" (Who says you can skive like that, recruit? You'd better stop daydreaming!)*

wan dan |wahn dtahn| Mandarin for "a finished egg". It means one is doomed or finished.

① *"Alamak, masuk two goals already! Wan dan leow!" (Oh god, they've scored two goals already! We're finished!)*
② *"I warn you, ah, the boss see you tuang like that, you sure wan dan!" (Let me warn you, if the boss catches you skiving like that, it'll be the end of you!)*
See also **habis**

wayang |wah-yahng| Originally a Malay word meaning "performance on a screen", in Singlish, it has come to mean an act of pretence.
⊡ *"Eh, we all saw you take his wallet. Don't come and wayang, okay?" (We all saw you take his wallet. Don't pretend you didn't do it!)*
See also **act blur, tok tok chiang**

wen |wurn| Singlish pronunciation of "won't", and is invariably followed by "one" or "lah". It is used to express an opinion that something is unlikely to occur.
① *Johnny: "You think Ah Beng will pass his 'O' levels?"*
Ah Seng: "Wen, lah." (No, he won't.)
② *"I know he said he would lend you his car, but I bet he wen one." (I know he said he would lend you his car, but I bet you he won't.)*

wen die / won't die |wurn dai| Singlish phrase used to reassure someone that something is not hazardous or troublesome. Derived from the Hokkien "buay si".
⊡ *"Injection only, lah! Dun scared! Wen die one!" (It's only an injection. Don't be scared. It won't kill you.)*
See also **die also won't die, dun scared, meng kia, long tio ooh sia**

whack In Singlish, "whack" retains its regular meaning of "hit", but it also has the additional meanings of acting in a reckless or careless manner, or eating something with relish.
① *"Last year, Singapore kena whack by SARS." (Last year, Singapore was hit by SARS.)*
② *"This is a serious job, okay, you cannot anyhow whack." (This is a serious job. You can't approach it in a careless manner.)*
③ *"Eh, the seafood buffet here is quite solid. Whack all the prawns, man!" (Wow, the seafood buffet here is quite good. Grab all the prawns!)*

what A Singlish sentence tag used by people who are in defensive situations.
⊡ *Ah Beng: "How come you borrow my shirt now got hole one?!" (When you borrowed my shirt, how did it end up with holes?)*
Ah Seng: "Borrow that time oreddy like dat, what!" (When I borrowed them, there were already holes!)
Ah Beng: "Then why you neh say first?" (Why didn't you say something then?)

Ah Seng: "You neh ask, what!" (Well, you never asked!)

what done? Eternal question asked by waiters and waitresses at local Western restaurants when someone orders a steak.

☐ *Ah Beng: "I want a sirloin steak."*
Waitress: "What done you want? Lare? Menium? Weww done?" (How do you wish your steak to be done? Rare? Medium? Well done?)

what for? The Singlish abbreviation of both "whatever for?" or "what did you do that for?" You could save you a syllable if you simply substituted "why", but that wouldn't be Singlish. Is used interchangeably with (wait for it) "for what?"

① *"Follow you go KL? What for?" (Follow you to Kuala Lumpur? Whatever for?)*

② *"What for you go and sign up with that MLM scheme?" (What on earth made you sign up with that multilevel marketing scheme?)*

See also **for what?**

what for tu donno An expression of bewilderment at another's actions. The closest English translation is "I have no idea why!".

☐ *"Ah Beng went to buy that condemn tech stock? What for tu donno!" (Ah Beng bought stock in that crappy tech company? I have no idea why he did that!)*

what talking you? Singlish for "what are you talking about?" A statement of incredulity or disbelief.

☐ *"Eh, Ah Beng where can pass 'A' maths? What talking you?" (How could Ah Beng pass his "A" maths exams? What are you talking about?)*

what-squat If someone asks you, "what?" in what you perceive to be a rude manner, it is customary to respond with "squat!" This childish exchange was popular in the 1970s but is now rare. See example below:

☐ *Tan: "Ah Lim, ah!!"*
Lim (irritated): "WHAT!!!"
Tan: "SQUAT!!!"
Lim: "I berak, you angkat!" (I shit, you carry!)
Tan: "I kencing you minum!" (I piss, you drink!)

where got A pithy expression akin to "how can this be", expressing exasperation, lament, disbelief or sometimes, outrage. It can also be used as an annoyed denial.

① *Beng: "Seng, you took my wallet, right?" (Seng, you took my wallet, didn't you?)*
Seng: "Where got?!" (I did not!)

② *"I always so nice to him but he say I kapo his wallet. I ask you,*

where got like that?" (I'm always so nice to him, yet he accused me of stealing his wallet. I ask you, how could he do that?)
3 *"A young man dying while in the prime of his life... Where got meaning?" (A young man dying while in the prime of his life... Where is the meaning in life?)*
4 *Ah Seng: "Eh, Beng ah, the file on inventory you put where, ah?" (Hey, Beng, where did you put the file on inventory?)*
Ah Beng: "Top cabinet." (In the top cabinet.)
Ah Seng (after frantically searching): "Where got?" (No, it's not!)
See also **where got? god in heaven, how can?**

where got? god in heaven The smart aleck retort to "where got?" due to the similarity in sound between "god" and "got".
· *Ah Seng: "Eh, Beng ah, the file on inventory you put where, ah?"*
Ah Beng: "Top cabinet."
Ah Seng (after frantically searching): "Where got?"
Ah Beng: "God in Heaven, lah! Arbuthen?"
See also **where got? how can?**

where got time? Anglicized version of the hybrid Malay-Hokkien phrase "mana ooh eng?", which is used to express incredulity at being asked to do something frivolous or unimportant when one has better things to do.
· *"Go and play golf? Where got time?" (Go and play golf? Who has the time?)*
See also **where got**

whole day A term used to describe having to do something for a really long period, though not necessarily 24 hours in duration.
1 *"Wah lau, convention that time, I whole day kena man reception counter. Damn sian, man!" (Man, during the convention, I had to spend all my time manning the reception counter. I was really bored!)*
2 *"You cho lifeguard, whole day can see girl in bikini. Song, man!" (If you get a job as a lifeguard, you can watch girls in bikinis the entire day. How pleasurable!)*
See also **whole life**

whole life Although sometimes used like an exaggerated version of "whole day" (above), "whole life" can also be used to comment (almost always negatively) on a person's recurring behaviour.
1 *"Ah Beng whole life hang out at the kopi tiam, do'wan to work." (Ah Beng spends all his time hanging out at the coffee shop, with no interest in working.)*
2 *"He whole life like to ji seow people. One day, sure kena hoot." (He always likes to annoy people. One day, he's bound to be beaten*

up.)

win liao / win oreddy From the Hokkien exclamation "yiah liao lor!", it marks the surrender of an argument or expression of unfairness, with a grudgingly friendly tone.

1 *"Wah, you win liao, lor! Ask me help you do so many things!" (Okay, you win! You've succeeded in getting me to help you with so many things!)*

2 *Ah Beng: "I insist I am right!"*
Ah Seng: "Yah lah, yah lah, you win liao lah!" (OK, OK, you win! You win!)

3 *Boss: "I'm going on off tomorrow, so I need you to faster type up all these documents." (Tomorrow's my day off, so I need you to type up all these documents quickly.)*
Secretary: "Like that win orredy lor." (Well, isn't that just dandy!)

world best Not just the best — the world's best. The ultimate. The top. Used mostly in the context of your favourite hawker stalls.

1 *"The Hokkien mee at Old Airport Road is world best, one." (The Hokkien mee at Old Airport Road hawker centre is the world's best.)*

2 *"Hwah, this one, world best char kway teow!" (Wow, this is the best char kway teow ever.)*

See also **chut mia, moh tuck teng**

worrage |wor-raych| Singlish pronunciation of "worried".

• *"Eh, you whole week go where, ah? I at home very worrage one, you know!" (Hey, where did you go the entire week? I was at home getting worried for you!)*

worth / wurf |wuhf| Singlish abbreviation of "worth it".

1 *"Wah, $100 for this kind of thing is very wurf what!" (Wow, $100 for an object like this is a really good deal.)*

2 *"They want to pay you in SingTel shares? Damn not wurf, man." (They want to pay you in SingTel shares? That's an improvident bargain.)*

wu liao |woo lee-ow| The Mandarin version of "boh liao", i e. "nothing better to do" or "idle".

• *"What for he go and do that sort of thing? Must be damn wu liao." (Why did he do that? He must have nothing better to do!)*

See also **boh liao, chiak pah boh sai pang, cho bo, itchy backside**

Xx

THERE are currently no "x" entries because in Singlish, "x" can always be replaced by "es", as in "eskew", "essciting" and "ess-ray".

Yy

ya ya Arrogant.
☐ *"Don't be so ya ya, I warn you." (Don't be so arrogant, I warn you.)*
See also **atas, dao, sombong, ya ya papaya**

ya ya papaya An arrogant person.
☐ *"Johnny is such a ya ya papaya." (Johnny is such an arrogant person.)*

yah lah! "I know!" Usually repeated for emphasis.
☐ *Beng: "Eh, don'ch angry leh, just kidding what!" (Hey, don't get angry! I was only kidding!)*
Seng: "Yah lah, yah lah, OK lah!" (Yeah, yeah, yeah! Okay! Whatever!)

yan dao |yen dtao| Hokkien for "handsome gentleman". Can be both noun and adjective. Often employed by female hawkers to curry favour with male customers. Almost always used in an ironic or insincere way.
☐ *"Yan dao, dun so kan cheong, can or not? Your kway png coming oreddy!" (Relax, handsome! Your chicken rice is on its way.)*
See also **lang loi**

yang-or Corruption of the Malay word "sayang", meaning "love" or "darling". A request to be loved or cuddled.
☐ *"I wan' a yang-or," said Ah Lian, pouting. ("I want a cuddle," said Ah Lian, pouting.)*

yat keok tek |yaht gkyok dtek| Cantonese term literally meaning "to kick with one leg". Can be used to describe a job where one has to do everything; can also refer to a jack of all trades, but not usually by choice.

☐ *"This is a small startup, so everyone must yat keok tek one." (This is a small startup, so everyone will have to pitch in and multitask.)*

yau kwee |yau gkwee| Hokkien term literally meaning "hungry ghost". It describes a glutton or avaricious person.

☐ *"Eh, don't take all the prawns from the buffet, leh! Why you so yau kwee?" (Hey, don't take all the prawns from the buffet! Why are you such a glutton?)*

yau mo gau chor? |yau moh gkau chaw| Cantonese for "did you make a mistake?" An expression of incredulity and surprise.

☐ *"Ha? You say Ah Beng got invited to join the Young PAP? You mo gau chor?" (Did you say Ah Beng was invited to join the Youth Wing of the People's Action Party? Are you sure you didn't make a mistake?)*

See also **ooh yia boh?**

you ask me, I ask who? An irritated response to someone pestering you with a question you are obviously in no position to answer.

☐ *"How come recession time our ministers' salary still so high? You ask me, I ask who?" (Why is it that our ministers' salaries are so high even during a recession? How am I supposed to know?)*

you think, he think, who confirm? One's exasperated response to a series of very tentative or fuzzy suggestions. An angry exhortation to arrive at a clear decision.

☐ *Employee: "I think maybe can do like that, but she think, maybe follow the other way better, but Mr Tan think lai dat how can..." (I thought maybe we could do it like this... but she thought, maybe it would be better if we followed the other way. But Mr Tan thought, how could we do it like that...)*

Boss: "You think, he think, who confirm?!" (You thought, he thought... Can someone please be more decisive?)

you think what A phrase that suggests you have made a naïve or simplistic assumption about a situation.

1 *"Eh, become scholar must work hard, lair! You think what!" (To be awarded a scholarship requires hard work. What did you think?)*

2 *"You think what, he got that scholarship because he study damn hard, ah? He got it because his lau peh donated a swimming pool to the university, lah!" (Do you really think he was awarded that scholarship because he studied hard? He got it because his father donated a swimming pool to the university!)*

your head Mild curse used to disabuse someone of his or her erroneous assumptions.
1 *Ah Beng: "You sure fail the test!" (You're sure to fail the test!) Ah Seng: "Your head, lah!" (Oh, buzz off!)*
2 *"She? Win Miss Universe? Your head, lah!" (Did you say she could win the Miss Universe title? You're out of your mind!)*

Zz

THERE are currently few "z" entries because in Singlish, "z" can always be replaced by "j", so, "Zoe" becomes "Joe", "zebra" becomes "jibra" and "zero", "jilo". Also, for those of you who are using hanyu pinyin spellings, words that seem like they could be spelled with a "z" may be found elsewhere, e.g.

- "zai" can be found under "tzai"
- "zha bor" can be found under "char bor"
- "zheng hu" can be found under "cheng hu"

We've chosen to do this for the benefit of our many non-Mandarin-speaking readers for whom the hanyu pinyin spellings are not intuitive.

zap The local term for "photocopy" or "Xerox".
"Cheh! This textbook so ex, I think I borrow from library and zap." (Huh! This textbook is so expensive! I think I'll borrow a copy from the library and photocopy it.)

zi bei |tze bpay| Mandarin for "low self-esteem".
"Until I got silicone implants, hor, when I wear tight T-shirt that time, always feel a bit zi bei like that." (Until I got silicone implants, I used to feel low self-esteem whenever I wore tight T-shirts.)

Why Singlish is Better than English

WHY do we insist on using the Queen's English, when Singlish is so much more economical and effective? Compare and see!

BRITONS	SINGAPOREANS
When going shopping…	
I'm sorry, Sir, but we don't seem to have the sweater you want in your size, but if you give me a moment, I can call the other outlets for you.	*No Stock!*
When returning a call…	
Hello, this is Mr Bean. Did anyone call me a few moments ago?	*Hello, who call?*
When someone is in the way…	
Excuse me, I'd like to get by. Would you please make way?	*Lai, siam! or Siam, hor! or Skews!*
When someone offers to pay…	
Hey, put your wallet away, this drink is on me.	*No-nid. (No need.)*
When asking for permission…	
Excuse me, but do you think it would be possible for me to enter through this door?	*(While pointing at door) Can or not?*

BRITONS	SINGAPOREANS
When asking to be excused…	
If you would excuse me for a moment, I have to go to the gents/ladies. Please carry on without me. I will only be a moment.	*Go toilet. Cannot tahan liao.*
When entertaining…	
Please make yourself right at home.	*Dun shy, leh!*
When doubting someone…	
I don't recall you giving me the money.	*Where got?*
When declining an offer…	
I'd prefer not to do that, if you don't mind.	*Do'wan.*
When deciding on a plan of action…	
What do you propose we do now that the movie's sold out & all the restaurants are closed?	*So how? Go where?*
When disagreeing on a topic of discussion…	
Err… Tom, I have to stop you there. I understand where you're coming from, but I really have to disagree with what you said about the policy.	*Talk cock lah, you!*
When asking someone to lower their voice…	
Excuse me, but could you please lower your voice, I'm trying to concentrate over here.	*Eh, tiam, can or not?*
When asking someone if he / she knows you…	
Excuse me, but I noticed you staring at me for some time. Do I know you? Or are you spoiling for a fight?	*See what? Kiam pak, ah?*

Singlish for the Traveller

Common Phrases in Common Situations

Arriving in Singapore

Hello, here is my passport.	*Nah.*
I'm afraid the photographer caught me on a bad day when he took my picture.	*Piang, my photo kana sai lai dat.*
Which way is baggage retrieval?	*Take bag, where?*
I have nothing to declare.	*Everything also dun have..*
This is only chewing gum.	*Gum only, what.*
Surely, there's nothing wrong with that!	*Cannot, meh?*
You can only buy specific kinds of gum from pharmacists and dentists and they have to take down my particulars upon purchase? That's ridiculous!	*Ha? Where got like that?*
If that's the case, how about if I just start chewing it here?	*Like that, I makan now, lor.*
You mean I'll still be fined?	*Like that still kena saman, ah?*
Oh dear.	*Seow leow.*
Darn.	*Na beh.*

Meeting and Greeting

Hello.	*Eh!*
Have you put on some weight?	*Wah, you fatter leow, hor!*
How are you?	*How, man? or* *How, da? or* *Ho bo?*
I'm fine.	*OK, lor.*
How is your family?	*Your fambly, how?*
I'm (they're) doing fine.	*Lai dat, lor.*
I heard you're doing well.	*Wah! You now damn big time, hor?*
Here's my business card.	*Nah.*
Do you wish to join me for a drink?	*Alcoholic: Want to togo?* *Non-alcoholic: Want to la kopi?*
I'd be delighted.	*Caaaan.*
Of course! Do you have to ask?	*Arbuthen?*
Have you eaten?	*Makan oreddy?*
Do you want to join me for a meal?	*Want to go makan?*
Don't be shy.	*Dun shy, leh!*
Let's go.	*On!*
That's excellent.	*Ho say!*
Thank you.	*Chankyewp.*
You're welcome.	*Dun mention.*
I have to go.	*Chao liao!*

At the Hawker Centre or Coffeeshop

Where shall we go for a meal?	*Makan go where?*
I'm open to suggestions.	*Anything also can.*
How about this place?	*Here can?*
Is this seat occupied?	*Here got people sit or not?*
Can I share the table with you?	*Can share?*
No, you can't share the table with me. This seat's reserved.	*Cannot. Chope already.*
Can't you see there's a packet of tissue paper here on the seat?	*You neh see here got tissue paper, meh?*
May I have a cup of coffee/tea without milk?	*Kopi-o/Teh-o!*
May I have a glass of iced Horlicks?	*Horlick peng!*
Do you want a hot drink/dessert or a cold drink/dessert?	*Hock one or koh one?*
Do you serve bread with kaya?	*Got loti kaya, not?*
This stall has received good reviews.	*This one tok kong one.*
I'd like a packet of noodles to go.	*Mee, one packet.*
I'd like three dollars worth of noodles.	*Mee, three dollar one..*
No chilli, please.	*Do'wan chilli.*
Not too spicy, please.	*Do'wan so hiam.*
More chilli please.	*More hiam.*
I do not want any cockles in my mee siam.	*Mee siam mai hum.*
Mee siam is never served with cockles.	*Mee siam where got hum one?*

You clearly haven't been to a hawker centre in ages, have you?	*You long-long neh come to hawker centre leow, is it?*
I'd like a bowl of pig innards, please.	*Spare parts, one bowl.*
I'd like a plain prata.	*Prata kosong, one.*
How long must I wait?	*Must wait how long?*
I have placed my order a long time ago, but the food still hasn't arrived.	*I order very long oreddy, lair. Still norchat come!*
Please make way, this bowl of soup is very hot.	*Siam ah! Sio ah!*
Bon appetit!	*Chiak! or Whack, ah!*
This is delicious!	*Shiok! or Shiok, sial!*
This stall is very dirty.	*Ee-yur.*
This food tastes horrible.	*Wah lau, damn cannot make it.*
How can this food pass muster?	*Lai dat, how can?*
What do you want for dessert?	*What lizard you wan', ah?*

At McDonald's

MCDONALD's in Singapore hires a lot of senior citizens as counter staff, many of whom are not very proficient in standard English. Here's how to order so the Auntie-Auntie can understand what the hell you want:

What you want	**How you pronounce it**
McDonald's	*Meh Donner*
Big Mac Meal	*Mee Mare Mew*
Happy Meal	*Hair Pee Mew*
French Fries	*Flench Fly*
Fillet O'Fish	*Feese Burger*
Mushroom Burger	*Mus-sloom Burger*
Chicken McNuggets	*Meh Narget*
Big Breakfast	*Bee Blare Fers*
Hot Cakes	*Whore Cakes*
Orange Juice	*Or Leng Joo*
Apple Pie	*Apper Pai*
Upsize	*Up Sai*

Entertaining at Home

Hello! Good to see you!	*Eh! Ho bo?*
This is a gift for you.	*Nah, give you!*
(Accepting a gift from the guest) Oh, you didn't have to get me anything. Why stand on ceremony?	*(Accepting a gift from the guest) Aiyoh, why so kek kee, no nid lah!*
How much did you pay for your house?	*Your house how much, ha?*
Wow, that's a lot!	*Piang eh, damn ex, man!!*
Your child is a little overweight.	*(Pinching the host's kid's cheek) Aiyoh, pooi-pooi, so cute!*
Which grade level in primary school is she in?	*She prembry what oreddy?*
She is about to sit for the Primary School Leaving Examination, isn't she?	*PSLE coming soon, hor?*
Which school will she be going to?	*What school you choose?*
What would you like to drink?	*You want to drink what?*
Make yourself at home!	*Dun shy, ah!*
How wide is your TV screen?	*Your TV how many inch one, ha?*
What will you be cooking tonight?	*Tonight you cook what, ha?*
Please wait a little while. You aren't hungry yet, are you?	*Wait a while, can? You not hungry yet, right?*
(If there are older family members present) Bon appetit, Auntie. Bon appetit, Uncle.	*(If there are older family members present) Auntie, eat! Uncle, eat!*
How much rice would you like?	*How much rice you want?*
So little? Are you on diet?	*So little? On diet, ah?*
Bon appetit! Please help yourself to the food.	*Eat, eat, dun shy!*

This is delicious!	*Hwah! Shiok man!*
Have some more food! You don't want to look undernourished, do you?	*Eat some more, lah! Skarly you look like teck koh, then you know.*
If you want a second helping, I have more in the kitchen in the back.	*Want some more, behind still got.*
I can't eat any more. I am full already.	*Aiyoh, full oreddy.*
(Without standing up) Do you need some help with the dishes?	*(Without standing up) Nid help, not?*
(Rejecting an offer of help with the dishes) It's not necessary, Flora, our domestic help, will wash all the dishes.	*(Rejecting an offer of help with the dishes) No nid, Flora wash can oreddy.*
May I take some food home?	*Can tar pao, not?*
(While accepting the Tupperware boxes of food) Oh, you really shouldn't.	*(While accepting the Tupperware boxes of food) Eh, pai seh leh.*
My parking coupon has expired. Got to go.	*Kupoon expire leow. I chao first.*
If you have time, feel free to visit me again!	*Free, come again!*

At a Posh Restaurant

Good evening. Do you have a reservation?	*Just now you got call, not?*
Yes, it's reserved under "Tan".	*Tan!*
Please wait a moment, while we attend to your table.	*Your name "Tan", so you "tan" a while, can?*
This way to your table, please.	*Lai! or Come!*
Here is the menu.	*Nah.*
What would you recommend?	*Here got what, ah?*
Our speciality is fine European haute cuisine.	*Ang moh chiak, lor.*
Would you recommend (point to dish on the menu)?	*Good or not?*
It's alright.	*Can, lah.*
The steak here is exceptional.	*Here the "steek" is tok kong, one.*
How would you like your steak to be done?	*What done you want?*
We also have a fine selection of pasta dishes.	*Here also got mee.*
Perhaps the fettuccine or linguine?	*Mee pok, mee kia also got.*
Would you care for some wine with your meal?	*Tiger beer for you?*
Would you care for some salt/pepper?	*(Pointing to shakers) Want?*
Would you care to sample our desserts?	*Want lizard, not?*
May I have the bill/check, please?	*Mai tan! (or just mime signing a cheque in the air)*
Wow, the prices here are really steep!	*Piang eh, damn ex, balls!*
I'd rather eat at a hawker centre.	*Hawker centre also better!*

Checking into a Hotel

Good day! Welcome to the Grand Hotel!	*(Silent stare)*
Did you have a pleasant flight?	*Flight OK, not?*
May I have your name?	*Name?*
The room is reserved under "Tan Ah Beng".	*Tan Ah Beng.*
Will you be paying by credit card?	*Card?*
Here is your key.	*Nah.*
Thank you.	*Chankyewp.*
What will the check out time be?	*Check out what time, ah?*
Can I check out later?	*Later, can or not?*
The porter will assist you with your bags.	*(To the porter) Oi! Take, leh!*
Are there any food establishments in the vicinity?	*Around here got what to eat, ha?*
Does the hotel have entertainment facilities?	*Here got KTV, not?*
Yes, we have many amenities for guests.	*Got. Everything also got.*
May I show you to your room, please?	*Lai!*
I say, this room is rather small.	*Lan eh! Why so kichi?*
I'm afraid I find the room unacceptable.	*Fail lah!*
I'll see what I can do to accommodate your wishes.	*See how, see how.*
Is this room more to your liking?	*This one, can?*
It's much better, thank you.	*Can.*
The towels are not to be taken with you when you leave.	*Eh, don't stun our towel, OK!*

Did you enjoy your massage?	*Your massage song, not?*
It was very good.	*Song-song kau Joolong!*
Can you explain to me these items on my bill?	*Eh? How come like this?*
I never drank those tiny bottles of whisky.	*Those kichi bottle, I neh drink one!*
That's impossible!	*Where got?*
I shall register a complaint with the relevant consumer protection agency, and it shall serve you right!	*I report you to Case, then you know!*

"Welcome back to our hotel, Mr Tan. This time, tolong-tolong, dun steal our towels, hor?"

At the Office / Doing Business

Can you help me photocopy these documents, please?	*Nah. Take and zap.*
Hello, Mr Tan's office.	*Hallo.*
Please hold the line while I transfer you to Mr Tan.	*Horn, ah.*
He's not in.	*Norrin.*
He's on medical leave.	*On MC.*
Would you like to leave a message?	*Got message, not?*
May I assist you with anything?	*Can I hepchu?*
This deal is important. Please deal with it with the utmost care.	*Eh, this one, ah, dun cock up, okay!*
Here comes the boss with an assignment.	*Boss come to arrow us oreddy.*
Darn, it looks like we'll have to indulge in a bit of dodging.	*Seow leow, must do Matrix oreddy.*
Quick! Let's get out of here.	*Faster! Take cover!*
Thanks to him, I got stuck with the assignment.	*Bloody sabo king! Now I kena arrow.*
He sure knows how to curry favour with the boss.	*He damn sah kah chua, one.*
Don't be so enthusiatic. You're beginning to make the rest of us look bad.	*Eh, dun so enthu, can or not! Don't spoil market, leh!*
It's crucial that you finish this assignment tomorrow.	*This one, tomorrow die-die must finish.*
I need it in a hurry.	*Chop chop kali pok.*
You can finish this assignment at your leisure.	*This job, own time own target also can.*
I'm really, really busy.	*Hwah, damn boh eng man!*
This job is really rough.	*Siong, ah! or* *Teruk, sial!*

How can you put up with such bad working conditions?	*How you tahan, ah?*
I have no choice. At least I have a job.	*Boh pian. Aiyah, no need to sell backside, can oreddy.*
I heard he's been passed over for promotion many times.	*I heard he now hentak kaki.*
Are these terms acceptable to you?	*Lai dat, can?*
Yes, they're fine. We have a deal!	*Caaaaan. Settle!*
I'll have to review them first.	*See how.*
I will have to bring it before the Board of Directors for their review first.	*Must surface to the Board first.*
I'm afraid I don't understand these clauses.	*These clauses I catch no ball.*
Why do these lawyers insist on using such difficult terms?	*Chao lawyer, write until so cheem.*
Let us celebrate the closing of the deal with champagne.	*Lai! Togo!*
Congratulations, you're sure to make a lot of money from this deal.	*Wah, now you bee tang chiak buay leow, ah!*
Just don't be arrogant when you're in management, alright?	*You go upstair that time, dun be atas, can?*
Well, that strategy backfired.	*Lum pah pah lan, man.*

Shopping

***CANIHEPCHU:** The only Singaporean Pokémon.*

Are you having a sale today?	*Today got sales, not?*
Can you direct me to the menswear section?	*Man clothes, where?*
Where is the fitting room?	*Fitting room where?*
May I assist you with your shopping?	*Can I hep'chu?*
Certainly.	*Can.*
I'm looking for a shirt for office wear.	*Got oppis shirt, not?*
Yes, we do.	*Got.*
I'm afraid we've run out.	*No stock!*
Do you have any other colours?	*Got other colour, not?*
I don't think this suits me.	*Wah! Damn argly, make me look like damn toot.*
Do you have any other sizes?	*Got other size?*
I'm afraid not.	*Dun have.*
This is the last piece.	*Last one oreddy.*
These items are discounted.	*This one got discount.*
Can you give me a better discount?	*Cheaper can or not?*

In School

Having to sing the National Anthem every morning is really boring.	*Every morning kena sing the Marikita, si beh sian.*
Hey, lend me your mathematics exercise book. I didn't do my homework, and I need to copy yours.	*Eh, borrow me your maths book to copy, can? I neh do my homework.*
What a damned swot you are! Why are you so competitive? What are you scared of?	*Chao mugger! Why so kiasu? Scared what?*
You're such an apple-polisher, forever buttering the teachers up.	*You bleddy sah kah chua! Whole life por teacher!*
Teacher, I need to go to the toilet.	*Cher, go toilet!*
It's very urgent.	*Urgent lah, cher!*
I'm not kidding!	*Neh bluff you!*
I skipped my physical education class last week.	*Last week, I tuang PE.*
Further, I played truant yesterday, and hung around Far East Plaza instead.	*Some more, yesterday, I pontang school and went Far East.*
But unluckily, I was caught.	*But I suay-suay kena caught.*
That's why I'm now in trouble.	*So now kena sai, lor.*
I'm afraid I might have to be held back a grade.	*Skarly I kena stayback.*

Attending Cultural Events

What shall we do this evening?	*Tonight do what?*
Let's attend a concert.	*Lai, go concert.*
What event are we attending?	*Come here see what?*
Wow, look at all the formally-dressed people.	*Piang, here got so many penguin.*
What a lot of pretentious, colonized Singaporeans.	*Wah lau eh, here got so many keng chio kia.*
Do you wish to purchase a programme?	*Wan' programme, not?*
Yes, thank you.	*Can.*
No, thank you.	*Do'wan.*
Were the tickets expensive?	*Ticket ex or not?*
I think you got scalped.	*You kena ketuk oreddy.*
Please turn off your mobile phones.	*Off your handphone, lah.*
I'm afraid I found the performance somewhat uninspired.	*Wah lau eh, damn sian, man.*
I'm afraid all of it was a little too complicated for me.	*Too cheem.*
I fell asleep.	*Koon leow.*
I would have preferred to stay home and watch TV.	*Stay home and watch TV oso better.*

Driving

Where are we going?	*Go where?*
Oh, let's just go cruising.	*Just KLKK, lah.*
Let's go!	*On!*
Did you remember to display a parking coupon?	*Got put kupoon, not?*
Can you turn on/off the radio?	*On/Off the radio, lah!*
Oh no! I've got a flat tire!	*Aiyah, tire pumchek!*
Don't worry, just drive the car forward.	*Kah kah lai! Meng kia, long tio ooh siah.*
Can you please slow down?	*Oi! You think you Formula One, is it?*
That driver is so inconsiderate — switching lanes without turning on his indicator!	*Na beh! Neh chut signal one!*
What an incompetent driver!	*Damn kayu driver!*
Why is this driver going so slowly?	*(To the driver) Eh, your grandfudder road, is it?!*
Oh no! My car has been hit!	*Seow leow! I kena langgar!*
What a bad accident!	*Wah lau eh, damn teruk accident, sial.*
Uh-oh, I've been spotted by the traffic police.	*Die, lah. Mata come oreddy.*
I'm sure to get a ticket.	*Sure kena saman.*
Is there a problem, officer?	*Wha'ppen?*
I'm sorry, officer, I didn't see the stop sign.	*Got stop sign, meh?*
Is this a serious offence?	*This one kena points one, not?*
Oh dear.	*Wah lau.*
Can I compound this offence on the spot?	*I pay now, can or not?*
No, no, this isn't an attempt at bribery!	*No lah, I neh try to bribe you!*

Look at my crappy car! How could I possibly afford to bribe anyone?	*Look at my lao pok chia! I where got money to bribe people?*
Can't you let me off this time?	*Panchan me this time, lah!*
I promise I won't do this again.	*I confirm wen do this again.*
Please believe me!	Neh bluff you one!
Those aren't handcuffs, are they?	*That one handcuff, ah?*
I'm finished.	*Liao, lah.*
Can you at least tell me the number of your police vehicle?	*Eh, your police car, what number, ah?*
I want to buy that number for the lottery. What do you think?	*Play 4D, lah. Arbuthen?*

At the Doctor's

Is there a doctor in the house?	*Here got doctor, not?*
Are you sure this is a clinic?	*This one clinic, meh?*
I thought with a queue as long as this, this was a branch of Singapore Pools.	*Piang, got so many people line up, I thought here sell 4D or what.*
I have a severe pain in my side.	*(Point to side) Here damn pain.*
No, I never engage in such hazardous activity.	*No, lah! I where got do this kind of thing?*
You want to take some of my blood?	*Take my blood, ah?*
That's a very painful looking needle.	*Your needle like damn pain, lai dat.*
You mean my illness is fatal?	*Mati, lah!*
What a sense of humour you have, doctor!	*Doc, you quite joker-type, hor?*
Wow, your bill is really high!	*Piang! How come so ex?*
Are you sure this isn't another of your jokes, doctor?	*Eh, dun ji seow me leh, Doc!*
With such high bills, I'm better off dead.	*Like that, die also better.*
At these charges, how about throwing in some Viagra?	*So ex, gimme some Viagra also, lah!*

Sporting Singaporeans

Watch the game? Please, it's really boring.	*See game, ah? Sian, lah!*
Our team is really crap.	*Our team kana sai.*
My grandmother plays better than them.	*My nenek also can whack them upside down.*
Okay, okay, I'll go!	*Okay, go lah, go lah!*
Don't ever accuse me of being unsupportive!	*Dun say I neh support-support a bit, okay?*
Anyway, the curry puffs at the stadium are quite good.	*The stadium kali pok not bad, lah.*
What a bloody sissy!	*Bapok!*
The referee is blind!	*Referee kayu!*
Cheats!	*Kelong!*
I can't believe we've spent so much money on training and still can't produce decent players!	*Wah lau, waste money only, our team!*
Go home!	*Balik kampong!*
I'm sure even I could play better!	*I play also better!*
What're you staring at?	*See what?*
Can't I express my own opinions?	*I say cannot, ah?*
Want to make something out of it?	*Kiam pak, ah?*
Do you think I'm intimidated by you just because you're a commando?	*You commando, I scared, meh?*
The only reason I'm not going to fight you is because I don't want to get you into trouble with your camp.	*I panchan you this time. Do'wan you to kena sign extra, mah. See you small only.*
Damn, can someone please call an ambulance?	*Na beh, call ambulance, leh!*

Romance

What a beautiful woman!	*Wah, she damn chio/jude, man!*
Hello, handsome!	*Eh, yan dao!*
Hello, I find you extremely attractive, would you care to go out with me?	*(Purse your lips and draw in air, making a loud, wet kiss)*
Shall we go on a date tonight?	*Tonight want to pak tor, not?*
Alright, what do you have in mind?	*Caaaan. Go where?*
I thought we'd start with dinner, then watch the midnight movie.	*Go and whack first, then kua meenite.*
Sounds good to me.	*On, lah!*
What time should we meet?	*Meet what time?*
If dinner is seven, then you can pick me up at half-past six.	*Dinner seven kolocks... less means, hor, happasix you come and fetch me.*
You're dressed very sharply.	*Wah, wear until so saht.*
You look pretty/handsome.	*So jude/hamsum.*
Shall we go dancing?	*Ai lumsing, mai?*
Or perhaps we could patronise a karaoke lounge?	*Or can go launge.*
What a romantic place!	*Wah, here damn lomance, one.*
Shall we make passionate love?	*Want to rabak-rabak, not?*
I don't understand. This has never happened before.	*Chey! How come like that?*
Clearly, it's been some time since you've engaged in this activity.	*You long-long neh do oreddy, hor?*
Can't you be a little more understanding?	*Dun like that, leh!*
How depressing.	*Lan lan, man.*

AND now to test whether all of you got catch any ball, we are proud to present the world's first Singlish test paper! Is your Singlish solid enough to pass the PSLE - the Powderful Singlish Language Examination? Try-try, wen die!

Coxford University Examinations Board

P.S.L.E.

POWDERFUL SINGLISH LANGUAGE EXAMINATION

PAPER I

Name:________________ School:____________________

Class: Prembry______ Secret Society:____________

Kind of Tattoo (please circle):

Dragon Eagle Tiger Snake Hello Kitty

Duration of paper: 56 minutes 2 seconds

INSTRUCTIONS TO CANDIDATES

THIS BOOKLET GOT MANY PAGES.

DUN OPEN THE BOOKLET OR TURN THE PAGE UNTIL WE TELL YOU.

YOU BETTER FOLLOW WHAT WE SAY.

IF NOT SKARLY YOU GET JILO, THEN YOU KNOW!

NEH BLUFF YOU ONE!

(For the answer key, see the end of the test paper. But only after you finish, okay! Dun play cheat!)

Grammar Cloze Passage (15 points)

Choose the correct tag from the following list to fill in the blanks in the passage below:

Hor Lah Lair Liao Man Meh

Yesterday ______(1), Auntie Neo went to the market. She went to buy fish, prawn and apple ______(2). And then ______(3), she ask the Fish Unker, "Eskew me, Unker, today the red fish how much?"

But the Unker, ______(4), he say, "The red fish, you can afford ______(5)? I think so better you buy the ikan billis." So of course Auntie Neo damn too lan ______(6). For no reason the chao Fish Unker see her no up, she oso donno why. Eh, dun see Auntie Neo so small-small, okay! She damn fierce one ______(7)! Sure wen let let the Fish Unker bully kichi one. Fish Unker got big knife, she oso not scared.

So Auntie Neo use her bag ______(8) - inside got a lot of apple, the big-big type one, ______(9)! She swing it in the air and hantam the Fish Unker until he gong-gong ______(10).

But then ______(11), suay-suay got one mata saw her. He immeelly come over and take her bag of apple and throw it on the ground. Hwah, all the apple inside become apple juice ______(12). Damn sayang, ______(13).

The moral of the story is, if you want to piah chui, then must buy cheaper type of apple

_____ (14). Dun say I neh tell you, _____ (15).

Grammar (5 points)

Each of the utterances below has a missing word. You have four choices. Only one of them is the correct answer. Make your choice by circling the correct letter.

16. I where got money to buy anything? We just go and ____________________, can or not?
a) look-look see-see
b) look-see
c) look and see
d) look-see look-see

17. Not say I say __________, hor, but, your boss new year also never give you ang pao. Why he so kiam, ah?
a) who
b) whom
c) what
d) whose

18. Eh, yesterday's homework you _____ do or not?
a) will
b) have
c) did
d) got

19. Eh, you not only clean your own boots, you also clean everybody else's boots. You a bit the siao ______, right?

a) on
b) off
c) up
d) with

20. Ah Beng very tricky one you know, at first very guai, then after two weeks on the job, start to ________ pattern oredy.

a) chutted
b) chuts
c) chutten
d) chut

Vocabulary (5 points)

21. You whole life want to tuang work, got so many excuse. One day say grandfather die, another day say dog die, pattern tzuay kuay __________!

a) ping pong
b) basketball
c) nintendo
d) badminton

22. Eh, you have a lot of time to complete the project, so, jangan ____________ can or not? Otherwise make everybody stress only!

a) emergency
b) tentative
c) tension
d) have a cow, dude

23. How come you donno your boss is having affair with the secretary? Everyone knows oreddy.
So ______________, lah, you!
a) sotong
b) spider
c) squid
d) seahorse

24. I don't know wha'ppen. I just heard a loud ___________, and then we lost communication!
a) goobaboom
b) kikaboom
c) vavavoom
d) chibaboom

25. Aiyoh, dun worry lah, this test is chicken ______________, man. I close my eyes also can score A!
a) backside
b) feed
c) fart
d) little

Comprehension Cloze Passage (20 points)

Choose the following words for each of the blanks. Each word can only be used once.

early-early	piah	hiao	too lan	cock
arbuthen	song	Dun	oreddy	pray-pray
chio	gila	kakis	suay	immeelly
hoot	bird	ji seow	do'wan	sai

Once upon a time, hor, in Bukit Gorblok got one auntie who was a real lao ______________ (26), always like to wear a lot of makeup even though she fifty year old ______________ (27). She also a bit ______________ (28), because she like to talk to her mirror. She always ask the mirror:

Mirror, mirror on the floor
Here got who is chio char bor?

And the mirror would tell her:

Auntie Auntie, neh bluff you
Here you are the tua ______________ (29) bu!

And the Auntie would be happy like ______________ (30). But then, hor, got one day, she ask the mirror:

Mirror, mirror on the floor
Here got who is chio char bor?

And this time, the mirror answer:

Auntie, Auntie, damn sorry
Downstair ah lian is more swee

Wah! Hear oreddy, the Auntie damn ____________(31) leow. So she ______________(32) went downstair and saw this pretty ah lian, who was called "White-White". (Why she call "White-White'? Because her skin damn white lah, ______________(33)?) The Auntie told White White to faster siam from Bukit Gorblok, but White White ______________(34). So Auntie said, "Nehmine! I later come and find you to settle!"

White-White hear oreddy, damn scared. So she immeelly phone her ______________(35), Ah Long, Ah Bong, Ah Song, Ah Tong, Ah Wong, Ah Chong, and Ah Gong - also known as the Seven Samsengs.

"Eh, got one lau char bor say she want to ______________(36) me, lair!" she cry-cry to the Seven Samsengs. "Lai dat how?"

"______________(37) scared," said Ah Long. "We all is expert at ______________(38) chui, one. We will also send a message to this auntie to dun ______________(39). She see this message, sure wen ______________(40) you again, confirm plus guarantee."

And so the next morning, the Auntie woke up, and

found one big pig's head hanging on her front door. The mirror also saw it and said:

Auntie, Auntie, make girl cry
That's why now you kena ______________ (41)!

Auntie hear this only, damn buay ______________ (42) and smash the mirror, saying:

Mirror, mirror, if you talk
Just make sure you don't talk __________ (43)!

And the last thing the mirror said before being thrown out in the rubbish:

Auntie, Auntie, si beh ______________ (44)
Why you ______________ (45) dun say!

ANSWER KEY

Grammar Cloze Passage

(1) hor
(2) lah/lair
(3) hor
(4) hor
(5) meh
(6) lah
(7) lair/man
(8) lah/hor
(9) lair/man
(10) liao
(11) hor
(12) liao
(13) man
(14) lah/lor
(15) hor

Grammar

(16)(d) look-see look-see
(17)(c) what
(18)(d) got
(19)(a) on
(20)(d) chut

Vocabulary

(21) (d) badminton
(22) (c) tension
(23) (a) sotong
(24) (d) chibaboom
(25) (b) feed

Comprehension Cloze Passage

(26) hiao
(27) oreddy
(28) gila
(29) chio
(30) bird
(31) too lan
(32) immeelly
(33) arbuthen
(34) do'wan
(35) kakis
(36) hoot
(37) Dun
(38) piah
(39) pray-pray
(40) ji seow
(41) sai
(42) song
(43) cock
(44) suay
(45) early-early

Editors' Biography

COLIN GOH and WOO YEN YEN are a husband-and-wife creative team who are award-winning filmmakers and multimedia producers. Together, they founded www.TalkingCock.com, a satirical website on Singaporean current affairs, which international traffic monitoring agency Hitwise has ranked as Singapore's #1 entertainment-humour website for 2 years in a row. It has been featured by Time magazine, the Economist, Wired and the BBC, and regularly gets over 3 million unique page views a month. From the website, they have also produced:

- "eAhLong.com", an award-winning short film;
- "TalkingCock SingingSong", a critically-acclaimed comedy and music CD;
- "TalkingCock the Movie", a feature length comedy that has been seen in numerous countries worldwide; and
- the bestselling Coxford Singlish Dictionary, a lexicon of vernacular Singaporean English that the Times of London has praised as "invaluable".

Their most recent feature film, "Singapore Dreaming", won the Montblanc Screenwriters Award at the San Sebastian International Film Festival, the Audience Award for Narrative Feature at the Asian-American International Film Festival in New York, and the Best Asian/Middle Eastern Film Award at the prestigious Tokyo International Film Festival. Praised by Variety as "a graceful satire on western capitalism in the east", it is now being screened around the world.

Colin is also a professional writer and cartoonist, as well as an attorney with qualifications in England, Singapore and New York, while Yen Yen is an Assistant Professor in the School of Education at Long Island University in New York, where she teaches curriculum development and the social foundations of education.